D1603551

WHO SHALL BE ABLE TO STAND?

FINDING PERSONAL MEANING IN

THE BOOK OF

REVELATION

WHO SHALL BE ABLE TO STAND?

FINDING PERSONAL MEANING IN

—— THE BOOK OF ——

REVELATION

S. MICHAEL WILCOX

DESERET
BOOK

SALT LAKE CITY, UTAH

Library of Congress Cataloging-in-Publication Data

Wilcox, S. Michael.
   Who shall be able to stand? : finding personal meaning in the book of Revelation / S. Michael Wilcox.
      p.   cm.
   Includes bibliographical references and index.
   ISBN 1-57008-870-5 (alk. paper)
   1. Bible. N.T. Revelation—Commentaries.   2. Church of Jesus Christ of Latter-day Saints—Doctrines.   I. Title.
   BS2825.53 .W55   2003
   228'.07—dc21   2002153647

Printed in the United States of America   70582-6988
Phoenix Color Corporation, Hagerstown, MD

10   9   8   7   6   5   4   3   2   1

CONTENTS

CONTENTS

THE POETIC BEAUTY
OF REVELATION

I have contemplated writing about the book of Revelation for many years. Writing tends to clarify my thinking and organize scriptural insights into a more compact wholeness of truth. I gain the greatest benefits from the exercise. I made a preliminary, general attempt long years ago; it was published, but the taste remained in my mouth, and I couldn't drop the fruit. The book of Revelation has fascinated me for as long as I can remember. As an English major, I have loved symbolism, metaphor, irony, figures of speech, and the mystery of underlying themes. Revelation scratches that literary itch in a most satisfying manner. The Old Testament has an equal fascination, and since Revelation relies so profoundly on the themes and realities of that oldest of books, I was drawn into its mystique and have been a captive ever since.

I have taught about Revelation and the Old Testament for many years, and they never lose their allure. I love to study and teach the other books of scripture too (God never wrote a bad book), but I suppose the Old Testament and Revelation, because of their symbolic, metaphorical nature, will ever hold a certain corner of my heart and mind. I long ago ceased to struggle against their charm and have surrendered completely.

Ecclesiastes' thesis on human vanity ends with the observation, "Of making many books there is no end." (Ecclesiastes 12:12.) Fearing that my own vanity would prove the sage true, I have hesitated to add to the already numerous publications detailing the majesty of Revelation. Each time I thought I had something to offer, another book would appear, or I would feel the timidity of a climber facing the Mt. Everest of scriptural exhortation, and I placed my own musings on the back burner, but I could never quite bring myself to turn the gas off. I could hear its soft, bubbling noises always in the distance. So the years have passed with other publishing projects, yet within the shadows a heart's desire awaited. Finally, with the encouragement of friends, fine editors, and family, the ideas that have lingered in my mind for decades began to push themselves out through my fingertips and onto a keyboard.

Decisions of what to include and what to leave out are painful. As a young man in love never tires of detailing the charms of his beloved's beauty, the graces of Revelation continue to attract me. I have decided not to deal with Revelation verse by verse, as this has been well done already. There are many fine, scholarly approaches from the background of language and other disciplines. It is the book's application to our lives and its poetic beauty that I will try to share. Because Revelation is daunting, I have decided to approach it in a conversational, informal tone. I have concentrated on keeping my thoughts simple, extracting the insights I hope will prove most valuable for everyday life. Obviously those ideas and truths that have come to mean the most to me will find dominance, so I claim no expertise on the totality of Revelation—only the acquaintance of a close friend who has come to treasure certain qualities of character in one with whom many years have been shared in intimate conversation. I write in the hope that those hours of familiarity will prove beneficial to others.

I offer one final note of caution. I recall sitting in an honors Shakespeare class at BYU during my undergraduate studies. The class was taught by Dr. Arthur Henry King, who had one of the keenest minds I encountered at BYU. I felt fortunate to be in his class and somewhat overwhelmed by the brilliance of my fellow students. One day while discussing certain passages in the poetry of Shakespeare, a number of students made strong assertions about their meaning. Dr. King allowed the comments to circulate for some time, then stepped in and explained the passages in such a way that we all realized we had been far too dogmatic and certain of our own interpretations to the exclusion of meaning and insight we had completely missed. Then he taught us one of the most important lessons of my university days. "In some matters," he said, "it is better to be intellectually uncertain rather than superficially sure. This will still leave us with a great deal to be certain about, while maintaining a humility to learn."

The book of Revelation has been dissected by brilliant minds, resulting in commentaries of edifying depth and perception. It has also been used to substantiate a rather large canon of nonsense. We will often need to accept a certain ambiguity about its images and passages. We will have to wait and see how the future plays out the script. Let us avoid being superficially sure about our own private views, allowing our enlightenment to expand as the mind searches and the Spirit directs.

THE KEY

T he Lord has often promised that if we would knock, he would open the doors of understanding and knowledge. Our desire to know eternal truth counts heavily with the Lord. The seeker will find, and those who ask will have answers provided. However, the Lord may respond in different ways. Sometimes he grants us an answer directly; at other times he gives us a key, anticipating that we will put it into the lock, turn it, and open the door for ourselves.

I approach Revelation in this manner. We need a key, and the Lord will provide one. A key works by a combination of notches that correspond to the inner workings of the lock. All are needed to open the door. So it is with Revelation, and that is why I prefer to speak of a single key to the book rather than a series of keys or aids in discerning the mind of the apostle when he described his visions. Some symbols will require that we draw upon all the elements of the key to produce the greatest understanding. With this in mind, let us design our key. There may be many other notches on the key than those I will describe, but these first six will be sufficient to help us open the door and take a good look inside.

THE JOSEPH SMITH TRANSLATION

The first notch is an obvious one—the Joseph Smith Translation of the Bible. Joseph Smith made numerous changes within the text of Revelation, greatly clarifying certain images and symbols. For example, he added several complete verses to the twelfth chapter, removing all doubt that the woman radiating the glory of the sun with the moon at her feet and crowned with twelve stars is the Church, and that the child she carries in her womb is the kingdom of God on the earth, or Zion. As our study progresses, we will pay close attention to the changes and additions made by the Prophet Joseph Smith.

MODERN SCRIPTURE

Scripture is the best commentary on scripture; therefore, the finest commentaries on Revelation have already been written. Other great prophets, such as Nephi, the brother of Jared, and Enoch, were also shown the grand scheme of world history, as was John the Beloved. Nephi was told, "The things which this apostle of the Lamb shall write are many things which thou hast seen." (1 Nephi 14:24.) It is helpful to see which symbol of Nephi's vision, for example, matches those of John. In Revelation, Christ is represented as a slain lamb; in Lehi's dream his symbol is a fruitful tree. In Revelation, a beast, a whore, and a great city fight the Church; in the visions of Lehi and Nephi, this role is played by the great and spacious building. Both sources speak of the apostasy in terms of a harlot.

Revelation speaks of billowing smoke from hell that gives birth to the locusts of war; in Nephi's vision, the influences of Lucifer are depicted as a mist of darkness that Nephi comprehends as he witnesses the wars between the Nephites and Lamanites. Enoch hears the earth mourn over the wickedness before the Flood, while John sees the sun clothed in black, like sackcloth, during the opening of the sixth seal. Examples like this are encountered often, and we must pay attention to them, for clarity inevitably follows.

The future is not the sole focus of John's Revelation, although it is the dominant one. Nephi's record informs us that John "shall see and write the remainder of these things; yea, *and also many things which have been.*" (1 Nephi 14:21; italics added.) We must keep in mind that some events may not directly correspond to the future. John is viewing an entire history that dates back to premortal times as well as forward to the final transformation of the earth into a celestial world.

Joseph Smith also made numerous inquiries concerning the last dispensations of history. In some cases, as in section 77 or 130 of the Doctrine and Covenants, the tie to Revelation is concise and obvious. In section 77 Joseph answered specific questions about individual symbols of Revelation. Here we learn the meaning of the sea of glass, the four angels, the sealing of the 144,000, and the book sealed with seven seals. Our understanding of Revelation is particularly enhanced with Joseph Smith's interpretation of the sealed book, for the bulk of Revelation rests upon this knowledge. Nephi tells us that he was not allowed to continue to write his revelatory experiences because John was assigned that task. He does, however, comment on what he was allowed to reveal. We must keep his words front and center also.

Other commentaries in modern scripture are not so easily detected, but they are just as important. Section 88, for instance, gives great insight about Revelation 8, which we discover by noticing that the sequence of events in both is similar. The same prophecies are often recorded by different prophets using unique, singular, and novel words. The choice of expressions, when examined closely, provides insight. John speaks of a great earthquake in Revelation 6; Doctrine and Covenants 88:87 states that the "earth shall tremble and reel to and fro as a drunken man," giving us a poetic hint to enhance our understanding. Whenever possible, we must examine modern scripture's equivalents to John's vision. This notch on our key is distinctive to Latter-day Saints, and it gives us great advantage.

OLD TESTAMENT ALLUSIONS

Perhaps the most important commentary on the book of Revelation is the Old Testament. Whenever I read a book on Revelation or listen to people speak on the subject, I think, "How much do they know about the Old Testament? How many years have they taught it? How many times have they read it thoroughly and deeply? Is their grasp of Old Testament themes equal to their interest in New Testament teachings?" If I do not receive satisfactory answers to these questions, my confidence in the person's ability to give meaning to the symbols and images of Revelation diminishes. Almost every chapter of Revelation contains allusions to the Old Testament. Without question, John assumed that his readers had a profound understanding of the stories, rites, history, and prophetic utterances of the Old Testament. When he alludes to "that woman Jezebel," or Balaam and Balak in chapter 2, for example, he assumes that we know who these people were and what they did. If we miss the allusion, we miss the meaning. By comparing the turmoil of the last days with the plagues of Egypt, John has a powerful lesson in mind, one we must grasp by association rather than direct exposition. The key to not fearing "the beast" and the image built to it, as described in Revelation 13, is found in perceiving the allusions to several stories in the book of Daniel. This is true of locust hordes, kings from the east, Armageddon, harvests and winepresses, weddings, mourning merchants, thundering trumpets, and crystal-clear rivers pouring from the throne of God.

Some allusions are easy to catch, while others are more subtle. Over the years, when teaching classes on the book of Revelation, I have tried to teach classes on the Old Testament at the same time. I have discovered many wonderful links between the two topics as I prepare lessons on them simultaneously. Whenever I struggle with a particular chapter or image, my first response is to conclude I have missed some aspect or moment in the Old Testament that would, if I noticed it, fill in a precious piece of information.

As you begin fitting the pieces of the Old Testament into the puzzle of Revelation, you will notice that what John leaves out is often as critical, or even more critical, than what he includes. Many times understanding Revelation will depend on turning to the Old Testament and receiving the entire subject to which John is alluding. Frequently inspiration, counsel, and insight will be found in verses of the Old Testament associated with the allusion. It is therefore essential that we find the allusions, turn to them, and read the entire account.

When Moroni first appeared to Joseph Smith, he taught him by explaining certain Old Testament passages. Those chosen, when put together, unfolded a panorama of the last days. I do not get the impression that they were necessarily placed in chronological order. From time to time, when reading Revelation, it is good to ponder Moroni's approach. I cannot help but think that John is being shown images revealed to former prophets, images that are explained to him or applied by him to events in the future. Perhaps Joseph Smith's words about Moroni would apply here: "He quoted many other passages of scripture, and offered many explanations." (JS—H 1:41.) Like pieces to a puzzle, the various descriptions are placed one by one until, when the puzzle is finished, we have a totality of prophetic insight.

POETIC IMAGERY

I cannot stress too much the notch of poetic imagery. We must approach Revelation with a different mind-set than the one we usually use. Perhaps an illustration will help. I was once given a calendar containing twelve "magic-eye" pictures, renditions of jungle animals. Magic-eye drawings are three-dimensional designs that, when looked at normally, appear only as a blotched set of colors with no apparent order. If we gaze at them as we do other pictures, we will never see the depth that is there. We must focus the eyes in a new way by looking beyond the picture. As the eyes assume a new focal point, suddenly we see the animals that are part of the picture. So it is with the images of Revelation. When reading it, we must leave our prose minds at the door and pick up our poetry minds. We should read Revelation the way we study serious poetry. With a new focus, the messages and truths suddenly appear, and we find ourselves saying, "So that's what it means!" This is much more difficult to do than to describe.

6

Poetry aims at awakening thoughts and feelings within us. It draws upon familiar objects, stories, and events, giving them added significance—imparting spiritual, moral, or ethical truths. More than one meaning can be held by a single image. Figurative language draws upon metaphor, allusion, symbol, personification, simile, irony, paradox, ambiguity, synecdoche, polysyndeton, and so on.

With each new image, we must stop and ponder. The very nature of symbolic, poetic writing forces the mind to ask questions. That is one of the main reasons the Lord employs this sometimes enigmatic method of bestowing his truths upon his wondering children. Our Father in Heaven wants us to use our minds, and nothing stimulates the mind quite like figurative language. Jesus was a master of this type of teaching, particularly the parable. The effectiveness of this manner of portraying truth is found in the fascination people have with understanding Revelation. I do not believe this interest comes from a desire to understand the last days as much as it does from the nature of John's approach. There is something compelling about red dragons, great images built to beasts, horses of varying colors stalking the land, falling stars, burning candlesticks, seals on foreheads, locusts with women's hair, seas turning to blood, and cities of pearl and gold. It is simply impossible to read Revelation casually; the mind wants answers, almost demands them. The closed door will always impel the curious to peek behind it. The Lord closed the door of Revelation, but he did not lock it! Mysteries summon and suggest solutions. There is something in the human psyche that cannot rest until the pieces fit and the clues make sense. How the Lord must smile as he watches us pore over Revelation, drawing upon all our powers of concentration, reflection, and study.

However, there are inherent dangers in dealing with poetic, figurative language. One of the most serious is the tendency to read it too literally. I do not wish to deny or diminish literal interpretations of Revelation. In the Lord's wisdom, he often places both literal and figurative together. Nephi, speaking of another deeply poetic book—that of Isaiah—told his questioning brothers that what he had read to them pertained "to things both temporal and spiritual." (1 Nephi 22:3.)

In this present attempt to offer help with Revelation, I will emphasize the figurative. Please do not assume by that emphasis that I am denying or challenging the literal, which may have been stressed by others. Because of the very nature of John's descriptions, I feel on safer ground with the symbolic. I have discovered over many years of teaching that more mistakes are made in reading a passage too literally than they are in reading too figuratively.

The New Testament itself offers this warning time and time again. Jesus told Nicodemus he needed to be "born again," to which he responded, "How can a man be born when he is old? can he enter the second time into his mother's womb, and be born?" (John 3:4.) The woman at the well, when offered "living water," replied, "Sir, thou hast nothing to draw with, and the well is deep: from whence then hast thou that living water?" (John 4:11.) When warned about the "leaven of the Pharisees," even Jesus' own disciples "reasoned among themselves, saying, It is because we have no bread." (Mark 8:15–16.) In each of these instances, the Savior's words were taken literally, and the spiritual edification was lost until Jesus opened the people's eyes to his true meaning.

Some of the greatest controversies of Christianity and the fallacies of the apostasy arise from too literal an interpretation.

When Jesus said, "I am in the Father, and the Father in me" (John 14:10), he was speaking figuratively, yet Christendom took his words at face value, and the three-in-one doctrine of the trinity was born. When Jesus said, "Take, eat; this is my body. . . . This is my blood" (Matthew 26:26–28), once again his words were understood literally, and the doctrine of transubstantiation had its foundations. Mistakes can be made and truth missed by a figurative rendition of scripture, but we are much more likely to err in the literal than the figurative, especially when dealing with something as symbolically rich as Revelation.

I have been surprised at times by how strongly people hold to an exclusively literal interpretation of certain passages, almost suggesting that a figurative reading borders on heresy. Often we need not choose either rendition, for both are present, but I have found that spiritual power usually lies with the figurative.

Since the dawn of the scientific revolution in the 1600s, the nature of language has changed. We demand more clarity of expression in our depictions of truth. Logic rules, and objective reporting is sought. This is the age of information and fact. Language was once more emotive, designed to produce feelings and states of soul as well as to impart information. The manner in which truth was presented was as critical as the truth itself. God is aware of these shifts in our world and adapts his revelatory methods and wording in accordance with our ability to perceive them. This the Lord himself acknowledged in the scriptures: "These commandments . . . were given unto my servants in their weakness, *after the manner of their language, that they might come to understanding.*" (D&C 1:24; italics added.) Therefore it is not surprising that the latest book of scripture is the Doctrine and Covenants. In our modern world, we are better able to receive truth in this line-upon-line, precept-upon-precept kind of revelation. If we are to fathom the rich depths of John's contribution to the scriptural canon, however, we will need to reason and think less scientifically and more poetically, less in modern exposition and more in the ancient flow of descriptive words. We will need to explore the power of language in an older mode, one that aimed at beauty and majesty of expression as much as the presentation of knowledge.

Every time I begin anew to read or teach the book of Revelation, I place firmly in my mind a statement made by Frederic Farrar, author of *The Life of Christ*. Speaking of the types of mistakes that often arise from misunderstanding New Testament language, Farrar wrote, "They would never have arisen if it had been sufficiently observed that it was a characteristic of Christ's teaching to adopt the language of picture and of emotion. But to turn metaphor into fact, poetry into prose, rhetoric into logic, parable into systematic theology, is at once fatal and absurd." (Frederic Farrar, *The Life of Christ* [Portland, Oregon: Fountain Publications, 1964], 564, n. 4.) So let us turn the intensity of our logical minds down considerably and turn up the light of our poetic, metaphorical thinking. We are much more likely to discover gems of truth in that light as we proceed with our examination of Revelation, for it shines with a greater brightness.

With each new image we will stop and ask ourselves some questions. For example, why did John depict Lucifer as a red dragon with seven heads? Why seven heads instead of one? What can we learn from the image of apostles and other Church leaders as stars? Why were the stars important in the ancient world? What is John telling us about our sixth-seal world by describing a black sun, a red moon, a quaking earth, and tumbling stars? Why do the mountains and islands flee? What does the sound of many waters teach us about the voice and character of God? Why do the locusts have men's faces, long hair like a woman's, and crowns on their heads? Why does a lamb speak with a dragon's voice? Reflecting on such questions is sure to have its rewards.

I would add one final caution. As we reflect on the images of John's vision, it is safest to assume John is describing to us exactly what he is seeing rather than something in the modern world with which he was unfamiliar and, therefore, tried to describe using things from his world. If someone asked, "Did he see modern attack helicopters and depict them as locusts that roared like 'many horses running to battle,' or did he actually see giant locusts with lion's teeth?" I would always favor the latter. I believe we are given an account of the very things John was shown. Our task is to find in reality what those symbols represent.

PARALLEL IMAGES

The fifth notch on our key is much like the fourth one. The images of Revelation often come in pairs. We are presented with two kingdoms, that of Christ and that of Lucifer. Lucifer is not very creative. His talent lies in deception, in transformation, in distortion. When I was young, I loved going into the fun house at Lagoon. Inside were curved mirrors that distorted my reflection. My legs would become tiny while my body was elongated. My head would widen and my hands drip with long, skinny fingers. The face staring back at me was my own, but it was deeply deformed. So it is with the kingdom of the adversary.

His is but a warped reflection of the Savior's kingdom. Since we are members of Christ's dominion, we are familiar with its dimensions and characteristics in reality and are, therefore, somewhat immune from making interpretative mistakes. Knowing that Satan's symbols are perverted reflections, we have an advantage in coming to understanding.

It does not require a close reading to notice this pairing of kingdoms. There are two women—the bride of Christ and the great whore. There are two cities—the New Jerusalem and Babylon. There are two harvests, both dominated by an angel with a sharp sickle; one gathers the white field, the other the grapes of wrath. There are two marks placed on the forehead— the seal of the living God and the mark of the beast. Our list could continue on and on, including horses, things that come out of the mouth, stars, keys, horns, armies, rising from the dead, and much more. There is a strong reason for these parallel images, and that leads us to our last notch.

Moral Warning or Encouragement

Though Revelation has a great deal to do with prophecy, I am not convinced that predicting the future is its primary purpose. John is helping us make choices. As we see the kingdom of the dragon set parallel to the kingdom of the Lamb, we are better able to detect the one and hold fast to the other. The final destinies of both are shown. We are able to side with the known winner before the battle ever begins.

Once again I quote from Frederic Farrar: "Keep hold of the certainty that the object of Prophecy in all ages has been moral warning infinitely more than even the vaguest chronological indication, since to the voice of Prophecy as to the eye of God all Time is but one eternal Present." (Farrar, *Life of Christ*, 542.)

Farrar speaks of moral warning, but I would add an additional word—that of encouragement. Revelation is a book of hope! When properly applied, its teachings bring peace and comfort to the reader. We should be as diligent in looking for these threads in the tapestry of John's vision as we are in ascertaining the signs of the times. Applying the book's principles may be more essential than revealing the mystery of its imagery.

I am also cautious about trying to create a detailed timeline of events. Other than the general chronological order of the seven seals, Revelation presents a total worldview, not a specific step-by-step calendar of events leading up to the return of the Savior. In the words of Yoda, the Jedi master of *Star Wars* fame, when instructing Luke Skywalker about seeing the future, "Difficult to see. *Always in motion is the future.*"

This is true of Revelation. The images turn and swirl in a kaleidoscope of power and truth, weaving into each other and shifting to create the greatest impact. The ultimate outcome is a preparation of purpose and a focus of finality, lest the "very elect" find themselves deceived. Prophetic writing sometimes portrays the same events multiple times but with different symbols. The book of Daniel is an excellent example of this. There, earthly political kingdoms are represented by a statue composed of different metals; by predatory beasts such as lions, bears, and leopards; by towering trees; and by animals with horns, such as rams and goats, that butt into each other in their quest for dominance over the herd. Daniel offers us four visions and dreams, but each one describes the same future reality.

The Holy Spirit comprehends all the mystery and charm of Revelation. If we seek for this wonderful gift, granted to all who covenant in the waters of baptism, our turning of the interpretive key should result in gratitude and rejoicing that the Lord has revealed to us the contents of a book that he himself is depicted as holding in his right hand. I suggest that you first read a chapter of Revelation and then turn to the present volume for ideas. Then return to the book of Revelation and see if applying the key has opened new doors.

THE KING OF KINGS

The first chapter of Revelation introduces us to the Savior, the source of the truths John will be shown. This is its main purpose. The setting of Revelation is also given, with instructions about our responsibility once we understand that the Lord has bestowed upon mankind such revelatory beauty. These truths had been shown to previous prophets, but they were instructed to seal up the knowledge for a future time.

We have all sat in sacrament meeting when the bishop read a letter from the First Presidency giving counsel to the Saints. The book of Revelation is just such a letter. It was addressed to seven branches of the ancient Church on the west coast of modern Turkey. You can locate six of the seven churches by studying the last map (number 22) in the map section of your Bible. Verse 11 gives us the names of the churches. Thyatira is not placed on the map, but it is located in the same general area.

John sent the Revelation in an epistle because of his imprisonment on the Isle of Patmos "for the word of God, and for the testimony of Jesus Christ." (Revelation 1:9.) The Romans often banished people they felt were troublesome to the stability of the empire. Although not identified on any map in the map section, the Isle of Patmos lies off the coast of western Turkey in the Aegean Sea, almost directly west of Miletus on map 22.

According to the Joseph Smith Translation, we are instructed to do four things with Revelation. The result of our efforts will be happiness, for that is implied in the word "blessed." Acknowledging that Revelation will require much more of the reader than other scriptures, the Lord wants us to know that the labor will be well worth the reflection: "Blessed are they who *read,* and they who *hear* and *understand* the words of this prophesy, and *keep* those things which are written therein, for the time of the coming of the Lord draweth nigh." (Revelation 1:3, JST; italics added.)

The first of the four responsibilities is relatively easy. It is well within our ability to "read" Revelation. Hearing and understanding what we read is more of a challenge. We may take some comfort in a phrase used repeatedly by the Lord in his messages to the seven churches: "He that hath an ear, *let him hear* what the Spirit saith unto the churches." (Revelation 2:7, 11, 17, 29; 3:6, 13, 22; italics added.) This phrase teaches that if we desire to learn and understand, if our ears are tuned and straining to listen, the Lord will impart truth through the Spirit. Our hunger for knowledge counts greatly with the Lord, who will know of our listening ears primarily because of our prayers asking for insight.

After quoting and explaining Isaiah (another prophet whose writings present some challenges), Nephi wrote, "I have spoken

these words, if ye cannot understand them it will be because ye
ask not, neither do ye *knock;* wherefore, ye are not brought into
the light." (2 Nephi 32:4; italics added.) On another occasion
Jesus quoted Old Testament prophecies to the Nephites, who
did not comprehend his counsels. He instructed them, "Ponder
upon the things which I have said, and ask of the Father, in my
name, that ye may understand." (3 Nephi 17:3.) Pondering and
asking show the Lord that our ears are ready. The Spirit then
responds with the affirmative "Let him hear!"

Belief is also critical in understanding eternal truth. In
Mosiah we read of the "rising generation" who did not "believe
concerning the coming of Christ. And now because of their
unbelief they could not understand the word of God." (Mosiah
26:1–3.) We sometimes do things backward. We say to the
Lord, "Help me understand and then I will believe." The Lord
responds, "Believe and I will help you understand."

The fourth thing required of us is to "keep" the counsels of
Revelation. This also leads to understanding. When we assure
the Lord that we will heed his counsels, act upon his instructions, obey his commandments, and apply his revelations, he
will grant us understanding. Perhaps the most critical factor in
mastering the images and symbols of Revelation is our willingness to put into practice the things we will be taught. The
emphasis is on living better lives rather than viewing apocalyp-
tic events. However, this is frequently impeded by our sometimes overly enthusiastic focus on knowing the future or placing a sensational spin on the signs of the times. We must
constantly remind ourselves that the main purpose of
Revelation is to help us make correct choices and discern
between the forces of good and evil. The Lord is not particularly interested in satisfying our curiosity about what is coming.

The worth of that knowledge, when it is imparted, is in its ability to help us make good decisions for our own lives. In a manner of speaking, it allows us to bet on the winner. Since the recompense centers on temporal security, everlasting joy, and eternal life, prophetic knowledge is extremely valuable.

The very humility created by our bewilderment before the swirling array of intertwining images acts in our favor. Humility is the chief factor in obtaining the learning the Spirit can bestow. "Because of meekness and lowliness of heart cometh the visitation of the Holy Ghost," Mormon testified. (Moroni 8:26.) And Brigham Young was told, "Let him that is ignorant learn wisdom by humbling himself and calling upon the Lord his God, that his eyes may be opened that he may see, and his ears opened that he may hear; for my Spirit is sent forth into the world to enlighten the humble and contrite." (D&C 136:32–33.)

I take comfort in these instructions. Perhaps our success with Revelation will depend less on scholarly pursuits of language or history and depend more on our humility, our willingness to apply what we learn, and our beseeching prayers to the Father. This, of course, makes perfect sense, for few people have the leisure or tools necessary for a scholarly study of Revelation. We must respect and be grateful for scholarship, but there are sharper tools with which we may dig beneath the surface to find gems of radiant truth.

THE PRINCE OF KINGS

The major theme of Revelation's first chapter is a reaffirmation of the Savior, of who he is and what he does for his people. As you read this chapter, and throughout Revelation, look for the descriptive attributes of Jesus. He is "the first begotten of the dead." (Revelation 1:5.) He is "the beginning and the ending . . . the Lord, which is, and which was, and which is to come." (Revelation 1:8.) In these preliminary verses, however, John seems to stress his title of "prince of the kings of the earth." (Revelation 1:5.) Later in Revelation, when Jesus comes in glory, he is "KING OF KINGS, AND LORD OF LORDS." (Revelation 19:16.)

Jesus is certainly the prince, king, and lord of all earthly monarchs, but there is a deeper meaning in these titles that directly relates to us. Immediately following this title, we read, "And unto him who *loved us*, be glory; who *washed us* from our sins in his own blood, and hath made us *kings and priests* unto God, his Father." (Revelation 1:6, JST; italics added.) Because of his love for us, and the cleansing power of his atonement (and we would add the saving ordinances of the temple), we too may become kings and queens. Paul tells us that *Melchizedek* is really a title that means "King of righteousness." (Hebrews 7:2.) Jesus is the King of all the kings of righteousness and their queens who will one day rule and reign with him. These ideas are further developed in the individual messages to the seven churches.

A related title may be worthy of reflection. The name of our Father in Heaven, we are told, is Elohim. In Hebrew, adding *im* to a noun makes it plural. Examples are *cherubim*, *Urim*, and *Thummim*. Since *El* is the Hebrew word for God, *Elohim* means "Gods." Perhaps we can relate this name to the titles of Jesus. As Christ is the King of Kings and the Lord of Lords, his Father is the God of Gods. As his children we have the potential to become like him. Doctrine and Covenants 132 indicates that some of our brothers and sisters who have preceded us in mortality are now "gods" in the eternal worlds. We belong to the race of the Gods. Our Father in Heaven is, therefore, a God of Gods.

Jesus, as King of Kings, will one day return "in the clouds with ten thousands of his saints . . . , clothed with the glory of his Father." (Revelation 1:7, JST.) The King of Kings will not only wash and anoint those who trust his mercy but will bring them with him when he returns to reign on the earth.

Most numbers in Revelation are symbolic, and we should exercise care in attaching too literal a meaning to them. Ten thousand was an extremely large number among ancient people (though not in our modern world, which speaks of trillions). Its connotation suggests myriads—so many they are almost numberless.

We see this number frequently in scripture. Nephi told his trembling brothers that they need not fear Laban and his fifty because the Lord was more powerful "than Laban and his fifty, yea, or even than his tens of thousands." (1 Nephi 4:1.) The casualty list of the last battle of the Nephites included the names of commanders with their "ten thousand." (Mormon 6:12–15.) In Micah we read that the Lord was not pleased with "thousands of rams, or with ten thousands of rivers of oil." (Micah 6:7.)

If one of the major purposes of Revelation is to give us encouragement, we receive it almost immediately. If myriads of people will return to reign with Christ—if tens of thousands are crowned kings and queens in his eternal realms—there is hope for each of us. Others have fought the battles of life and come away conquerors. By maintaining a firm faith in Christ, might not we anticipate our enlistment in that triumphant assembly of kings and queens?

GOLDEN CANDLESTICKS

The first major image of Revelation begins in verse 12 with the words, "And being turned, I saw seven golden candlesticks." As if John anticipated our trouble with symbolic representations, he jump-starts our thinking by telling us plainly in verse 20 that the seven candlesticks represent the seven different churches to whom the epistle is addressed. The word "candlesticks" reflects the King James translators' familiarity with wax candles. What John actually saw, however, was a seven-branched menorah with a bowl at the top of each branch. Each bowl held olive oil, into which a wick was placed and then lit, providing light. *Lamps* might be a better translation.

In the Sermon on the Mount, Jesus described his disciples as the light of the world, saying that people do not "light a candle, and put it under a bushel, but on a candlestick; and it giveth light unto all that are in the house." (Matthew 5:15.) Olive oil was a source of light and also of healing. In the parable of the Good Samaritan, oil was poured into the wounds of the beaten man. (See Luke 10:34.) To this day the olive has strong associations with peace. Light. Healing. Peace. These are all attributes of the Spirit. Ancient kings, prophets, and priests were all anointed with olive oil. This suggested that no leader had the right to rule others unless he was guided by the Spirit. In Revelation, the seven churches must be filled with the Spirit that they might bring light, healing, and peace to the world. The challenge has not changed for us today.

The next verse tells us where Christ is in relation to his churches: "And in the midst of the seven candlesticks one like unto the Son of man." (Revelation 1:13.) He is not an absentee ruler but dwells in the very midst of his people. That is why in chapters 2 and 3 he knows the specific strengths and problems of each church. Temples today suggest this same truth: the Savior dwells with his people. I can see his house shining across the valley in the darkness each morning as I drive to work. He will help us fulfill our responsibility to be a light to the world. His messages to the churches contain correcting counsel that must be heeded lest their candlestick be "remove[d] . . . out of his place." (Revelation 2:5.)

All the words that describe the Savior emphasize one central attribute. We might ask ourselves what these phrases have in common: "golden girdle," "hairs white like wool," "white as snow," "flame of fire," "fine brass burned in a furnace," and "countenance as the sun shineth in his strength"? (Revelation 1:13–16.) Each suggests purity. White is also a token of victory or triumph. The two ideas go hand in hand. Is it not purity of life that brings spiritual and moral victory?

John describes the voice of Christ "as the sound of many waters." (Revelation 1:15.) I frequently ask my classes when we reach this point to close their eyes and hear in their imagination the sound of many waters. I then ask them to tell me what they are listening to. I get three answers. Some hear the waves of the sea rolling to shore, some hear a mountain stream rushing from high peaks, and some hear the thunder of waterfalls cascading down the rocks. It doesn't matter which they hear, for all suit the purpose of the poetic description. In each case the sound is a powerful one, impossible to ignore. Yet when I ask them how they feel when they hear these sounds of water, they respond with words like "Peaceful!" "Calming!" "Soothing!" "Healing!" The voice of God is powerful but instills solace.

SEVEN STARS

"And he had in his right hand seven stars." (Revelation 1:16.) As in the case of the candlesticks, we are told what the stars represent: the angels of the seven churches. (See Revelation 1:20.) The Joseph Smith Translation changes this explanation, replacing the word "angels" with "servants." This leads us to understand that the stars are the leaders, the bishops, of the seven churches. When I served as a bishop I found great comfort in this verse, knowing that the Savior would uphold me. My confidence in each bishop I have had over the years has also increased because of this tender image of support.

In a later image, the Church is shown as a radiant woman crowned with twelve stars. The most natural interpretation of the stars is the twelve apostles. Why might apostles, in particular, be symbolized by stars? In the ancient world people used the stars for navigation. People looked to them for direction because they were constant and unchanging. On the central west tower of the Salt Lake Temple, about halfway up, you can see the Big Dipper carved into the granite. These stone stars represent the priesthood, who will show us the way, just as we use the Big Dipper to find the North Star. The local leaders must be constant in order to direct their members. The Savior's upturned hand is a testimony of his willingness to succor them.

The power of John's use of parallel images can be seen at this point. In the twelfth chapter Lucifer is rendered as a red dragon. Notice that his followers are also depicted as stars: "And his tail drew the third part of the stars of heaven, and did cast them to the earth." (Revelation 12:4.) We are familiar with this verse and recognize it as the expulsion from heaven of Lucifer and his followers. Christ upholds his stars, his followers, while the adversary drags down those who choose him as their leader. As stars fall, they lose their light. The blaze of a meteorite may dazzle us for a moment, but we cannot take our bearings by it. When I meditate on these truths, I cannot help but sense an irony of the modern world, in which three groups are called stars: athletes, movie celebrities, and musical entertainers. The irony is deeper when we think of how much these groups influence the standards and directions of the age. Yet we would hardly call these groups constant and unchanging. If we want to get our moral, ethical, or spiritual bearings, we will be wise to look to the stars in the hands of the Savior—to those who crown his church.

As we get further into Revelation, we will notice that Christ calls himself "the bright and morning star." (Revelation 22:16; see also 2:28.) Venus, though a planet, is often referred to as the morning star because it is the brightest one in the sky and the last to fade with the intense light of the rising sun. It should not surprise us that Satan is also shown as a star, but each time he is falling. "And there fell a great star from heaven, burning as it were a lamp." (Revelation 8:10.) "I saw a star fall from heaven unto the earth." (Revelation 9:1.) The first syllable, *Luc*, in the name of Lucifer means "light." *Fer* comes from a Latin root meaning "to carry." Lucifer was once the light-bearer, but when he fell, his light was extinguished, leaving only darkness—a darkness outside the light glowing from the Father and Son. The choice for mankind is obvious if we would have the courage to make it. We can follow the fallen star or the morning one. Sadly, though, Jesus is "the light [that] shineth in darkness; and the darkness comprehended it not." (John 1:5.)

THE TWO-EDGED SWORD

The image of the Savior continues with the phrase "and out of his mouth went a sharp twoedged sword." (Revelation 1:16.) This is not a difficult symbol to fathom. Numerous sections of the Doctrine and Covenants begin with this image: "I am God; give heed unto *my word*, which is quick and powerful, sharper than a two-edged sword." (D&C 6:2; italics added.) Joseph Smith once said, "Truth will cut its own way." (*Teachings of the Prophet Joseph Smith*, selected by Joseph Fielding Smith [Salt Lake City: Deseret Book, 1976], 313.) Nephi chided his rebellious brothers by alluding to the sword of truth. "The guilty taketh the truth to be hard, for it cutteth them to the very center." (1 Nephi 16:2.) Apparently, one of the edges of Christ's words of truth is for the righteous. It penetrates to the very soul and moves them to action, testimony, and faithfulness. The other edge is for the wicked and rebellious. It, too, pierces deeply. If repentance is not the result, they oppose its source more vehemently. One way or the other, the truth tends to move us to action, either supportive or opposing. Do we not read that the Pharisees, after hearing Peter's testimony, "were cut to the heart, and took counsel to slay [him]." (Acts 5:33.)

Let us here apply once again the notch of parallel images. In two other places in Revelation we read the words "out of his mouth." Both refer to Lucifer and his minions. In the twelfth chapter, a serpent tries to destroy the Church represented by a woman: "And the serpent cast out of his mouth water as a flood after the woman, that he might cause her to be carried away of the flood." (Revelation 12:15.) In the sixteenth chapter we read, "I saw three unclean spirits like frogs come out of the mouth of the dragon, and out of the mouth of the beast, and out of the mouth of the false prophet." (Revelation 16:13.) If the sword from the mouth of Christ represents his truths, his gospel, then by contrast the flood and the frogs must signify the lies, falsehoods, and apostate doctrines of the devil. We will deal with these images in greater detail in the context of their individual chapters.

THE KEY OF DAVID

Overwhelmed by the vision of Christ, who appears "as the sun shineth in his strength," John falls "at his feet as dead." Yet with all Christ's majesty comes a sweet tenderness that removes all fear. Notice the gentleness implied in the Savior's touching of the bowing apostle. "And he laid his right hand upon me, saying unto me, Fear not; I am the first and the last: I am he that liveth, and was dead; and, behold, I am alive for evermore." (Revelation 1:16–18.) This last statement introduces the keys that we might picture held in the Savior's other hand. Jesus confirms that he has "the keys of hell and of death." (Revelation 1:18.)

Nephi included in his writings a discourse given by his brother Jacob. In this speech, Jacob referred to an "awful monster" he called "death and hell." He then clarified his meaning. Death meant "the death of the body," and hell meant "the death of the spirit." (2 Nephi 9:10.) The fall of Adam resulted in these two deaths. The resurrection overcomes the first of these two deaths; the atoning blood of Christ's mercy overcomes the second.

In each of the messages to the seven churches, the Lord repeats one of the elements from the first chapter's introductory representations. The keys of death and hell are called "the key of David" in the message to the church of Philadelphia. With this key Christ "openeth, and no man shutteth; and shutteth, and no man openeth." (Revelation 3:7.) John is quoting Isaiah in this verse. (See Isaiah 22:22.)

Isaiah described the replacement of one of the king's leading ministers, one who had access to the king. If you wanted entrance to the king's presence, this man, because of his authority, could secure you an audience. Because the new official's name was Eliakim, which means, "God shall cause to arise" (see Isaiah 22, footnote 20a), Isaiah used the event as a foreshadowing of the resurrecting power of the coming Messiah, who would hold a key that would open the door to a much higher majesty than the court of David's descendants.

If we wanted to see the CEO of a major corporation, we could not just walk through his office door and up to his desk. We would need to get by his secretary. In a sense, she has the key to open the door to his presence.

Death and hell, like a heavy door, bar us from the presence of our Father in Heaven. But Christ's victory over them placed in his hands the key that can open that door. No one returns to the Father without the permission of the holder of the key. He can shut as well as open, but notice the wonderful words that follow the Isaiah quotation in the third chapter of Revelation: "I have set before thee an open door, and no man can shut it." (Revelation 3:8.) I can think of few promises of the Savior that penetrate me as deeply as this pronouncement. I have had it engraved in bronze, and it hangs on my office wall. The Savior has chosen to open the door, and it will remain open throughout eternity. We may choose not to walk through its portals, as Mormon taught, because of "a consciousness of guilt" (see Mormon 9:3–4), but the door swings inward, inviting the repentant and faithful to enter.

Revelation begins with the dignity of Christ, with the reassuring comfort of his watchful care over his people. Since some of the images that follow in later chapters are more foreboding, the sweet calm of the introductory one sets the tone we must maintain as we move through the visions of Christ's beloved disciple. The Savior loves us. His life and motives are pure. He will wash and anoint us that we may share authority in his dominions. He is in our midst. He will uphold the leaders we are asked to follow. His mouth will continue to speak the ennobling words of truth. His voice calms like running water. His touch is one of tenderness and reassurance. He has opened the door to our Father in Heaven, and only our own volition can keep us from his welcoming embrace.

Thus in the very first chapter we are introduced to a theme that will be repeated over and over again. The apostle of Patmos testifies in every chapter that God is involved in the affairs of men. He is not an absentee Lord, nor forgetful of us in his occupation with other worlds. As Enoch once stated, "Were it possible that man could number the particles of the earth, yea, millions of earths like this, it would not be a beginning to the number of thy creations; and thy curtains are stretched out still; *and yet thou art there; and thy bosom is there, and also thou art just; thou art merciful and kind forever.* (Moses 7:30; italics added.)

TO HIM THAT OVERCOMETH

C hapters 2 and 3 of Revelation contain the individual messages the Savior offers to the seven churches. We worship Jesus for many reasons; not least among them is the intimate attention he gives to his people. Although he has created "worlds without number," his attention is also focused on the sparrow that falls. This quality of the Savior's divinity, which ministers to his creations "one by one" (3 Nephi 11:15), intensifies our faith, for we know that his keen awareness of the details of our lives allows for maximum mercy and personalized counsel. "All things are numbered unto me," he says, "for they are mine and I know them." (Moses 1:35.)

The problems faced by the churches are not unique to their time but continue to challenge faith and activity today. But we also have the same promises offered for those who "overcome" those problems. As Christ speaks to the churches, we see a pattern for correcting problems involving others. This chastening pattern reveals the Savior's character; it also provides an example for our own families or callings. The prototype consists of three basic steps:

1. Praise for the positive.
2. Correction of the negative.
3. Promises offered if the transgressions are overcome. (These promises are often directly related to the problem being faced.)

Praise before correction creates an atmosphere where the transgressor is more likely to respond favorably to the censure that follows. Promises extended after the rebuke leaves hope and motivation to apply the given counsel. Many times, I have regretted not following this divine format. Often in our human weakness we go directly to number 2 with vigor, passing lightly over numbers 1 and 3, if we touch on them at all. As you read the second and third chapters, pay attention to this general configuration. Also bear in mind that components from the first description of the Savior in chapter 1 are repeated, thus giving them added significance. These are definitely qualities the Lord wants us to understand about his nature.

EPHESUS

Ephesus is praised for her "works . . . labour . . . patience." She has also resisted the deceptions of false "apostles," the teachings of an apostate group called "the Nicolaitans," and "not fainted" under apparent opposition. (Revelation 2:2–3, 6.) For these things she is praised. She is corrected for having "left [her] first love" and accordingly admonished to "do the first works." (Revelation 2:4–5.)

One of the chief metaphorical relationships between the

Savior and his church is that of a bride and bridegroom. This comparison is especially strong in the Old Testament and in Revelation. I let my mind run back to the time in my life when I was immersed in "first love." Those days of courtship, engagement, and sharing the companionship of new life in marriage were some of the sweetest in memory. My life was centered on the woman I loved. I tried to please her, brought her gifts, and wanted to spend my whole time in her company. Her needs were paramount in the circle of my concerns. First love suggests a priority position in the heart. There is something compelling about first love and the works that go with it. Even a casual survey of the Savior's attention to us, his bride, will reveal his eagerness to act according to the demands of first love.

When the fullness of the gospel draws us into a covenant relationship with the Savior, we often respond in a religious way to the exigencies of first love. With hearts full of gratitude, we direct our attention to pleasing the Lord, offering him the "works" of obedience, faithfulness, service, and prayer. We are naturally "anxiously engaged in a good cause." (D&C 58:27.) Far too often in marriage, as well as in devotion to God, time takes its toll, and the early joys once expressed in acts of kindness to each other fade quietly and slowly away. Emotion, though often demandingly intense, is not stable. Love, as well as faith, must be maintained by an act of the will. We desire the ability to endure and take the necessary actions to ensure love's continuation. Our love is reinforced by daily commitment and selflessness. If consistent attention is not riveted to the bond, it will die, and our rationalizing minds begin to justify its death by assuming that we made a wrong choice in the first place, thus blaming our own failure to nourish faith or love on circumstances beyond our control. This is as true of testimony as it is of marriage.

Should the Saints in Ephesus find the motivation to overcome this natural human tendency, by throwing off their growing apathy, they will have the promise of enduring love with God: "To him that overcometh will I give to eat of the tree of life, which is in the midst of the paradise of God." (Revelation 2:7.) We learn from Nephi that the tree of life represents God's love. The promise for overcoming is linked directly with the needed correction. It is also linked to the words Jesus used in his initial introduction to the Saints of Ephesus. He now repeats the loving image of holding the stars in his hand and dwelling in the midst of the candlesticks.

SMYRNA

The Saints of Smyrna faced intense persecution and struggled under the burden of poverty. The Savior here assures them he is aware of these challenges. "Fear none of those things which thou shalt suffer," he tells them. It is all part of the testing of life. As he comforted Joseph Smith in Liberty Jail with the certainty that his trials would last "but a small moment" (D&C 121:7), the Lord tells the suffering Saints of Smyrna that their tribulations will last "ten days" only, meaning a short time. If they will remain faithful even "unto death" a "crown of life" awaits them: "He that overcometh shall not be hurt of the second death." (Revelation 2:9–11.) The repeated aspect of Christ's character as found in the first chapter addresses their present crisis, for he reassures them, "These things saith the first and the last, which was *dead, and is alive.*" (Revelation 2:8; italics added.) Death is not the culmination of life. Jesus himself suffered the full fury of persecution's rage, but the consummation of Calvary was brief—the dawn of eternal life awaited him in the Garden Tomb.

The pattern of chastening is broken somewhat in this message. There are no problems to correct but rather encouragement to be given, lest the present sufferings turn the Saints from their chosen path. The rewards that await them will far outweigh the present difficulties. Though physical death may be their fate, spiritual death (second death) will forever be avoided. We learn from the Book of Mormon that to die the second death means to die "as to things pertaining unto righteousness." (Alma 12:16; see also Helaman 14:18.)

Once again the promise for overcoming is linked to the situation at hand. The truth we are to receive from Smyrna is the realization that the promised crown more than equals the present cross. Paul, who knew something of suffering for the truth's sake, told the Roman Saints, "I reckon that the sufferings of this present time are not worthy to be compared with the glory which shall be revealed in us." (Romans 8:18.) Since Paul suffered tremendous persecution during his life (see 2 Corinthians 11:23–33) yet was also "caught up to the third heaven" (2 Corinthians 12:2), we may trust his conclusion regarding their comparison.

The reassuring belief that eternal joys outweigh mortal stress is comforting, but the Savior offers another counsel. We might miss it in a quick reading of the text. After speaking of the people's poverty, the Lord adds, "but thou art rich." We need not wait for future crowns, the Savior seems to say; the knowledge, fruits, and blessings of the gospel provide their own present rewards.

I grew up in San Bernardino, California. Because I was small, I was often the object of bullying. In addition, I shared all the insecurities of a teenager and carry numerous unpleasant memories of the fears I harbored during those years. I went to junior high school and high school afraid nearly every day. When I left for college, I never looked back.

Occasionally I return to my hometown, and the pilgrimage always brings back the memories of the adversities of the past. I must admit I sometimes indulge in the syrupy-sweet, sickly pleasure of self-pity. One year while entertaining these thoughts, the Spirit whispered a wholly unexpected truth: "You were the luckiest boy ever to grow up in San Bernardino, California." The message came so emphatically that I could not pass it off as inconsequential. However, I did not believe what I was hearing, and I argued with the Lord. "Not so! Not so!" I countered, reminding the Lord of many sad moments. Then came the reality I needed to hear. It is the same certainty offered to the Saints of Smyrna in those four single-syllable words, "but thou art rich." The Lord countered my objection with, "You had the gospel of Jesus Christ in all its fullness, and a mother who knew it was true and taught it to you."

Perhaps for the first time in my life, I saw my youth through the eyes of God, and he was right. Though persecution even unto death raged for the church at Smyrna, they were still the richest people in the Roman Empire; they had the gospel—and that gospel not only blessed their present lives but would also give them eternal life if they remained on the narrow path they were asked to walk.

Pergamos

Pergamos is commended for its constancy in the face of martyrdom: "Thou holdest fast my name, and hast not denied my faith, even in those days wherein Antipas was my faithful martyr." (Revelation 2:13.) Their problem lies in the acceptance of certain worldly doctrines and practices by some of their members, particularly immorality. Some also harbor sympathy with the Nicolaitans, whose beliefs the Lord "hate[s]." Lest these deceptive beliefs spread, they must be addressed.

In offering his correcting advice, the Lord refers to the Old Testament story of Balaam and Balak, found in Numbers chapters 22 through 24 and 31. Reference is made to this story in Jude and 2 Peter also. (See 2 Peter 2:15–16; Jude 1:11.) It is most helpful in coming to a full understanding of Revelation to read the story. Balaam, eager to receive the honors of men and the rewards they offered, went against the protective counsel of God. Though for a time he was true to the messages imparted through him to Balak, the Moabite king, in time his lust for worldly honors corrupted him as he tempted the Israelites with the immoral beliefs and practices of a fallen Canaanite world.

In the context of today, a modern Balaam would be eager to compromise the teachings and positions of the Church to obtain the honors of men. Modern Balaams are keenly interested in "political correctness" at the expense of doctrinal purity. In Pergamos, those corrupting influences related to the looser morals of the Greek world. The Balaams of today want the Church to change its views on such subjects as abortion, marriage, homosexuality, and the roles of men and women. The Proclamation on the Family signals the righteous response of the Church to the pressures of a Balaam-directed view.

The Lord introduced his message to Pergamos by reminding them that the counsel given them comes from "he which hath the sharp sword with two edges." (Revelation 2:12.) The sword from the mouth of the Savior is truth. Notice that the proper way to combat the "doctrine of Balaam" is with the truth:

"Repent; or else I will come unto thee quickly, and will fight against them with the sword of my mouth." (Revelation 2:16.) Worldly philosophies are best opposed with the truth. Speaking of the false educational ideas that from time to time rival the faith of the Saints, Spencer W. Kimball once said, "We do not resist such ideas because we fear them, but because they are false." (Spencer W. Kimball, *Teachings of Spencer W. Kimball* [Salt Lake City: Bookcraft, 1982], 400.)

Since it is false ideas that must be overcome in Pergamos, the promise for overcoming is, once again, related to their problem. Knowledge is the central theme of the blessings that await them: "To him that overcometh will I give to eat of the hidden manna, and will give him a white stone, and in the stone a new name written, which no man knoweth saving he that receiveth it." (Revelation 2:17.)

Moses revealed to the children of Israel that manna was given them so they might learn "that man doth not live by bread only, but by every word that proceedeth out of the mouth of the Lord." (Deuteronomy 8:3.) As the sword is an image of God's words and truth, so too was the manna. "Hidden manna" means sacred knowledge not given to the world. A modern example of hidden manna is the knowledge we receive in the ordinances of the House of the Lord.

The white stone also suggests the reception of deeper knowledge concerning God's wisdom. Fortunately for us, the Prophet Joseph Smith spoke about the white stone in the Doctrine and Covenants: "The white stone mentioned in Revelation 2:17, will become a Urim and Thummim to each individual who receives one, whereby things pertaining to a higher order of kingdoms will be made known; and a white stone is given to each of those who come into the celestial kingdom." (D&C 130:10–11.)

As stated earlier, in Hebrew, adding *im* to a word makes it plural. *Ur* means light, so *Urim* means "lights." *Thummim* is the plural of *perfection,* rendering the word *perfections.* The Urim and Thummim is a revelatory instrument that enables the bearer to receive light in all its perfections. In the scriptures, light is interchangeable with truth, wisdom, intelligence, knowledge, spirit, and glory. (See D&C 88:66; 93:36.) It can bestow hidden manna. If we reject the false wisdom and knowledge of the world, even though it represents the popular, accepted thinking of the day, higher truth and greater intelligence will be available.

The Lord mentioned a new name that would be associated with the white stone. In section 130 of the Doctrine and Covenants, Joseph Smith called this new name a "key word." (D&C 130:11.) These are sacred matters not appropriately discussed in a published work. However, since the idea of a new name is a repeated aspect of Revelation and a common scriptural practice, some general comments are in order.

A new name can suggest a number of different realities. It connotes a new station or major change in life, such as birth, marriage, or baptism into Christ's family. Names are received in each situation. It suggests a beginning, a cleansing, a fresh start, a renewal or awakening. Anyone who has done genealogy understands the connection between the old practice of christening (naming) a child and the cleansing ordinance of baptism. New names may also suggest a graduation of some sort, a testing period completed, the proving of an initiate. The dubbing of a knight in the medieval world is an example of this type of naming. In Genesis, Jacob's name was changed to Israel after he wrestled with an angel and prevailed with God. Abram became Abraham and Sarai became Sarah after long years of faithful obedience and righteousness.

All of the above may apply to the new name mentioned several times in Revelation, but perhaps the closest corollary would be the crowning of a king or queen. The new name becomes the coronation name. This application is also seen in religious offices or priestly names. For instance, in the Catholic Church each new pope assumes a different name. Many of the promises offered to the churches for overcoming worldly obstacles contain coronation imagery. Those of Smyrna receive a crown; those of Thyatira rule over many kingdoms: those of Laodicea are seated on a throne. The new name promised the Saints of Pergamos is also associated with knowledge, for once in a position of authority and dominion, a ruler receives enlightenment unique to the new appointment.

The name is not revealed, for it is sacred; it is given by God to the worthy individual and is not to be shared with the world. Sacred things brought out for open discussion may be compromised or cheapened. The new name is to be treasured, for it promises a renewed life and an ultimate coronation in the future. Those who receive such a name know their destiny. They know who they are, and that knowledge becomes a protective shield, an inner assurance to warm the heart, an intimate friendship between God and his children.

THYATIRA

Thyatira is commended for her "service, and faith, and [her] patience, and . . . works; and the last to be more than the first." Apparently the waning enthusiasm for the gospel found in Ephesus has no place in Thyatira. Her flaw is similar to that of

Pergamos: "I have a few things against thee, because thou sufferest that woman Jezebel, which calleth herself a prophetess, to teach and to seduce my servants." (Revelation 2:19–20.) The seduction centered, as in Pergamos, on certain practices of the Greek world. Jesus introduces himself to Thyatira by reminding them of the pure aspects of his nature. As he is pure, he would have his church free of corruption.

We might stop and ask ourselves a question at this juncture. Is the woman's name really Jezebel, or has the Lord alluded to Ahab's corrupting wife, Jezebel? I favor the latter reading. When arriving at this point in your study of Revelation, you might want to review the life of this Old Testament queen. John anticipates that we know the story of Jezebel and how she introduced the worship of Baal into the religious beliefs of Israel. She is the female counterpart, in some ways, to Balaam. If we know the details of her life, the Lord's words to the Saints of Thyatira contain a deeper warning than their surface implies.

Jezebel was cast out of a window to her death at the command of Jehu, who later purged Israel of Ahab's and Jezebel's descendants. (See 2 Kings 9–10.) Jezebel's daughter, Athaliah, was also executed in Jerusalem. In Revelation, the Jezebel of Thyatira will be "cast into hell," says the Lord, "and I will kill her children [her followers] with death." (Revelation 2:22–23, JST.) Of course, the death referred to here is a spiritual one. Knowing the fate of Jezebel and her family gives a certain ironic power to the message offered the Saints of Thyatira.

The promises for overcoming have been considerably changed by Joseph Smith. We will need to turn to the Joseph Smith Translation for the corrected version of the verses: "And to him who overcometh, and keepeth my commandments unto the end, will I give power over many kingdoms; and he shall rule them with the word of God; and they shall be in his hands as the vessels of clay in the hands of a potter; and he shall govern them by faith, with equity and justice, even as I received of my Father." (Revelation 2:26–27, JST.)

This reading is much more benign than that found in the King James translation of Revelation, and it encompasses a more eternal fulfillment. The timeless dominions promised the faithful will be ruled with the majesty of God's word, not the rod of the hand that beats and drives in the manner of earthly kingdoms. With the skill of a potter softly shaping his clay, the "overcoming" monarchs of eternity's endless kingdoms will guide and form their realms with equity and justice. They will be able to do this for they will have Jesus as their model and teacher: "And I will give him the morning star." (Revelation 2:28.) In the clear light of that radiance, worlds without number will continue to roll into existence through the gentle tutoring of One who learned his own kingly demeanor from his Father.

SARDIS

The problem in Sardis appears to be one of shallowness and hypocrisy. The expression "thou hast a name that thou livest, and art dead" suggests that in Sardis they have the reputation of being Saints, the title of Saints, but inwardly the light of devotion is almost extinguished. They are Saints in name only.

The correction comes first in this message, rather than following a point of praise, but in Sardis only a few things remain to commend, and even these areas of faith need strengthening. (See Revelation 3:2–3.) After the correction, however, with kindlier tones, the Savior speaks of those who do not fall under the earlier general condemnation: "Thou hast a few names even in Sardis which have not defiled their garments; and they shall

40

walk with me in white: for they are worthy. He that over-cometh, the same shall be clothed in white raiment; and I will not blot out his name out of the book of life, but I will confess his name before my Father, and before his angels." (Revelation 3:4–5.) Defiling one's garments means the breaking or ignoring of covenants. The clean garments of our covenants will one day result in celestial garments of white where companionship with Christ will be its own reward.

A key word we can center on in the instructions to Sardis is "name." When we become members of Christ's kingdom, our names are written in his book of life. Our quest is to keep them there. If we will be members in thought, word, and deed as well as in name, not only will they remain in Christ's book, but he will also speak our names in gladness before his Father. This confessing of his followers' names can be read in two ways: (1) a pleading in our behalf, as is found in Doctrine and Covenants 45:3–5 ("Father, spare these my brethren that believe on my name, that they may come unto me and have everlasting life"), or (2) the fellowship suggested by Paul, who wrote, "Both he that sanctifieth and they who are sanctified are all of one: for which cause he is not ashamed to call them brethren." (Hebrews 2:11.)

PHILADELPHIA

Much to the joy of the Saints of Philadelphia, the Lord mentions no corrections for them. They receive only praise and encouragement. They have kept his word and refused to deny his name, for which he will keep them in the future times of trial and temptation.

The Lord makes several promises to strengthen them for the times to come: "Him that overcometh will I make a pillar in the temple of my God, and he shall go no more out: and I will write upon him the name of my God, and the name of the city of my God, which is new Jerusalem, which cometh down out of heaven from my God: and I will write upon him my new name." (Revelation 3:12.)

Paul referred to Peter, James, and John as "pillars" of the Church. (See Galatians 2:9.) A pillar holds the weight of the building. If we keep in mind the beauty of Greek and Roman edifices, the image becomes more striking. The word suggests responsibility, leadership, and weight in Christ's dominion. It also suggests permanency, especially when coupled with the phrase "he shall go no more out." This is the last testing period. As Paul said of his own life, the battle is almost won; the race nears its end, the open door issues an inviting welcome, the celestial radiance already warms the face. Once admitted back into the temple of our Father, we will never leave again. There will assuredly be much to learn, but the outcome in our own minds will never again be in doubt.

I remember what comfort I felt as a doctoral candidate preparing to take my orals when I realized this would be the last test I would ever take. It gave me a sense of confidence, for the end was in sight. Only one final hurdle was left to clear. I prepared for it with vigor, energy, and excitement. What wonderful hope is found in those simple words "go no more out."

To place a name on something is to claim it as one's own. If we have the name of our God upon us, then we belong to him. To carry the name of a city or nation denotes citizenship in that city or nation. The new name of Christ is his coronation name. It is mentioned in chapter 19 of Revelation in connection with his wearing many crowns and coming in glory to rule and reign on the earth. (See Revelation 19:11–16.) To have this name upon us implies that we will share in his coming glory as members of his ruling family.

King Benjamin signifies that the day will come when we will be called forth by the Savior, and he will call us in his own name—the name we took upon ourselves in baptism and renewed each Sabbath in the sacrament. He counsels us on how to maintain forever the imprint of all those names mentioned to the Church in Philadelphia. "Remember to retain the name written always in your hearts," he urges, "that ye hear and know the voice by which ye shall be called, and also, the name by which he shall call you. For how knoweth a man the master *whom he has not served, and who is a stranger unto him, and is far from the thoughts and intents of his heart?*" (Mosiah 5:12–13; italics added.) Our constant focus on the Father's will, our Savior's commands, and the laws of Zion allows the names to impart all desired blessings.

LAODICEA

If the Saints at Philadelphia receive no reproof, those of Laodicea obtain no approbation. They are the recipients of the severest admonition: "Thou art neither cold nor hot: I would thou wert cold or hot. So then because thou art lukewarm, and neither cold nor hot, I will spue thee out of my mouth." (Revelation 3:15–16.) The zeal of Laodicea has been quenched in a new thirst, that of wealth, fine clothes, and the vain things of life. "Increased with goods," they feel they "have need of nothing." (Revelation 3:17.) There is nothing like wealth and success to silence the ardor of faith. They are not against God's kingdom; they just feel it is now an extraneous element of their lives. Moses warned the children of Israel that "goodly houses" and the multiplication of temporal blessings inevitably lead to "forget[ting] the Lord." (Deuteronomy 8:11–14.)

Among all the problems of the seven churches, the Laodiciean hindrance is one to which we, in our affluent age, must pay close attention. "Buy of me gold tried in the fire," the Lord counsels, "that thou mayest be rich; and white raiment that thou mayest be clothed." (Revelation 3:18.) We know from the Doctrine and Covenants that the riches of which the Lord speaks are those of knowledge and wisdom, for he offers this counsel several times: "Seek not for riches but for wisdom, and behold, the mysteries of God shall be unfolded unto you, and then shall you be made rich. Behold, he that hath eternal life is rich." (D&C 6:7; 11:7.)

In Doctrine and Covenants 121 the Lord instructs his priesthood leaders about reproof. At times correction is required, but afterward we must show an "increase of love," lest the corrected one "esteem [us] to be his enemy; that he may know that [our] faithfulness is stronger than the cords of death." (D&C 121:43–44.) The Lord always obeys his own rules, and we find a perfect example of this counsel in the last verses of Revelation 3. Though he has bluntly and without hesitation rebuked Laodicea, he ends with love: "As many as I love, I rebuke and chasten: be zealous therefore, and repent." This is followed by one of the most famous verses in Revelation: "I stand at the door, and knock: if any man hear my voice, and open the door, I will come in to him, and will sup with him, and he with me." (Revelation 3:19–20.)

The divine humility pulsing from this image is sometimes overwhelming. Two doors are described in Revelation 3. In verse 8 we see the Lord's door. It is open, inviting, welcoming; it will not be shut. The door in verse 20 is the door to our hearts and lives. It is shut, but rather than waiting for our needs to drive us to his door, the Savior comes gently knocking at our own. Not only does he knock, but he also calls out, softly imploring us to open that we may share in a feast of love, truth, and friendship. Several ideas come to mind here. We may not open the door because we do not recognize the voice that calls out to us. Remember, King Benjamin indicated that the Savior must be close to the thoughts and intents of the heart. We have heard his calling voice so many times in the past that we open quickly, for he is a trusted friend.

Another idea is found in Luke's gospel. Luke recorded an earlier teaching of the Savior about his knocking at our doors, one that magnifies Christ's divine humility four-fold. (We will make reference to it again in the closing chapters of Revelation when discussing the wedding supper of the Lamb.) It is given in the same context as the Laodicean fascination with wealth: "Sell that ye have, and give alms; provide yourselves bags which wax not old, a treasure in the heavens that faileth not, where no thief approacheth , neither moth corrupteth. For where your treasure is, there will your heart be also. Let your loins be girded about, and your lights burning; and ye yourselves like unto men that wait for their lord, when he will return from the wedding; that when *he cometh and knocketh,* they may open unto him *immediately.* Blessed are those servants, whom the lord when he cometh shall find watching: verily I say unto you, that *he shall gird himself, and make them to sit down to meat, and will come forth and serve them.*" (Luke 12:33–37; italics added.)

Luke's account gives us added insight as to why the door in Revelation 3:20 is shut. If an honored, respected guest suddenly showed up at our door and began to knock, what condition in the house might move us to call out, "Just a minute!" instead of opening "immediately." I can imagine the hurried rush to straighten things out, picking up items on the floor, cleaning and adjusting the room so it is suitable for visitation. An immediate opening of the door suggests that the room is spotless, ready to receive a long-awaited and beloved guest.

The reward for this constant vigilance is inestimable. The guest has brought a feast with him. More amazing still, not only does he provide the feast, but he also "girds himself," bidding us to sit that he might serve those who responded to his knocking and opened the door to his considerate calls. We will talk about the contents of the feast in a later chapter of Revelation. It is well worth the opening of our doors.

But the shared supper is not the only promise extended to the Laodiceans if they shift their zealous search for riches to that of eternal truths: "To him that overcometh will I grant to sit with me in my throne, even as I also overcame, and am set down with my Father in his throne." (Revelation 3:21.) The wealth of the universe is offered in exchange for the wealth of this world. Only those who are truly blind would choose the temporal over the eternal, but then the Savior's chastening words told the Laodiceans that in reality they were "wretched, and miserable, and poor, and blind, and naked." (Revelation 3:17.)

THE WHOLE GREATER THAN THE PARTS

Each of the concerns facing the members of the seven churches of Asia are shared, to a greater or lesser degree, by you and me today. The strength to overcome them is offered by the Savior, and we will receive an endowment of power by contemplating all of the promises together. We may feast upon the fruit of the tree of life, eternally partaking of the Savior's love in his paradise. The hidden manna of never-ending truth will be manifest continually before our eyes. With the Savior as our example, we will mold and shape our own eternal dominions, ruling them with God's words and receiving the joy of their progression. We will hear Christ speak our names with joy in the presence of our Father while dressed in robes made white with his atoning blood. Their names will be upon us, and as citizens of the New Jerusalem we will enjoy the company of all the Saints from dispensations past, holding positions of responsibility and trust. We will sit on the throne of the King of Kings and God of Gods. For these blessings and many more, can we not open the door when we hear the voice of the Master?

Since many of the images and events of Revelation that follow in succeeding chapters are quite sobering, portraying the trials, sufferings, and difficulties that so often dominate mortal life, it is imperative that we keep always before us the promises outlined in the individual messages to the seven churches. We look beyond the storms to the rainbow of light awaiting those who endure. Chapters 2 and 3 thus provide a context of hope to strengthen us as we proceed through the rest of Revelation.

❦

THE FATHER AND
THE SON

Chapter 3 of Revelation ends with an invitation for all who overcome to sit upon the throne of Christ as he sits upon the throne of his Father. Even though a heading separates chapters 3 and 4, they obviously share a continuation of thought. A door is opened, and John is invited to pass through it that he might see "things which must be hereafter." The first thing he sees, however, is "a throne . . . set in heaven." (Revelation 4:1–2.) Since a throne is promised the faithful, this vision follows naturally the messages to the seven churches, and it is designed, among other things, to encourage and inspire hope. It is as if the Savior were saying, "Here is the goal for which you are laboring!"

The Father takes center stage in chapter 4. The Son's role with the Father dominates chapter 5. These two chapters, working together, form the preface to the main revelation that follows. The Father and Son are the sources of the knowledge that will be given to John and, through him, to all of us. These chapters teach that God is the ultimate power in the universe. His will *will* be accomplished on earth as it is in heaven, when all is said and done. We can appeal to him for help when all earthly thrones fail us or when confronted with the false supremacy of temporal sovereignty.

The description of the throne of God the Father is, point for point, similar to that in the vision of Ezekiel. (See Ezekiel 1.) What would the Father have us understand about Him as revealed in these visions? Both Ezekiel and John describe the glory of the Father using images of light, rainbows, and precious gems. God is a being of light, is the source of light, and lives in the midst of light. *Light* in the scriptures is synonymous with *truth* and *intelligence*. The word *crystal* is used in both Ezekiel and later chapters of Revelation. Like a prism splitting the light of the sun into its many rainbow colors, God's throne is resplendent in the multifaceted beauty of eternal truth. The world's rulers may puzzle in darkness or seek answers by the dim light of human exigencies, but the Father is the most enlightened of all monarchs. Where he dwells there is only brilliance, only clarity. There are no shadows.

John's rainbow is "like unto an emerald," emphasizing green, the color of life. Ezekiel's displays the full colors "as the appearance of the bow that is in the cloud in the day of rain." (Revelation 4:3; Ezekiel 1:28.) Since a rainbow presents light in one of its most beautiful manifestations, a rainbow surrounding the Father is most appropriate. One aspect of eternal truth and the attributes of the Father appear to be displayed here. The rainbow has strong associations with the mercy of the Father. This is seen as early as the flood. In the midst of storm, God's light, truth, and mercy ever bend back to the earth, touching it softly in healing wonder. Because of the nature of all that follows in Revelation, the memory and message of the encircling rainbow must be held firm in the heart's holding place of highest aspirations.

THE TWENTY-FOUR ELDERS

In the vision, the throne of the Father consists of three things, represented by the twenty-four elders, the sea of glass, and the four beasts. According to Doctrine and Covenants 77, the twenty-four elders "had been faithful in the work of the ministry and were dead; who belonged to the seven churches." (D&C 77:5.) The Joseph Smith Translation makes an important change. These elders are not sitting "round about the throne" but "in the midst of the throne." (Revelation 4:4, footnote a.) They have crowns on their heads, for they rule and reign with the Father and are dressed in white, signifying victory and purity.

God's throne includes, first and foremost, exalted beings. This is his work and his glory, and its fruits are prominently displayed. Hope and encouragement come from understanding that these beings came from the seven churches. These are ordinary members of the kingdom, coming from its many scattered branches. If we were to see a vision of the paradise of God, the celestial kingdom, and within those glorified confines we saw members of our own wards enjoying eternal life with the Father—members we served with, home taught, and sat next to in sacrament meeting—would that not inspire us to believe in our own everlasting possibilities? If Brother Allred, Sister Curtis, and the Thomas family were there, might not God's mercy embrace my family also? Have we not strived to be faithful as they were faithful? Would not our hope increase even more to see members from each of the wards of our stake?

The number "twenty-four" may impart additional strength to these thoughts. It is a number associated with priesthood in the Old Testament. Even today, twenty-four teachers comprise a full quorum. In 1 Chronicles, "the sons of Aaron" were separated by David into twenty-four different divisions, each taking turns with the ordinances "of the house of God." (1 Chronicles 24:1–19.) All were invited to participate and thus exercise their priesthood equally at the temple. The number twenty-four may suggest an elder from each of the divisions that were designated by family lineage.

The seven lamps burning before the throne add to the idea of the exalted station of man also, for Joseph Smith substitutes the word "servants" for "Spirits" in verse 5, one from each church. They are burning lamps of fire before the throne, adding their own eternal light to the general blaze of heaven, as do both the Father and the Son.

Let us skip down a few verses to see what the twenty-four elders do: "The four and twenty elders fall down before him that sat on the throne, and worship him that liveth for ever and ever, and *cast their crowns before the throne*, saying, Thou art worthy, O Lord, to receive glory and honour and power: for thou hast created all things, and for thy pleasure they are and were created." (Revelation 4:10–11; italics added.)

As members of the Church, we assert the truthfulness of Joseph Smith's teaching that the destiny of man is to become like God—to do what God does, sharing God's power and knowledge. Our Father in Heaven does three major things of which we are aware: he begets children, he creates worlds where they may learn and progress, and, in time, he exalts them, thus providing for their eternal happiness.

If you and I fulfill the measure of our creation, we will

follow our Father's example. I am therefore deeply impressed by the actions of the twenty-four elders in placing their crowns at the feet of the Father. It suggests the prime motivation that will cause us to do the works of God throughout the eternities. Surely, you and I will beget, create, and exalt that our own eternal children may find happiness. Do we not then present those worlds to our Father in Heaven to add to his glory, honor, and power? We will participate in this great work in the spirit of gratitude, love, and devotion to One who offers to us his own throne. Our crowns for his throne—the exchange of kings, but surely we receive the deeper blessing in this sharing of dominions, this celestial order of consecration.

THE SEA OF GLASS

Joseph Smith taught that the sea of glass "is the earth, in its sanctified, immortal, and eternal state." (D&C 77:1.) Later he added, "This earth, in its sanctified and immortal state, will be made like unto crystal and will be a Urim and Thummim to the inhabitants who dwell thereon." (D&C 130:9.)

Students are sometimes troubled by these descriptions, asking questions like "Will there be color?" "Won't it be too much of one thing?" Sometimes they have linked the crystal earth with another prophecy that speaks of the mountains being leveled and the valleys raised. The combination projects an image of one great glass Kansas in their minds. I try to remind them that we are living on a fallen, telestial, world and that the future world will be an exalted, celestial one. If we loved the beauty and variety of this one, the "new heaven and new earth" will be even more wonderful. The Lord has also promised that when "the old things shall pass away," we will lose nothing of his original creation, for "the heaven and the earth, and all the fulness thereof, both men and beasts, the fowls of the air, and the fishes of the sea; and not one hair, neither mote, shall be lost." (D&C 29:23–25.)

Crystal and glass are often used to represent God's celestial world, for they are not susceptible to decay or change. If we buried a glass bowl in the earth and dug it up a thousand years later, it would not have deteriorated. Crystal also suggests purity, a clarity born of the heat of refining fires. When the earth is sanctified, all the impurities that once had dominion upon it will be gone, and this extends to every object of creation.

The fact that the earth serves as a Urim and Thummim is also wonderfully instructive. As we learned earlier, *Urim* means "lights" and *Thummim* means "perfections." The whole earth, and everything on it, will exist and be understood in all its perfections. If we can live worthy of that celestial sphere, the truths of each living thing, every law of nature, every life cycle from the smallest insect to the greatest whale, from the tiniest crystals in the depths of the earth to the laws of continents and the forces of weather will be manifest to us. As glass is transparent, so too will this earth cease to hide its secrets—secrets that once required long years of research, testing, experimentation, and observation to uncover. A crystal earth, a Urim and Thummim world, is a sphere of light, truth, intelligence, beauty, perfection, purity, and endless, open knowledge. Before the throne of God such worlds turn through the eternities.

THE FOUR BEASTS

The four beasts John was shown are part and parcel of the sea of glass, as if the Lord magnified a part of that totality of creation and showed John a tiny sliver of it. When Joseph Smith was asked the meaning of the four beasts, he answered, "They are figurative expressions, used by the Revelator, John, in describing heaven, the paradise of God, *the happiness* of man, *and of beasts,* and of creeping things, and of the fowls of the air." (D&C 77:2; italics added.)

When I was a boy, I loved small animals and other living creatures. I was especially fond of "creeping things," the lizards, snakes, frogs, crabs, insects, and rodents I would bring home after foraging through the fields or along the seacoast. My mother never told me to take my treasures out of the house. She stooped down to my level, cupped her hands beneath mine, and asked, "Which of Heavenly Father's little creatures did you bring home today, Son?" I grew up believing that God was wonderful because he created a playmate as marvelous as a lizard. It often pained me to see other boys treating cruelly a living thing. A deep part of me loves God intensely because he is concerned about the "happiness of creeping things." We worship a Father who wants butterflies and beetles, geckoes and giraffes, swallows and seagulls to be merry. Did not his son remind us that not even sparrows fall without our Father's notice?

The four beasts were "limited to four individual beasts, which were shown to John, to represent the glory of the classes of beings in their destined order or sphere of creation, *in the enjoyment of their eternal felicity.*" (D&C 77:3; italics added.) "Felicity" is a certain kind of happiness. The word suggests celebration—holiday happiness. It is the joy of festivals, feasts, and jubilees. School is out! Graduation has arrived! The vacation has begun! Every schoolchild knows this euphoria. In his love for his creations, man as well as beast, the Father provides ceaseless delight. A great part of that enjoyment comes from the freedom and knowledge granted them, which is represented by the eyes and wings: "Their eyes are a representation of light and

54

knowledge, that is, they are full of knowledge; and their wings are a representation of power, to move, to act, etc." (D&C 77:4.) What great doctrine we are being taught here! Liberty and light, freedom and intelligence, when properly applied, are the true sources of felicity. They are offered to each and every mote of creation.

If we come to understand, even in a small degree, God's designs and feelings for his "workmanship," our own respect for all life increases. We have been given "dominion over the fish of the sea, and over the fowl of the air, and over every living thing that moveth upon the earth." (Genesis 1:28.) I think it worthy of reflection that the Lord specified animals, not land or earthly resources, as the subject of our dominion. From the vantage point of John's revelation, it is easy to see that *dominion* means to care for all things in an appreciative, solicitous manner, even as God cares for them. As we do this, we will be more hesitant to take life unnecessarily, more willing to accommodate our own need to subdue the earth at the expense of other species that inhabit it.

The particular beasts chosen may have been selected because of their representative associations. The lion is called the king of beasts and causes us to think of wild creatures; the calf's innocence turns the mind to the usefulness and friendship of domestic animals; the face of a man suggests thought; and the eagle's dignity and swiftness represents the free world of birds. Strength, gentleness, intelligence, and movement are all incorporated to stand for the world of animals.

As I ponder the three things that constitute the throne of God, exalted people, sanctified worlds, and glorified animals, I find it easy to understand why the four beasts "rest not day and night, saying, Holy, holy, holy, Lord God Almighty, which was, and is, and is to come. . . . Those beasts give glory and honour and thanks to him that sat on the throne, who liveth for ever and ever." (Revelation 4:8–9.) Are we not also glad that such a Being will always exist, eternity to eternity, worlds without end?

THE BOOK WITH THE SEVEN SEALS

I n the right hand of God John sees a "book written within and on the backside, sealed with seven seals." (Revelation 5:1.) The book, undoubtedly a scroll, has writing on both sides of the parchment. In one of the most critical commentaries on the book of Revelation, Joseph Smith tells us what the book represents: "It contains the *revealed will, mysteries, and the works of God;* the hidden things of his economy concerning this earth during the seven thousand years of its continuance, or its temporal existence." The seven seals, therefore, correspond to the seven dispensations of time. "The first seal contains the things of the first thousand years, and the second also of the second thousand years, and so on until the seventh." (D&C 77:6–7; italics added.)

One is sought for who is worthy to open the book, loose its seals, and look thereon. No one is found worthy, not even the "strong angel," and John weeps. John's sorrow is not from thwarted curiosity about the contents of the book. Let us ask ourselves, What is the work and the will of God concerning this earth in each of its dispensations? Since his work and glory center on the immortality and eternal life of man, he desires that all mankind be redeemed from the Fall; have the opportunity, through the exercise of their moral agency, to choose eternal life; and, in time, inherit this earth in a sanctified, glorified, and purified state. This must be done without the violation of eternal law or agency, for God will not break his own rules. God's wisdom consists of his ability to bring about his will, to establish "his economy," without intruding on the agency of man. Man can accomplish his designs by impinging on agency, but God will not do so.

Joseph Smith stated the resolve of the Father as it was revealed to him in the following manner: "Therefore, it [the earth] must needs be sanctified from all unrighteousness, that it may be prepared for the celestial glory; for after it hath filled the measure of its creation, it shall be crowned with glory, even with the presence of God the Father; that bodies who are of the celestial kingdom may possess it forever and ever; for, for this intent was it made and created, and for this intent are they [God's children] sanctified." (D&C 88:18–20.)

A SLAIN LAMB—HIS HORNS AND EYES

The weeping John is comforted with the knowledge that "the Lion . . . of Juda, the Root of David, hath prevailed to open the book and to loose the seven seals thereof." (Revelation 5:5.) These are both titles for Christ. In today's language we would probably use the word *branch* instead of *root*, as Jesus was a descendant of David, a branch of his family tree. Jesus alone has the power necessary to see that the Father's desires for this world and its inhabitants are accomplished. He alone can vindicate agency, cleanse the world, overcome evil, and prepare the earth for its celestial future. The visions that follow in the succeeding chapters of Revelation tell the story of the Savior's enemies and how he will overcome them as the Father wishes.

How will Christ accomplish the Father's foreordained will concerning this earth? The answer is found in the next image shown to John: "I beheld, and, lo, in the midst of the throne and of the four beasts, and in the midst of the elders, stood a Lamb as it had been slain." (Revelation 5:6.) The Father's work and will is accomplished in the sacrifice of Jesus. Not as a "lion" do we see his power, but in the innocence and purity of a sacrificial lamb. His atoning mercy is mightier than even "strong" angels. Angels can shake the earth, Alma testified, and they can unleash the winds of destruction, as we will see later in Revelation, but only the Savior could redeem and overcome death. The meekness of a lamb is proved the mightiest power of all. Speaking of the atoning power to cleanse and sanctify, Isaiah called Jesus, "the arm of the Lord," proclaiming that God would "bare his holy arm in the eyes of all the nations; and all the ends of the earth shall see the salvation of our God." (Isaiah 52:10; 53:1.) One bares his arm in order to reveal strength.

Though the weight of mortality's redemption rested on Jesus alone, he would have help in accomplishing the Father's will. The Lamb was shown "having twelve horns and twelve eyes, which are the twelve servants of God, sent forth into all the earth. (Revelation 5:6, JST.) The message of Christ's salvation, which must penetrate every corner of the globe, will spread through the instrumentality of the apostles. We have already discussed the symbolic representation of an apostle as a star; here they are depicted as horns and eyes.

A horn is an extension of an animal's head and symbolized

59

power in the ancient world, like a sword or tool in the hands of a man. Mighty kingdoms or kings were sometimes called horns, as in Daniel 8 or Zechariah 1. In the blessings Moses gave to the tribes, he spoke of Joseph's lineage, comparing them to a bullock whose "horns are like the horns of unicorns [wild oxen]: with them he shall push the people together to the ends of the earth." (Deuteronomy 33:17.) This referred to the gathering of scattered Israel, and the animal's horns are being used as a tool. The head moves the horns, and Christ is the head of his Church, but his apostles are the tools that he uses to spread his gospel, thus sharing in the preparations of the earth and the accomplishment of the Father's will. (See also 1 Samuel 2, footnote 1c.)

Eyes receive light and direct the path or direction of the body. Each conference we sustain fifteen men as prophets, *seers*, and revelators. A full spelling of the word seer would be *see-er*, meaning one that sees. A revelator is one who reveals. The two words together suggest that see-ers reveal what they see. Receiving light and truth for the Church and having a clear vision of God's work (as eyes), the apostles help execute God's will (as horns), providing stable, constant guidance (as stars) for the Saints through the troubled, turbulent history of the world, which will be shown in the continuing chapters of Revelation. Those who have been through the House of the Lord will have additional knowledge to understand the apostle's role as eyes and horns of Christ.

Joseph Smith indicated that the book in the Father's hand also contained the "mysteries . . . of God . . . the hidden things of his economy." (D&C 77:6.) Since he is one with his Father, Jesus knows the Father's mind. He knows the great plan of salvation. He is familiar with all the laws governing creation.

These may be hidden to man but not to the Son of Man. They can be revealed to the seers. Thus Christ has the knowledge to execute the Father's will, the ability to accomplish it through the purity of his life, and the compassionate willingness to see it through to the end. He also has the assistance of his apostles, and to a larger extent all the faithful members of his kingdom. The Father's determination will not be completed until Jesus presents this world to him as a fit abode for celestial beings, even the Father himself, and that is precisely how Revelation ends.

As the Enlightenment developed during the sixteenth and seventeenth centuries, the idea was spread that God had wound up the universe like a clock and was now content to let it run its course. He was no longer deeply involved in the affairs of men. Nature moved along its determined configurations. Revelation asserts that this is not so. God is still intimately involved in his children's destiny, and though his acts are sometimes hidden or mysterious to us, he has prepared all from the beginning to the end and has chosen One to execute it to the last crossing of a *t* or dotting of an *i*.

THE NEW SONG

Knowing it is his Father's desire, Jesus takes the book from his hand. From that moment, the hosts of heaven know that the Father's work will be accomplished. The earth will inherit celestial glory. Sometimes it appears that evil is triumphant. The Lord himself said, "All flesh is corrupted before me; and the powers of darkness prevail upon the earth, among the children of men." (D&C 38:11.) As the seven seals are opened, revealing the history of the world and its dominion of war, famine, plague, hatred, greed, cruelty, apostasy, destruction, pride, and all the other evils we have seen through the long, sad litany of human woes through the ages, we must keep firmly in mind what is implied in that dramatic moment when the Lamb receives the Father's commission and takes the book into his hands. There must be no doubt, lest we foolishly choose the wrong side in the continuing struggle between righteousness and iniquity. Evil will not win; goodness will achieve the mastery. The earth will not diminish in nuclear winter but rise in millennial splendor. Christ, not Lucifer, will claim the earth, and his claim will stand.

With this understanding, the weeping of John is turned into song. There is no need to fear or despair. The twenty-four elders now hold harps for the singing of the "new song" and also "vials full of odours, which are the prayers of [the] saints." (Revelation 5:8.) These are prayers of gratitude that come with the security of ultimate victory. The victory is not only for man but also for the rest of creation; therefore "every creature which is in heaven, and on the earth, and under the earth, and such as are in the sea, and all that are in them" (Revelation 5:13) join in the song of praise.

Even in the idiomatic expressions of our own age, we speak of singing a new tune. It implies that a change has taken place. A new song is a victory song, indicating that things on the earth are not as they were before. Its singing almost always centers on righteousness overcoming opposition. In the Old Testament we see people singing victory songs after the defeat of the Egyptians in the Red Sea (See Exodus 15) and after the demise of Sisera's forces by Deborah and Barak (see Judges 5). Hannah sings a type of new song in 1 Samuel 2, as does Mary in Luke 1. So sure are the hosts of heaven that Christ will bring to pass the Father's designs for his creations that the heavens burst into song at the very taking of the book. "Thou art worthy to take the book, and to open the seals thereof," the song begins, "for thou wast slain, and hast redeemed us to God by thy blood out of every kindred, and tongue, and people, and nation; and hast made us unto our God kings and priests: and we *shall* reign on the earth." (Revelation 5:9–10; italics added.)

The new song is a love song as well as one of triumph. Alma asked his straying members if they had once "experienced a change of heart, and . . . felt to sing the song of redeeming love," did they feel the same way still? (Alma 5:26.) This fits the idea of the new song perfectly, for what greater transformation is there, what more wonderful conquest, than the "mighty change" of heart that leads us to "have no more disposition to do evil, but to do good continually"? (Mosiah 5:2.)

When the Savior went into the spirit world, while his body was in the tomb, a great multitude of the righteous had gathered, awaiting his arrival. They knew that he would soon release them from the bondage of the grave and that they would rise with him in his resurrection. Suddenly "the Son of God appeared, declaring liberty to the captives who had been faithful. . . . And the saints rejoiced in their redemption, and bowed the knee and acknowledged the Son of God as their Redeemer and Deliverer. . . . Their countenances shone, and the radiance from the presence of the Lord rested upon them, *and they sang praises unto his holy name.*" (D&C 138:18, 23–24; italics added.)

Words to the new song were revealed to Joseph Smith and can be found in section 84 of the Doctrine and Covenants, verses 98 through 102, but it is not the words that carry the potency of the event but the emotion of gratitude, love, and joy. Later in Revelation we learn that "no man could learn that song" except those who have been "redeemed from the earth" and have followed "the Lamb whithersoever he goeth." (Revelation 14:3–4.) The words may be given to us in the scriptures, but only love can tune the harp of the heart and bring forth the melodies of gratitude.

"What doth it profit a man if a gift is bestowed upon him, and he receive not the gift?" the Lord asked. "He rejoices not in that which is given unto him, neither rejoices in him who is the giver of the gift." (D&C 88:33.) If we receive the gifts of God, and they are many, no one will need to teach us how to sing the new song, for our souls will open and the divine music issue forth. I have for years loved the last verses of section 128 of the Doctrine and Covenants. Here Joseph Smith, while pondering on the blessing of the Restoration, sang his version of the new song for all of us to share. As in Revelation 5, the Prophet Joseph invites all creation to join in his singing:

"What do we hear in the gospel which we have received? A voice of gladness! A voice of mercy from heaven . . . Courage, brethren; and on, on to the victory! Let your hearts rejoice, and be exceeding glad. Let the earth break forth into singing. Let the dead speak forth anthems of eternal praise to the King Immanuel. . . . Let the mountains shout for joy, and all ye valleys cry aloud; and all ye seas and dry lands tell the wonders of your Eternal King! And ye rivers, and brooks, and rills, flow down with gladness. Let the woods and all the trees of the field praise the Lord; and ye solid rocks weep for joy! And let the sun, moon, and the morning stars sing together, and let all the sons of God shout for joy! And let the eternal creations declare his name forever and ever!" (D&C 128:19, 22–23.)

From time to time we feel a foretaste of the joy John and Joseph expressed. Sometimes during the singing of a sacrament song or while listening to the Tabernacle Choir, our hearts fill and spill over with emotion. Words like these become deeply personal, as though we had created them ourselves: "Oh, it is wonderful that he should care for me enough to die for me! Oh, it is wonderful, wonderful to me!" "Oh, love effulgent, love divine! What debt of gratitude is mine, that in his off'ring I have part and hold a place within his heart." "Then sings my soul, my Savior God, to thee, How great thou art! How great thou art!" "Come thou fount of every blessing; tune my heart to sing thy grace; Streams of mercy, never ceasing, call for songs of loudest praise." (*Hymns* [Salt Lake City: The Church of Jesus Christ of Latter-day Saints, 1985], nos. 193, 187, 86; *Hymns* [Salt Lake City: The Church of Jesus Christ of Latter-day Saints, 1948], no. 70.) Then the new song renews us with the certainty of fulfilled hope. Then we have the confidence, the vibrant conviction, that all will be well, both in our individual lives and also in the world.

The words of the new song tell us something about the character of Jesus: "Worthy is the Lamb that was slain to receive power, and riches, and wisdom, and strength, and honour, and glory, and blessing." (Revelation 5:12.) Most people cannot receive these things and then use them in perfect balance for the benefit of others. Power, wealth, knowledge, and glory are often corrupting, most often being turned to the selfish benefit of the holder. Christ, however, employs all these things within their proper boundaries and governed by the charity and compassion he has, not only for his brothers and sisters but for all creation. Hence, not only do God's children praise him, but so does "every creature" in heaven, on earth, or in the sea.

There are a number of songs throughout the book of Revelation. We must pay attention to these spontaneous utterances of praise and adoration. They lighten the mood and encourage the righteous armies of the Lamb. Song is the natural flow of faith. In the hymns of a people we will fathom the depth of their convictions and the soul of their religion. Next to scripture, the LDS hymnal is a study in the truthfulness of our religion. The quality of song measures the temper of religion's heart and conversion's endurance. Truth will ever tune the voice with singing. There are many popular strains of music in the churches of the world, including our own, but the songs of Revelation are not based on sentiment or nostalgia but on deep, soul-filling faith. They are essential in the fight against the darkness of the dragon. When the soul sings out its harmonies to God, as if recalling heaven's memories, the foundations of evil tremble.

With the joy of song in our hearts, we are now ready to open the book and view the great battle with the dragon as it unfolds from seal to seal. Yet behind all the horrific scenes of lion-toothed locusts, falling stars, and images built to the honor of devouring beasts, we hear the never-fading echoes of the new song, instilling its whispers of ultimate peace and glory.

REVELATION 6

❧

THE FOUR HORSEMEN

Strictly speaking, the revelation John is going to receive
begins in chapter 6 with the opening of the first six
seals. The Lamb is going to "reveal" the contents of the
book he received from the right hand of the Father,
hence the name "Revelation." Chapters four and five provide
the setting for the opening of the seals that governs the rest of
Revelation. The first four seals are in the past, the fifth represents the present generation of John, and the sixth and seventh
seals look to the future. We can study the first five seals, searching for specific historical context, or we can generalize them,
looking for major earth patterns. I prefer the second approach.
Nephi wrote several times that the words of Isaiah lent themselves to "likening." The breadth of application allowed is seen
in Nephi's introductory words before quoting Isaiah 2–14: "Now
these are the words, and ye may liken them *unto you and unto
all men.*" (2 Nephi 11:8; italics added.) Much of Revelation's
power lies in our ability to follow Nephi's counsel by likening

the images of Revelation "unto all men" throughout all time. Revelation deals with ideologies, premises, and ethics so consequential that we see in them all of history. This is also true of the sixth and seventh seals.

John is shown four horsemen riding four colored horses, each controlling their respective seals. Roots of this image are found in both chapter 1 and 6 of Zechariah, particularly chapter 6, where different colored chariots are depicted. Today we think of horses and chariots primarily as modes of transportation, but in biblical times the commanding association was one of war, conquest, and triumph. In literary lore, particularly tales of epic proportions, the horse of a conqueror or legendary leader was as important as its rider, having names that survived in written memory. It is not coincidental that Jesus chose a donkey rather than a horse for his triumphal entry into Jerusalem. In light of the fact that the four horsemen arise from the imagery of Zechariah, it is interesting that it is Zechariah who used the word "lowly" when prophesying that Christ would bring "salvation . . . riding upon an ass, and upon a colt the foal of an ass." (Zechariah 9:9.) Had he ridden in on a horse, particularly a white one, Pilate would undoubtedly have been more concerned that the Jewish leadership's charge of treason against Rome had substance.

In Zechariah 1, the horsemen report on the conditions of the world as they are sent by the Lord to "walk to and fro through the earth." (Zechariah 1:8–11.) In Zechariah 6, it is implied that the four chariots have control over the nations and people they ride against. Both ideas are useful for understanding John's riders. We will be shown the conditions of the earth and the paramount controlling forces that govern it. The choice of four horsemen instead of seven, therefore, lends itself to the idea of the four directions of the compass, meaning that the whole earth is involved in John's descriptions. The state of the world throughout much of its past is about to be reviewed. Their colors also suggest different directions, for the association of the cardinal points of the compass with varying colors has deep, widespread, and ancient roots.

THE WHITE HORSE

White is the color of conquest or victory. The crown the rider wears is akin to the laurel-leaf garland seen on the statues of Roman emperors or those given to victors in Greek athletic contests. Most LDS commentaries identify the rider as Enoch, and the conquest he has won as the establishment of Zion. This interpretation is enhanced by reading Moses 7, where Enoch is shown wielding tremendous power against the enemies of Zion. (See Moses 7:13.)

If we choose to see the white horse in more general terms, using a less literal fulfillment, grouping it more fully with its three companions, it can symbolize the idea of *conquest*. I lean to this reading of the first seal. This shifts the emphasis more to one of a desire for power and the unrighteous seeking of it, Enoch being a lonely exception. From the very beginning of history, commencing in the first dispensation, men have sought to conquer each other. In the same chapter of Moses that speaks of Enoch's righteous mastery, we read of various peoples destroying each other. "Giants" are mentioned in the generations of both Enoch and Noah. (See Moses 7:15; 8:18.) We would use the word *warrior* instead of *giant* today. This was an age of "mighty men, which are like unto men of old, men of great renown." (Moses 8:21.) In this sense the white horse still stalks the land, and the idea of conquest leads naturally to the red horse's dominance as shown in the second seal, as we shall see.

THE RED HORSE

"And from that time forth there were wars and bloodshed among them." This early description of man is found in the context of Enoch's vision of future animosity and hatred, a violent generation whose wickedness would bring on the Flood. "Look, and I will show unto thee the world for the space of many generations," the Lord told him. (Moses 7:4, 16.) He saw that Satan "veiled the whole face of the earth with darkness; and he [Lucifer] looked up and laughed, and his angels rejoiced." But God grieved over the fury of his children, stating, "They are without affection, and they hate their own blood." (Moses 7:26, 33.)

The desire to go "forth conquering, and to conquer" (Revelation 6:2) inevitably leads to war. Therefore, John is shown "another horse that was red: and power was given to him that sat thereon to take peace from the earth, and that they should kill one another: and there was given unto him a great sword." (Revelation 6:4.) War drives history forward as it sweeps the globe from the back of the red horse. God does grant unto man agency; and though nothing on earth happens without the Lord's allowance, it is man's brutality, selfishness, pride, and hatred that give the rider of the red horse "power . . . to take peace from the earth." The sword has often been a symbol of war, so it is fitting that the rider wields a great one.

THE BLACK HORSE

The opening of the third seal reveals a black horse, whose rider holds "a pair of balances in his hand." (Revelation 6:5.)

These are the type of scales still used in many parts of the world for weighing grains, legumes, and other items of food. A voice declares the price of wheat and barley. A "measure" is equal to about two pints, and a penny is a day's wage. Barley was less expensive and was considered a poor man's bread. The voice also proclaims that the oil (olive trees) and the wine (vineyards) are not to be hurt. The scales coupled with the words of the voice let us know that the black horse brings famine. This is further verified in the opening of the fourth seal when the destruction of the black horse is repeated using the straightforward phrase, "to kill with . . . hunger." (Revelation 6:8.) Leviticus contains a warning from the Lord to Israel about the consequences of rebellion: "When I have broken the staff of your bread, ten women shall bake your bread in one oven, and *they shall deliver you your bread again by weight*: and ye shall eat, and not be satisfied." (Leviticus 26:26; italics added.)

One need only look to an area of the world where war is being waged, or to any past period in history, to recognize that famine is often the fellow-rider with the sword and the lust for conquest. The black horse follows on the heels of the red as the red follows on the heels of the white. We begin now to see that the opening of the seals does more than identify a problem specific to that age; it portrays the commanding sorrows that always result from succumbing to the temptations of a fallen world. Conquest, war, and famine have ever been the lot of mortality's children. The fourth and the fifth seal will help round out the history.

THE PALE HORSE

In the scriptures, three sources of misery are described as traveling together. Amulek warned the citizens of Ammonihah that their wickedness would result in destruction: "Yet it would not be by flood, as were the people in the days of Noah, but it would be by *famine*, and by *pestilence*, and the *sword*." (Alma 10:22; italics added.) Our pale horse is ridden by "Death, and Hell followed with him." (Revelation 6:8.) Death is a general term, but in this case it is strongly associated with epidemics of pestilence, plague, and disease. During the Middle Ages, Europe and Asia were often swept by bubonic plague, which they called the "black *death*." In wartime more soldiers and civilians are killed through sickness and disease than the confrontations of the battlefield. Famine weakens once-healthy bodies as the seeds of conquest and the sword are sown in the whirlwind. Death and hell also suggest physical and spiritual death, as discussed in an earlier chapter.

"Therefore hell hath enlarged herself," Isaiah wrote, "and opened her mouth without measure." (Isaiah 5:14.) Following patiently behind the preceding horsemen, hell collects her wages. Sadly, so many innocent victims also suffer needlessly. Mormon taught, "Thus we see that the devil will not support his children at the last day, but doth speedily drag them down to hell." (Alma 30:60.)

The pale horse is not a ghostly white but rather a sickly green, as the Greek word for it indicates. Even today, when someone is unwell, we might say, "You look a little green; are you feeling all right?" It is an unhealthy color, not the vibrant green of living things, but a poisonous, yellow-tinged, venomous color, the hue of decay, spoilage, and degeneration. Life is slowly draining away, leaving only the shadow of a once-sustaining vitality.

"Power was given unto *them* over the fourth part of the earth, to kill with sword, and with hunger, and with death, and with the beasts of the earth." (Revelation 6:8; italics.) These words are reminiscent of the Lord's warning in Leviticus, where "wild beasts," "a sword," "the pestilence," and "bread deliver[ed] . . . by weight" are mentioned. I have often pondered if the pronoun "them" in Revelation 6:8 refers to death and hell or the four horses, since they are repeated in this sentence. (See Leviticus 26:19–26.) At various points in Revelation, fractions are used. We should be wary of reading them too literally. Generally they indicate a large portion, a great amount, or many. We are most familiar with this idea in the expression used, for example, by King Lamoni's father when defeated by Ammon. "If thou wilt spare me," the king cried, "I will grant unto thee whatsoever thou wilt ask, even to *half of the kingdom*." (Alma 20:23; italics added.) Herod also used this expression after Salome's dance, which resulted in the beheading of John the Baptist. (See Mark 6:23.) "Over the fourth part of the earth" suggests that the rider has sway over a great area. As has been noted, the red (sword), black (hunger), and pale (death or pestilence) horses are repeated in the last part of the above verse with the addition of "the beasts of the earth."

Ezekiel was told by the Lord, "When the land sinneth against me by trespassing grievously, then will I stretch out mine hand upon it." He then mentioned four agents that are used. They are "famine. . . . noisome beasts. . . . a sword. . . . pestilence." Grouping them in one verse, the Lord tells Ezekiel, "How much more when I send my four sore judgments upon Jerusalem, the sword, and the famine, and the noisome beast, and the pestilence." (Ezekiel 14:13–21.) These same four judgments are mentioned together in connection with the fourth seal. It seems reasonable to conclude that each of the four is sent to a quarter of the earth, and that each different-colored horse stands for one of the four. The entire earth is involved, in all its ages—not just a portion of it or a particular time period. Joseph Smith's insight about the seals representing the history of the earth is now seen as extremely critical to understanding and application.

The white horse of conquest appears to be repeated in the noisome beasts. Beasts are added to the list of forces seen during the fourth seal. Daniel was shown a vision in which he saw future conquering political empires rising out of the sea: "And four great beasts came up . . . diverse one from another." Babylon was a lion, Persia was a bear, Greece was a leopard, and Rome was described as "dreadful and terrible, and strong exceedingly." (Daniel 7:3–7.) We will return to this vision of Daniel later in Revelation, for it is key to understanding chapter 13. For the present, it is sufficient to note that each of these animals subdues according to its strength. They are predators, exploiting weaker, more defenseless animals. The "law of the jungle," eat or be eaten, has applied throughout history from the very beginning to both individuals and nations.

It is in this light that we are able to see the most powerful fulfillment of Isaiah's prophecy that "the wolf . . . shall dwell with the lamb, and the leopard shall lie down with the kid; and the calf and the young lion. . . . And the cow and the bear shall feed." (Isaiah 11:6–7.) Simply put, the Soviet Unions and the Nazi Germanys will stop invading and devouring the Hungarys and Polands of the world. Might will no longer make right. But, as John saw with the opening of the fourth seal, the dominant world theme for many dispensations would be that of jungle law.

THE SOULS UNDER THE ALTAR

When the fifth seal is opened, we are not shown another ominous horseman, further substantiating the idea that the four cor-

ners of the earth are suggested earlier. In Zechariah the four colored chariots are dispersed to the cardinal points of the compass.
Conquest, war, famine, pestilence, and marauding empires have
descended upon humanity from every direction and in every age.
We must be careful not to limit the horsemen exclusively to their
own seal. There have been famines and plagues in the first as well
as the fourth dispensation, just as war and new subjugating
empires have come and gone throughout the sad disharmony of
history. We are being shown the manner in which Lucifer rules
the world when man gives him the ascendancy. He has been in
the saddle long enough, though. This will all change in the seventh seal, as Joseph Smith wrote: "The world itself presents one
great theater of misery, woe, and 'distress of nations with per-
plexity.' All, all, speak with a voice of thunder, that man is not
able to govern himself, to legislate for himself, to protect himself,
to promote his own good, nor the good of the world. . . . The
world has had a fair trial for six thousand years; the Lord will try
the seventh thousand Himself." (*Teachings of the Prophet Joseph
Smith*, 250, 252.) Until that time, however, the horsemen haunt
the land, and the earth mourns under the tread of their hooves.

Has the Lord abandoned the earth to this woeful state? Does
he make no attempt to turn the tides of history? Is he content
to watch the desolations of the marauding quartet, waiting
patiently for the seventh seal to arrive? The answer is given in
the fifth seal: "I saw under the altar the souls of them that were
slain for the word of God, and for the testimony which they
held." (Revelation 6:9.) In every age our Father in Heaven has
sent righteous men and women, prophets and apostles, to warn,
exhort, teach, encourage, and testify. But as John himself knew,
there is stiff resistance to the accustomed order of the day. The
fifth seal depicts the frequent fate of those who challenge the

status quo. Lucifer is not anxious to dismount and abandon the field without a fight. Prophets and holy men have been slain in every dispensation, but it is appropriate that the fifth seal represent the martyrs, for Christ himself, the greatest martyr to truth, would share the fortune of his prophets and apostles during the fifth seal's act in the drama of life.

John sees these martyrs under the altar of sacrifice before the temple. Certain sacrifices of the Jewish religion required that the animal's blood be used in different ways. Sometimes it was sprinkled or dabbed on the object, clothing, or person that was the center of the ritual. In some rituals the blood was collected in a bowl and poured out at the foot of the altar of sacrifice. (See Leviticus 4 for examples.) Pouring out the blood suggests a freely willed, total commitment of life to the Lord. It was often associated with the removing of sin. The souls John saw under the altar had freely given the Lord their all. Their offering was directly related to their desire to remove evil from the world. They poured out their lives at the altar of God. In one of the most famous Messianic prophecies of Isaiah, Jesus "poured out his soul unto death." (Isaiah 53:12.) This expression carries shadows of the same idea.

The slain martyrs cry out to God, asking a question that has burned in the minds of righteous people century after century from Habakkuk and Malachi in the Old Testament (see Habakkuk 1 and Malachi 3) to Joseph Smith in Liberty Jail (see section 121): "How long, O Lord, holy and true, dost thou not judge and avenge our blood on them that dwell on the earth?" (Revelation 6:10.)

God gives them all white robes, suggesting that their warning testimony has cleansed them from the blood and the sins of their respective generations (see Jacob 1:19 for an example of a prophet's testimony rendering him clean); then he answers their question: "It was said unto them, that they should rest yet for a little season, until their fellowservants also and their brethren, that should be killed as they were, should be fulfilled." (Revelation 6:11.)

There would be no immediate end to the persecution and killing of the righteous. The Father would continue to send them, and they would continue to pour out their blood at the foot of his altar. These martyrs can include the many thousands killed during times of religious persecution in the early Christian era, through the religious wars of the Reformation, right up to Joseph and Hyrum Smith. John Taylor said of Carthage, "Their innocent blood, with the innocent blood of all the martyrs under the altar that John saw, will cry unto the Lord of Hosts till he avenges that blood on the earth." (D&C 135:7.) They also include those, like the daughters of Onidah, who lived centuries before the opening of the fifth seal and foreshadowed future ages of martyrdom. These women and many others were "offered up because of their virtue; they would not bow down to worship gods of wood or of stone, therefore they were killed." (Abraham 1:11.)

How long will evil prevail in mortal ascendancy over the fortunes of the righteous? We will see that the sixth seal will give no relief, although effective protection will be offered. No, the answer to six dispensations of opposition will not come until Christ returns to cleanse and sanctify the earth in the seventh seal of its temporal existence.

OPENING THE SIXTH SEAL

The sixth seal brings us to our own time and dispensation. Since we are living during this seal, it would stand to reason that we recognize our own age in the visionary descriptions of it. John sees a world where all things are in commotion, where stability is overturned. Seven areas come under this general impression as the seal is opened: (1) a quaking earth, (2) a blackened sun, (3) a blood-red moon, (4) falling stars, (5) opening heavens, (6) shifting mountains and islands, and (7) people seeking places to hide.

These images are repeated numerous times in many other scriptures both modern and ancient. They originate in the writings of Joel. (See Joel 2:28–31.) We have a tendency to interpret them almost exclusively in their literal fulfillment. We speak of, and look for, earthquakes that will shake whole continents; an eclipsed sun or one darkened by the smoke and pollution of destruction and war; a moon turned red through the haze of that same heaven-filled debris; and meteorite showers and sinking islands.

I do not wish to discount the literal fulfillment of any ancient prophecy. Nephi told his wondering brothers that the words of Isaiah had both "temporal and spiritual" fulfillment. (See 1 Nephi 22:3.) The turmoil of the sixth seal may have literal as well as poetic fulfillment, but because of the nature of the writing style in Revelation, we would be foolish to examine the literal at the expense of the figurative. If we read these images with emphasis on the poetic, the symbolic, we will recognize our own day and realize that we see the fulfillment almost every year, and certainly throughout the last century. So let us examine the less prosaic—more metaphorical—meaning and see if it does not impart significant insight that will perhaps strike with greater power than past readings.

License to read these particular prophecies in a more figurative setting is somewhat enhanced when we realize that Peter quoted Joel's original words immediately after the resurrection of Jesus, indicating they were being fulfilled during his time period. (See Acts 2:16–20.) Yet during Moroni's first visit to Joseph Smith, he quoted the same passage from Joel, stating "that this was not yet fulfilled, but was soon to be." (JS—H 1:41.) Figurative readings lend themselves to multiple fulfillments in many different times. There need be no contradiction between Peter's affirmation and Moroni's promise.

DARK AND UNSTABLE

If the scene presented to John were opened to our view, we would immediately notice that darkness was dominant. There would be little light with a black sun, a red moon, and falling stars. The sixth seal is a time of darkness, when the deeds of the wicked are shadowed in black. Jesus told Nicodemus, "This is the condemnation, that light is come into the world, and men loved darkness rather than light, because their deeds were evil. For every one that doeth evil hateth the light, neither cometh to the light, lest his deeds should be reproved." (John 3:19–20.) Applying the Savior's insights to the generation of the sixth seal, and in truth to all previous generations, we come to understand that the deeds done by this generation will encompass great evil.

It is also a time of great instability, or, as Joseph Smith put it, "All things shall be in commotion." (D&C 88:91.) Notice that the major aspects of creation are mentioned—earth, sun, moon, stars, heavens. We are missing the sea, but it is mentioned in other places in Revelation, and Joseph Smith includes it in his rendition of this prophecy, with the words "the waves of the sea heaving themselves beyond their bounds." (D&C 88:90.) Normally the earth is firm, not shaking; the stars are constant and never depart from their accustomed cycle in the night sky. Mountains are supposed to be immovable, and the moon shines with soft light. Instability and deeds of darkness certainly coincide with our era. With this general tenor of the times, let us now look at the images more closely.

The Earth Quakes and the Stars Fall

We can discover at least two ideas while exploring the image of earthquakes. Because John's description of the sixth seal is found in many other places in scripture, it gives us the opportunity to compare wording and poetic expressions. The scriptures thus comment on each other, giving us handles with which to grasp truth.

Joseph Smith said the "earth shall tremble and reel to and fro as a drunken man." (D&C 88:87.) Isaiah described the generation of the Restoration using images of drunkenness also. Those who are drunk are out of control, cannot walk correctly, have trouble seeing clearly, and are impaired in judgment. (See Isaiah 28:7–8.) We will return to these images when speaking of the wine cup that is offered to the world by the great whore of chapter 17. We can also find three phrases in other scriptures that tell us more about the earth reeling like a drunken man.

Nephi's description of the last days included this description: "They shall war among themselves, and the sword of their own hands shall fall upon their own heads, and they shall be *drunken with their own blood*." (1 Nephi 22:13; italics added. See also Revelation 17:6 and Isaiah 49:26.) The Jaredites were "*drunken with anger*, even as a man who is drunken with wine" (Ether 15:22; italics added) just prior to their final mutual annihilation. Anger and hate are often the cause for being out of control in blood and murder, blinded by desires of revenge.

Nephi further stated, "In the last days, or in the days of the Gentiles—yea, behold all the nations of the Gentiles and also the Jews, both those who shall come upon this land and those who shall be upon other lands, yea, even upon all the lands of the earth, behold, they will be *drunken with iniquity* and all manner of abominations." (2 Nephi 27:1; italics added.) The whole earth trembles and reels under the influence of blood, anger, iniquity. The headlines of any week during the past hundred years would fit this description. We have seen holocausts involving millions, and "ethnic cleansing" is the new descriptive title of the day.

SHAKING THE NATIONS

There is, however, a more compelling idea associated with the quaking earth that is seconded by the falling stars. Both are essentially teaching the same message. John says that the "stars of heaven fell unto the earth, even as a fig tree casteth her untimely figs, when she is *shaken* of a mighty wind." (Revelation 6:13; italics added.) The verb *to shake* was used by Jesus when he spoke the words of this same sixth-seal prophecy: "The stars shall fall from heaven, and the powers of the heavens shall be shaken." (Matthew 24:29.) Joel also included both heaven and earth in his version of these events, saying, "The heavens and the earth shall shake." (Joel 3:16.) The key word in all of these verses is "shake," coupled with the idea that the shaking will cause things to fall.

The reason we fear earthquakes is not so much the shaking of the earth but what that shaking produces. Buildings, bridges, roads, and rocks tumble to the ground. At this point we can ask ourselves what it is that God wants to tumble to the ground. What will be the result of the shaking? Haggai, and Paul's commentary on Haggai's words, provide an answer: "Thus saith the Lord of hosts; Yet once, it is a little while, and I will shake the heavens, and the earth, and the sea, and the dry land [indicating all creation]; and I will *shake all nations, and the desire of all nations shall come.*" (Haggai 2:6–7; italics added.) The "desire of all nations" is a reference to the Savior. It is the nations that must be shaken prior to the appearance of the Son of Man.

Paul reminded the Hebrews of how the Lord's voice caused the earth to tremble when He spoke to them from Mount Sinai, then drew upon the words of Haggai to speak of a future shaking of earth and heaven and its purpose: "See that ye refuse not him that speaketh. For if they escaped not who refused him that spake on earth, much more shall not we escape, if we turn away from him that speaketh from heaven: Whose voice then shook the earth: but now he hath promised, saying, Yet once more I shake not the earth only, but also heaven. And this word, Yet once more, *signifieth the removing of those things that are shaken,* as of things that are made, that *those things which cannot be shaken may remain.* Wherefore we receiving a kingdom which *cannot be moved,* let us have grace, whereby we may serve God acceptably." (Hebrews 12:25–28; italics added.)

Paul's phrase, "things that are made," connotes things made by man. These temporary creations will tumble. These prophecies are another way of stating what Daniel interpreted in Nebuchadnezzar's dream of the great statue. It represented various kingdoms of the world. Remember that a "stone was cut out *without hands*" that smote the feet of the image and brought it crashing to the ground. The stone is The Church of Jesus Christ of Latter-day Saints, the Lord's kingdom on earth. The stone then "became a great mountain, and filled the whole earth." (Daniel 2:34–35; italics added.) No human hands crafted the Restoration; only those of God could instill such beauty, truth, and permanency.

In the last century, as Haggai indicated, we saw nations fall. Two of the most obvious were Nazi Germany and the Soviet Union, but smaller, less dramatic examples are almost too numerous to name. When all the shaking is done, one kingdom, one nation, will remain—that of Zion or the kingdom of God. Paul and Daniel would have us understand and find comfort in the knowledge that we are part of that kingdom.

The Lord ended section 84 of the Doctrine and Covenants with yet another version of the major sixth-seal image, urging his servants to raise the warning voice: "Go ye forth as your circumstances shall permit . . . unto the great and notable cities and villages, reproving the world in righteousness of all their unrighteous and ungodly deeds, setting forth clearly and understandingly the desolation of abomination in the last days. For, with you saith the Lord Almighty, I will *rend their kingdoms*; I will not only shake the earth, but the starry heavens shall tremble. . . . I will come and reign with my people." (D&C 84:117–19; italics added.)

Nephi, who ever loved words that were "plain" and easy to understand, stated the main objective of the quaking earth and falling stars: "Behold, that great and abominable church, the whore of all the earth, must tumble to the earth, and great must be the fall thereof. For *the kingdom of the devil must shake*, and they which belong to it must needs be stirred up unto repentance, or the devil will grasp them with his everlasting chains." (2 Nephi 28:18–19; italics added.)

The Lord often speaks of "earthquakes in divers places." (Matthew 24:30, JST.) These are called the "signs of the times."

83

A sign's main purpose is to call attention to something or point us to a future destination or place. Perhaps, in addition to thinking these signs point to the return of Jesus, let us ponder the transitory nature of worldly kingdoms, organizations, religions, and businesses. Do they not also testify that even those things we believe to be as unmovable as the earth itself or the stars above us may tumble if they are not part of our Savior's realm and reflect his righteousness? When we witness the destructive force of an earthquake, or meditate on a night lit by shooting stars, they are a reminder that ultimately anything that is not eternal will be removed. Let us not set our hearts upon the temporal but rather lift our eyes, raise our voices, and offer our arms to The Church of Jesus Christ of Latter-day Saints, for it is the one kingdom that will be left standing, the one star that will continue to shine, when the shaking stills and the "desire of all nations" finally comes.

THE SUN BECAME BLACK

Two ideas can be deduced from Revelation's image of a darkened sun. Let us turn again to the Prophet Joseph Smith's language: "The sun shall *hide his face,* and shall *refuse* to give light." (D&C 88:87; italics added.) The sun can't choose to hide its face, nor can it willingly refuse to give light. This phrase employs a common literary technique called *personification,* which is attributing human characteristics to an object. Insight can come if we ask ourselves what might cause human beings to hide their faces or refuse to look upon something.

Occasionally when watching the evening news, the network will announce that the following footage may be disturbing to some viewers. I have noticed that every time this happens, my wife changes the channel or leaves the room. She does not wish to see scenes of human misery or cruelty. She is hiding her face. A person might turn away from an act of wickedness, thus refusing to countenance it. We also use the expression "to bury our face in our hands." This is often done because of sorrow, anguish, or shame. When the sun hides its face and refuses to shine, it does so because the deeds of men are so disturbingly hateful, cruel, and evil. Human suffering and misery during the sixth seal will be great and painful, not only to experience but also to see.

The stars are personified as well as the sun in other versions of this prophecy. In the Doctrine and Covenants we read, "and the stars shall *refuse* their shining." (D&C 34:9; italics added.) Isaiah and the Savior personify the moon as well as the stars, attributing to them the power to choose whether or not to give their light: "The stars of heaven and the constellations thereof shall not give their light: the sun shall be darkened in his going forth, and the moon shall not cause her light to shine." (Isaiah 13:10; see also Matthew 24:29.) Joel follows this same pattern: "The stars shall withdraw their shining." (Joel 2:10; 3:15.)

A second meaning for a black, eclipsed sun is inherent in the wording used in Revelation itself: "The sun became black as sackcloth of hair." (Revelation 6:12.) The color black and the word *sackcloth* provide poetic clues. Both are associated with mourning. Describing the destruction of the land in an earlier era, Jeremiah wrote, "For this shall the earth mourn, and the heavens above be black." (Jeremiah 4:28.) The wickedness of men makes the heavens mourn.

Enoch saw a vision of the weeping Lord, who contemplated the wickedness of men, their inevitable suffering, and their final destruction, and asked, "How is it that the heavens weep, and shed forth their tears as the rain upon the mountains?" (Moses

7:28.) In this vision the earth was personified as Enoch looked upon it: "He heard a voice from the bowels thereof, saying: Wo, wo is me, the mother of men; I am pained, I am weary, because of the wickedness of my children. When shall I rest, and be cleansed from the filthiness which is gone forth out of me? When will my Creator sanctify me, that I may rest, and righteousness for a season abide upon my face?" (Moses 7:48.) These same words with only minor changes could be uttered by a sun dressed in black sackcloth, mourning and weeping over the trespasses of men, which he sees constantly.

THE MOON BECAME AS BLOOD

The general impression of wickedness during the sixth seal is augmented with the image of a blood-red moon. Certain colors are associated with human moods. Blue suggests depression and sorrow, as does black. Yellow depicts joy, happiness, or light-heartedness, and we speak of someone being green with envy or jealousy. Blood-red is the color of anger. The moon is angry. Joseph Smith's wording of the cosmic drama of the sixth seal describes anger in the falling of the stars, which "shall become exceedingly angry, and shall cast themselves down as a fig that falleth from off a fig-tree." (D&C 88:87.) Anger is a part of the last days in two ways. People themselves are angry, and the heavens are angry at the scenes played out before them.

Doctrine and Covenants 88 describes the moon as being "bathed" in blood. (D&C 88:87.) A similar idea is portrayed in Isaiah when the Lord speaks of his return to the earth: "My sword shall be bathed in heaven. . . . The sword of the Lord is filled with blood." The Lord's sword then falls upon the earth, "for it is the day of the Lord's vengeance." (Isaiah 34:5–6, 8.)

Once again indignation at wickedness is the point of the figurative language.

THE HEAVENS OPENED

The Joseph Smith Translation rewords the image of the heavens "depart[ing] as a scroll," rendering it like this: "The heavens opened as a scroll is opened when it is rolled together." (Revelation 6:14, JST.) Depending on which word we focus on, the opening heavens can suggest several things. If we center our thoughts on the word "scroll," the idea of *reading* the heavens seems appropriate. These are signs of the times, given to us that we may read the "handwriting on the wall," so to speak.

If we shift our attention to the word "rolled," we get the image of storm clouds rolling through the heavens. We have all seen the approach of thunderstorms. The clouds are black, boiling, and turbulent. We speak of such storm clouds also in terms of anger. The Greek word for the opening of the heavens suggests that they are split, separated, or torn. Today, if someone said to us, "The heavens just opened on us while we were driving home," we would assume the person had been caught in a severe storm. Threatening, dark, rolling heavens add to the overall impression of the scene John describes for us. It fits well with falling stars, a black sun, and a red moon.

THE MOUNTAINS AND ISLANDS MOVE

The moving mountains and islands contribute to the impressions already created by the trembling earth and the shaking heavens. The common denominator is the instability and shifting of things that are normally permanent and constant. However, we get an additional detail about the troubled times when we consider that mountains and islands were frequently used as places of refuge and safety. Castles and fortresses were most often built on the tops of hills, and history abounds with stories of islands resisting the advances of conquering armies. Medieval lords dug moats around their castles to create an island defense. When in danger, one could escape to the island or mountain and find relative immunity from disturbances otherwise indefensible. Jesus counseled his disciples, "Let them who are in Judea, flee into the mountains." (Matthew 24:13, JST.)

Yet, in Revelation, the mountains and islands are also on the move. In Revelation 16:20 the Revelator uses the words "fled away" to describe the islands. Where does one run for safety when even the refuge is fleeing? There are no safe places; there is nowhere to hide, nowhere to run. Isaiah issued a similar warning in his generation, using language that echoes Revelation: "Fear, and the pit, and the snare, are upon thee, O inhabitant of the earth. And it shall come to pass, that he who fleeth from the noise of the fear shall fall into the pit; and he that cometh up out of the midst of the pit shall be taken in the snare: for the windows from on high are open, and the foundations of the earth do shake. . . . The earth is moved exceedingly. The earth shall reel to and fro like a drunkard, and shall be removed like a cottage; and the transgression thereof shall be heavy upon it; and it shall fall, and not rise again." (Isaiah 24:17–20.) Notice how many repeated elements are in these words and how strongly they suggest the removing of worldly kingdoms because of transgression. In an earlier entry Isaiah asked, "What will ye do in the day of visitation, and in the desolation which shall come from far? to whom will ye flee for help? and where will ye leave your glory?" (Isaiah 10:3.)

In the Doctrine and Covenants, the Lord urges the Saints

to build Zion, that they might have "a city of refuge, a place of safety for the saints of the Most High God." This will be necessary because of the distressing conflicts that burst out continuously across the globe: "Every man that will not take his sword against his neighbor must needs flee unto Zion for safety." (D&C 45:66, 68.) In a chaotic world of ethnic cleansing, terrorism, war, refugees, and brutality, God has provided one mountain, one island, that will not move: "And there shall be gathered unto it out of every nation under heaven; and it shall be the only people that shall not be at war one with another." (D&C 45:69.) As Saints, we need not be overwhelmed by the darkness of the seal in which we live—we need to build Zion.

HIDING FROM THE LORD

The last of our seven images concerning the sixth seal describes people of every station and class of life seeking a hiding place from the "wrath of the Lamb." They call to the mountains, "Fall on us, and hide us from the face of him that sitteth on the throne." (Revelation 6:15–16.) The first desire to hide from the Lord takes us back as far as Adam and Eve in the Garden of Eden. They had partaken of forbidden fruit and were not particularly desirous of meeting with God when he called for them. Even in the often-brazen world in which we live, people still try to hide the things they do from the sight of others. They do this for a number of reasons, shame and guilt being the most prominent. This is true of rulers of nations and of the lowliest of servants. Perhaps the call for the mountains to fall upon them suggests the magnitude of the sins of that generation. Fig leaves will no longer do; there is too much to hide. Now mountains and rocks are needed as a covering.

If we read John's description of our day less literally, we see that every feature points to the same conclusions. We can also see its fulfillment in our own generation. We need not wait for debris-filled skies, a massive earthquake, or meteorites. We are already in the midst of the scene. There may yet be a more exacting fulfillment, and the Lord is not limited in his ability to fulfill temporally as well as spiritually, but if we will look with different eyes for just a moment, we can understand how clearly and closely John detailed our own era.

Perhaps more important (and this is critical), when we use the lens of poetic metaphor to examine the opening of the sixth seal, finding the answer to the question in the last verse of chapter 6 becomes paramount. It is not for a future time, when natural eyes stare at a blood-red moon or feet feel the rolling earth beneath them. It is for here and now. In this shaking, rolling, moving, angry, fleeing, hiding, drunken world, "who shall be able to stand?" (Revelation 6:17.) When we find the answer to that question, we will know how to survive in our present conditions, whether we ever see a mountain move or an island sink. We will receive John's counsel on where to focus our energies, hopes, and faith. That answer is found in chapter 7. Here the great, overarching work of the sixth seal is offered to the Saints for their protection, uplift, and salvation.

WHO SHALL BE ABLE TO STAND?

J ohn almost always follows scenes of distress and trouble with those of joy and hope. This provides relief from the building tension, thus increasing the power of each new component of the Revelation. While reading Revelation it is good to be reminded that a main purpose of the vision is to encourage as well as to warn. The shifting of tension is a manifestation of literary wisdom used by great authors to maintain the intensity of language and dramatic effect for the reader. Shakespeare, in particular, was a master of this technique. The importance of chapter 7, therefore, is to teach those who live during the turbulent times of the sixth seal what they must do to find protection and acceptance with God.

John is now shown "four angels standing on the four corners of the earth, holding the four winds of the earth, that the wind should not blow on the earth, nor on the sea, nor on any tree." He is then shown another angel who has "the seal of the living God." This angel calls out to the first four, "Hurt not the earth, neither the sea, nor the trees, till we have sealed the servants of our God in their foreheads." (Revelation 7:1–3.)

Throughout Revelation, plagues and destructive forces are described as falling on earth, sea, trees, grass, sun, moon, stars, creatures of the sea, rivers, fountains of waters, and air. Each of these is mentioned in Genesis as part of the creation of the earth. John intends these to represent the whole of creation and not merely each specific element. This is particularly true when different aspects of the creation follow each other in successive verses, as in chapters 8 and 16. A part standing for the whole is a figure of speech called synecdoche. It is used frequently in other books of the Bible, so we should not be surprised to find it in one of the most literarily crafted books of the canon.

Let us begin with some of the broader parameters of this vision, then move to the more specific. Joseph Smith tells us that these angels have "power over the four parts of the earth, to save life and to *destroy*." They see that the gospel is spread to "every nation, kindred, tongue, and people," and they can "seal up unto life, or . . . cast down to the regions of darkness." (D&C 77:8; italics added.) In the book of Daniel, angels with this authority are called "the watchers." (Daniel 4:17.) They bring down nations or raise them up according to the wisdom of God. We may infer from this, therefore, that no nation will stand in the way of the sealing of God's servants. Those who do will be brought down, softened, or changed that the work of sealing may continue to fruition. We have seen this in our own age, most recently, for example, in the falling of the Berlin Wall and the removal of the Iron Curtain.

Joseph Smith also comments on the angel from the east who places the seal. "This is Elias," the Prophet states, "which was to come to gather together the tribes of Israel and restore all things." (D&C 77:9.) *Elias* is a title that has numerous meanings, many of which may apply here. (See "Elias" in the Bible Dictionary.) Its broadest application to our present discussion is seen in a statement by Jesus to his apostles: "Who is Elias? Behold, this is Elias, whom I send to prepare the way before me." (Matthew 17:13, JST.) Thus, the Restoration, with its many returning messengers, keys, ordinances, and truths, may be considered, as a whole, an Elias designed to prepare the way for the Savior's return. On another occasion Joseph Smith said, "The spirit of Elias is to prepare the way for a greater revelation of God." (*Teachings of the Prophet Joseph Smith*, 335.) The angel with the seal is sent to seal God's servants because that sealing will be crucial in preparing the world for the return of her eternal King.

PROTECTION FROM THE DESTROYER

The winds held back by the four angels are the winds of destruction; when let loose, they will come from every direction. The wind as a harbinger of woe is a common biblical as well as a broader cultural idea. The seal is to provide protection. This concept has several roots in the Old Testament, the best-known being the story of the Passover. In this example, lamb's blood placed on the door forbade the entrance of "the destroyer." (Exodus 12:23.) The symbolism is not too difficult to grasp. The atoning blood of the Savior has power to defend against the threatened destruction desired by Lucifer, who is aptly named "the destroyer." Later in Revelation, Satan is called by names that mean destruction. (See Revelation 9:11.) In Exodus the blood on the door's frame is called "a token." (Exodus 12:13.) The destroyer had no power to enter the house where the token was placed.

An even stronger source for John's vision is found in Ezekiel chapter 9. The destruction of Jerusalem is imminent because of its wickedness. Ezekiel is shown six men who have "charge over the city." They draw near "every man with his *destroying* weapon in his hand." One of them is "clothed with linen, with a writer's inkhorn by his side." (Ezekiel 9:1, 2; italics added.) The fact that one of them is dressed in linen suggests that he is a priest. (See Ezekiel 44:17–18.) He is instructed by the Lord to "go through the midst of the city, through the midst of Jerusalem, and set a *mark upon the foreheads* of the men that sigh and that cry for all the abominations that be done in the midst thereof." (Ezekiel 9:4; italics added.) Since they are troubled by wickedness, those who will receive the mark are the righteous. The mark is to be placed by one who holds the priesthood.

The Lord then commands the other men to follow after and destroy all who do not have the mark on their foreheads. He also instructs them to "begin at my sanctuary." (Ezekiel 9:6.) Interestingly, the final cleansing of the earth prior to Christ's return, according to the Doctrine and Covenants, also begins at the Lord's house, "first among those among you . . . who have professed to know my name and have not known me." (D&C 112:26.)

Exodus, Ezekiel, and Revelation share the same pattern. A seal, mark, or token is placed on the righteous to protect them from the destroyer, destroying weapons, or winds of destruction. Later in Revelation, we learn that the seal is the "Father's name." (Revelation 14:1; see also 22:4.) Seals in biblical times could be on a signet ring, but most often they were small cylinders that could be rolled in soft clay or wax, inscribing the name of the owner on his property. Today we put our names on things

94

we own, especially if they are of worth to us. Those who are sealed in Revelation 7 belong to the Father.

Drawing upon all the stories studied so far, we begin to see a common thread and an apparent application. At what place do the words *token, mark, name, seal, sign,* and *symbol* all come together? In the temple. That is where the priesthood can seal the Lord's righteous Saints in the same protective manner as in Exodus or Ezekiel. This makes perfect sense, for those who make covenants in the temple offer themselves as living gifts to God. When we present something to the Lord, we call it consecration. When we offer the Lord all that we have and are, all of our gifts and talents, all of our time and resources, he responds by placing his name upon us. Now the winds can blow, and we need not fear. Now the earth can shake, but our feet are firm on a solid foundation. Now the destroyer can roam, but he will have no power over us.

Being endowed is as critical to us as it was for the children of Israel to place the lamb's blood on their doors. The great work of the sixth seal, therefore, is the gathering of the righteous into the fold of the lamb through missionary labor, then perfecting them that they might consecrate themselves in the Lord's house. We need not fear and tremble or lose hope. We can be positive. We need not sensationalize the signs of the times. We can be about our Father's business, his errand, confident in the knowledge of his watchful care.

At the beginning of the Restoration, the Lord spoke of the conditions of the earth and the anxiousness of the angels to unleash the winds they control. "All flesh is corrupted before me," the Lord revealed, "and the powers of darkness prevail upon the earth, among the children of men, in the presence of all the hosts of heaven. . . . and the angels are waiting the great command to reap down the earth, to gather the tares that they may be burned; and, behold, the enemy is combined." (D&C 38:11–12.)

How do we find protection in such a world, where darkness prevails and evil is combined? The answer is offered in the dedicatory prayer of the first temple built in this dispensation. Observe how many elements of John's vision come together in Joseph Smith's dedication: "We ask thee, Holy Father, to establish the people that shall worship, and honorably hold a name and standing in this thy house, to all generations and for eternity. . . . That no combination of wickedness shall have power to rise up and prevail over thy people *upon whom thy name shall be put in this house*." (D&C 109:24, 26; italics added.) Earlier in the same prayer, Joseph asked the Father to allow His servants to leave His house "armed with thy power, and that thy name may be upon them, and thy glory be round about them, and thine angels have charge over them." (D&C 109:22.) There is something comforting in knowing that the identical angels who watch the nations and control the four winds, also have power "to seal up unto life." (D&C 77:8.)

OF EVERY TRIBE—OF EVERY NATION

Since we are the children of the Lord, he allows us free access to his house just as our children have free access to the rooms of our homes. This understanding may offer us some help in applying and comprehending some of the meaning behind the 144,000. They are composed of 12,000 from each tribe of Israel. Numbers in Revelation are rarely meant to be read at face value. Anciently, squaring a number magnified, completed, and perfected it. As discussed earlier, 10,000 was an enormous number for biblical peoples. The number 144,000 implies a vast and complete amount—many people. Verse 9 then adds "a great multitude, which no man could number, of all nations, and kindreds, and people, and tongues." (Revelation 7:9.) Dan is not mentioned, and though Joseph is included in the tribal account, so is Manasseh, his son. This is apparently an error of translation. "Manasseh" should in all probability read "Dan." In the Old Testament, Dan is often mentioned in connection with Asher and Naphtali, as they were all assigned to the north side of the camp of Israel while wandering in the wilderness. (See Numbers 2:25–29; Deuteronomy 33:22–24.) They also lived next to one another in the north of the land of Canaan. Notice that the other two tribes mentioned in Revelation 7:6 are Asher and Naphtali. I mention this because I know someone whose patriarchal blessing said that her lineage was of Dan, and she was troubled that Revelation 7 excluded her.

Joseph Smith associated the sealed of God with temple work when he wrote, "I am going on in my progress for eternal life. It is not only necessary that you should be baptized for your dead, but you will have to go through all the ordinances for them, the same as you have gone through to save yourselves. There will be 144,000 saviors on Mount Zion, and with them an innumerable host that no man can number." (*Teachings of the Prophet Joseph Smith,* 366.) The 144,000 would have entrance into the Lord's house and the opportunity to participate in its most holy ordinances, both for themselves and their ancestors.

In section 77 of the Doctrine and Covenants, the Prophet said that the 144,000 "are high priests, ordained unto the holy order of God, to administer the everlasting gospel." He also said these would be "ordained out of every nation, kindred, tongue, and people." (D&C 77:11.) They would necessarily hold the Melchizedek Priesthood.

During Old and New Testament times, only the Levites could administer in the temple ordinances. They could go into the "holy place," where they would place bread on the table, light the lampstand, and burn incense on the altar before the veil. The holy place in their temple corresponds most closely to the terrestrial room in our temples today. Behind the veil of the temple rested the Ark of the Covenant. Only the high priest could pass through this veil into the Holy of Holies, which corresponds most closely to our celestial room. He did this but once a year, on the Day of Atonement, when he made an offering that cleansed Israel from their national sins, or the sins of their generation. In order to enter this most sacred area, he had to be of the lineage of Aaron.

In the Church today, every tribe of Israel may hold the priesthood, so by biblical standards, they all have the right to enter the holy place, the right to participate in temple sacrifices and ordinances. Yet, by virtue of that same priesthood, they can also enter the Holy of Holies, passing through the veil like the ancient high priest. Perhaps John was shown the wonderful extension of temple blessings to a much wider priesthood. What wonder the ancients would feel if they returned today to visit the Church. Every single tribe is allowed to hold the priesthood. All are invited into God's presence, into the holiest places of the temple. All may, through their faithfulness, receive the fullness of the priesthood, holding every exalting blessing of the temple. One way of looking at the 144,000, therefore, is in the light of these advantages. I am sure that the ancients would continue to marvel as they realized that women were no longer limited to the outer Court of the Women but were also invited into the holiest center of the Lord's house.

Would that wonder not increase even more if they could see

that these blessings were no longer restricted solely to the house of Israel but to all nations? Isaiah prophesied of such a day: "The sons of the stranger, that join themselves to the Lord, to serve him, and to love the name of the Lord, to be his servants, every one that . . . taketh hold of my covenant; even them will I bring to my holy mountain, and make them joyful in my house of prayer: their burnt offerings and their sacrifices shall be accepted upon mine altar; for mine house shall be called an house of prayer *for all people*." (Isaiah 56:6–7; italics added.)

UPON THE FOREHEAD

This brings us to the seal that is placed upon the foreheads. Two Old Testament scriptures give us some insight about this topic, and they contribute to the idea that the temple commands the center of the sealing mentioned in chapter 7. They will also be helpful when we examine the opposite image—the mark of the beast introduced in chapter 13.

Perhaps the single most important scripture to the Jewish faith is found in Deuteronomy. "Hear, O Israel: The Lord our God is one Lord: And thou shalt love the Lord thy God with all thine heart, and with all thy soul, and with all thy might. And these words, which I command thee this day, shall be in thine heart: and thou shalt teach them diligently unto thy children, and shalt talk of them when thou sittest in thine house, and when thou walkest by the way, and when thou liest down, and when thou risest up. And thou shalt bind them for a sign upon thine hand, and they shall be as *frontlets between thine eyes*." (Deuteronomy 6:4–8; italics added.)

Applying the Lord's words literally, the children of Israel prayed with phylacteries attached to the forehead and hand. Practicing Jews today still pray in this manner. Inside the small boxes that constitute the phylactery are the verses from Deuteronomy. This was to remind them that all their thoughts, desires, and actions, all they lived for or strived to obtain, must be guided by their total commitment to the Lord. He was their God, and they had consecrated themselves to him. The seal in the forehead suggests that the lives of the 144,000 and the great multitude from every nation were guided by this devotion.

As we look at the Israelite high priest, we find another layer of meaning. Before entering the Holy of Holies, he was clothed in his priesthood robes and other official dress. On his head he wore a mitre, or cap, on which was a special emblem: "And thou shalt make a plate of pure gold, and grave upon it, like the engravings of a signet, HOLINESS TO THE LORD. . . . And it shall be upon Aaron's forehead . . . and it shall be always upon his forehead." (Exodus 28:36–38.) In Leviticus, the gold "plate" is called "the holy crown." (Leviticus 8:9.)

The word *holy* means consecrated, dedicated, and hallowed. Aaron had given himself to the service of God, and his whole being was consecrated. Therefore, upon his forehead was placed the same words we place on our temples when they have been dedicated to our Father in Heaven's service. By virtue of our covenants in the Lord's house, we may assume that the words "Holiness to the Lord" are symbolically or spiritually written on our foreheads. Since we have given ourselves to him, he puts his name, his seal, upon us, and he will watch over his own. If we are true to our covenants, the Lord's promised protection will remain with us throughout our lives, in spite of all the winds that blow.

THE SHOUT OF PRAISE

In time those same temple covenants will lead to the fullest blessings of priesthood, to our calling and election being made sure. We shall become the "kings and priests" (or queens) John spoke of in earlier chapters. Until then, we may deeply appreciate the wonder of our time—this marvelous sixth seal in which the light that pours down upon humanity surpasses the darkness that prevails in the world. We must be up and doing, sharing the gospel in the four corners of the earth, confident that the same angels who hold the winds of destruction will prepare the way for the spread of the truth until temples are found among every nation, kindred, tongue, and people. Then the sixth seal can pass into memory and the seventh proceed to its glorious climax.

With this in mind, it is easy to understand why the heavens again break forth in holy shouts of praise in the next verses of chapter 7, "saying . . . blessing, and glory, and wisdom, and thanksgiving, and honour, and power, and might, be unto our God for ever and ever, Amen." (Revelation 7:12.) As John sees the renewing songs of praise issuing from the great multitude, he is asked, "What are these which are arrayed in white robes? and whence came they?" John returns the question and is answered, "These are they which came out of great tribulation, and have washed their robes, and made them white in the blood of the Lamb." (Revelation 7:13–14.)

The Lord is aware of the tribulations of his Saints, even "great" trials. He understands it is not easy to live in the chaotic world of the sixth seal. Yet he knows that the work he has assigned us is edifying and will extend blessings to past generations. He knows that the rewards he has prepared for those who endure will more than surpass the challenges thrown against us. Though our weaknesses may allow some of the stains of the world to rest upon us, the Lamb's sacrifice will remove them through baptism, the renewing blessing of the sacrament, and the cleansing power of the ordinances of the temple.

If we remain worthy to enter his house here on earth, if we live in such a way that we may always enjoy the peace of the temple's celestial room, one day we will "serve him day and night in his temple: and he that sitteth on the throne shall dwell among [us]." That temple will encompass not only a celestial room but also a celestial world. Then "they shall hunger no more, neither thirst any more; neither shall the sun light on them, nor any heat. For the Lamb which is in the midst of the throne shall feed them, and shall lead them unto living fountains of waters: and God shall wipe way all tears from their eyes." (Revelation 7:15–17.)

Since many of these promises are repeated at the ending of the seventh seal, we will explore them in fuller detail when we arrive at those verses. (See Revelation 21:3–6.) It is sufficient to conclude that our dispensation, our seal, offers more reason to rejoice than to worry, more cause for gratitude than brooding. We will watch for the signs of the times, knowing what they foreshadow, but our vision will linger more often and more fully on the widening circle of sealed nationalities and the future peace of those who have been asked to pass through tribulation.

OPENING THE
SEVENTH SEAL

The rest of Revelation allows us to look into the final chapter of the Father's book. It begins with "silence in heaven about the space of half an hour." (Revelation 8:1.) Other than, perhaps, the birth of the head of a dispensation, it would be difficult to designate an event that marked the closing of one seal and the opening of another. This is apparently not true of the seventh seal, however. With the help of the Doctrine and Covenants, it is possible to determine the defining period when the sixth seal ends and the last seal commences. Since there is so much speculation and debate about this matter, it might be worthwhile to consider it before discussing the half hour of silence.

THE SIGN OF THE SON OF MAN

When the Savior was asked by his disciples to teach them about his return, he said there would be a last great sign in the heavens after the days of the darkened sun, moon, and stars. As did John, Jesus also indicated they would be days of trial: "After the tribulation of those days, and the powers of the heavens shall be shaken, then shall appear the sign of the Son of Man in heaven; and then shall all the tribes of the earth mourn. And they shall see the Son of Man coming in the clouds of heaven, with power and great glory." (Matthew 24:37–38, JST.)

Doctrine and Covenants 88 also mentions this great sign, but the half hour of silence spoken of by John is included in the prophecy. Verses 87 through 92 speak of the sixth-seal turmoil as discussed in the last chapter. Then we read, "And immediately there shall appear a great sign in heaven, and all people shall see it together." (D&C 88:93.) Verse 94 announces the end of the apostasy, a concept we will discuss when we get to Revelation 17. Verse 95 then quotes Revelation 8:1: "There shall be silence in heaven for the space of half an hour; and immediately after shall the curtain of heaven be unfolded . . . and the face of the Lord shall be unveiled." (D&C 88:95.)

The general order of events is established in section 88 of the Doctrine and Covenants. It is the same order seen in Revelation, with the addition of the heavenly sign that precedes the half hour of silence. We can conclude that the last act of the sixth seal or the first act of the seventh, if you prefer, will be the great sign in heaven that all people will see. The practical value of understanding this is obvious. It should put to rest the barrage of theories we often hear that try to establish the timing of the Savior's coming at the beginning of the last dispensation. The work of the sixth seal is not completed yet, nor have we received the last great sign.

Joseph Smith indicated that the world would not understand the importance of this sign. After repeating the general description of the sixth seal, he said, "Then will appear one grand sign of the Son of Man in heaven. But what will the world do? They will say it is a planet, a comet, etc." (*Teachings of the Prophet Joseph Smith*, 287.) Just as the Nephites tried to explain away the sign of Christ's first coming, the sign of his Second Coming will go unheeded by most of the world. (See 3 Nephi 2:1–2.)

The first coming of Christ was announced by the appearance of a new star and a day, a night, and a day of light in the New World. We do not know what the sign will be at the beginning of the seventh seal, but in God's great economy, we may be amazed to see a repetition of the first sign. Perhaps Zechariah hinted at such a repetition when he wrote of the Second Coming, "It shall come to pass in that day, that the light shall not be clear, nor dark: but it shall be one day which shall be known to the Lord, not day, nor night: but it shall come to pass, that at evening time it shall be light." (Zechariah 14:6–7.) Of course, this prophecy may be interpreted in other ways, and I do not wish to be dogmatic; I simply find it interesting and worthy of reflection.

THE SILENCE OF HEAVEN

We can discover a number of ideas as we ponder the meaning of the silence in heaven. The most obvious is a *dramatic silence*. This is a silence that creates anticipation. We have probably all sat in an auditorium before a symphony begins. We hear the noise of spectators entering and the conversations and preparations on the stage. Noise and bustling activity dominate the hall as the musicians tune their instruments. Often the orchestra will give a final, single note that announces to everyone that the conductor is ready to enter. After that note, everyone is hushed, and a period of silence follows. We could compare the last great sign in the heavens to that final quieting note. All are quiet as we await the conductor. On a battlefield a similar phenomenon may happen. The noise and confusion of the battle is everywhere. Suddenly all grows quiet as the guns cease and the shouting dies down. All ears now strain for the tiniest sound. Something is about to happen, and all wait in expectation.

In the case of Revelation, the angels are waiting for the Lord's command to prepare the tares for the burning. Since things have deteriorated so greatly, how long will he wait? Surely some action is forthcoming. This aspect of anticipatory silence is augmented by the story of the crossing of the Red Sea. Moses told the children of Israel, "Stand still, and see the salvation of the Lord. . . . The Lord shall fight for you, and ye *shall hold your peace*." (Exodus 14:13–14; italics added.) "Be still, and know that I am God," wrote the Psalmist. (Psalms 46:10.) Zephaniah's words about the Second Coming convey the same idea: "Hold thy peace at the presence of the Lord God: for the day of the Lord is at hand." (Zephaniah 1:7.)

A second explanation is a *silence of pain*. The Lord told Joseph Smith that "the powers of darkness prevail upon the earth, among the children of men, in the presence of all the hosts of heaven—which causeth silence to reign, and all eternity is pained." (D&C 38:11–12.) We have all been in a stadium when our favorite team was losing to its arch-rival. There is nothing to cheer about, just a pained, numbing silence. The prevailing darkness of the earth is distressful to the righteous beings of heaven. Enoch saw that Satan "veiled the whole face of the earth with darkness." He then saw the Lord weeping for the suffering and wickedness of his children; the Lord told him,

"The heavens weep, yea, and all the workmanship of mine hands." (Moses 7:26, 40.)

A third impression for the half hour of quiet is a *silence of finality*. The Lord's Spirit withdrawing from earth leaves it devoid of heaven's healing voices. When the Lord finally comes, he will speak to the nations using words identical to those he gave the remaining Nephites and Lamanites during the three days of darkness, with a detailed list of all the voices he had used to try to bring them to repentance:

"O, ye nations of the earth, how often would I have gathered you together as a hen gathereth her chickens under her wings, but ye would not! How oft have I called upon you by the mouth of my servants, and by the ministering of angels, and by mine own voice, and by the voice of thunderings, and by the voice of lightnings, and by the voice of tempests, and by the voice of earthquakes, and great hailstorms, and by the voice of famines and pestilences of every kind, and by the great sound of a trump, and by the voice of judgment, and by the voice of mercy all the day long, and by the voice of glory and honor and the riches of eternal life, and would have saved you with an everlasting salvation, but ye would not." (D&C 43:24–25.)

The Lord has nothing more to say. He has exhausted every voice available in trying to turn his children from their chosen path. He will be silent only a short time longer. The silence is given to allow mankind one last chance to repent, which leads us to our last meaning of silence.

The *silence of longsuffering* is consistent with the Lord's character. In Psalms the Lord gives us a list of human sins that pain him, then speaks of the silence of patience: "But unto the wicked God saith, What hast thou to do to declare my statutes, or that thou shouldest take my covenant in thy mouth? Seeing thou hatest instruction, and castest my words behind thee. When thou sawest a thief, then thou consentedst with him, and hast been partaker with adulterers. Thou givest thy mouth to evil, and thy tongue frameth deceit. Thou sittest and speakest against thy brother; thou slanderest thine own mother's son. These things hast thou done, *and I kept silence*; thou thoughtest that I was altogether such an one as thyself: but I will reprove thee, and set them in order before thine eyes." (Psalms 50:16–21; italics added.)

Sometimes as a parent, when my children were quarreling, I would not step in immediately and stop their arguments. I kept quiet, hoping they would solve the problem themselves. This did not mean I approved of their conflicts or that I was indifferent, but I wanted to give them every chance to learn and develop their own family skills, to arbitrate their own difficulties.

Peter accentuates the silence of longsuffering in his explanation as to why the Savior "delayeth his coming until the end of the earth." (D&C 45:26.) He acknowledges that in the last days there will be "scoffers" who will mock the belief in the coming Messiah, saying, "Where is the promise of his coming? for since the fathers fell asleep, all things continue as they were from the beginning of the creation." (2 Peter 3:3–4.) In other words, "We have been waiting for him for thousands of years and he has not arrived. He is not going to come, so let us eat, drink, and be merry."

Peter corrects their foolish thinking. The Lord's time is not ours. He "is not slack concerning his promise, as some men count slackness; *but is longsuffering to us-ward, not willing that any should perish, but that all should come to repentance.*" (2 Peter 3:9; italics added.) Though pained with man's cruelty and iniquity, the Lord will hold his peace a little longer. His silence is often effective. Just prior to the destructions in 3 Nephi, which took place in the first part of the thirty-fourth year, a large number of the people repented. "And there were many in the commencement of this year (the thirty-third) that were baptized unto repentance." (3 Nephi 7:26.) Had he come a few months earlier, what would have been their fate?

It is often difficult for the righteous to endure those moments of silence; they cry out as Joseph Smith did in Liberty Jail (see D&C 121:1–6) or as Habakkuk, who asked, "How long shall I cry and thou wilt not hear! even cry out unto thee of violence and thou wilt not save! . . . Therefore the law is slacked and judgement doth never go forth: for the wicked doth compass about the righteous." (Habakkuk 1:2–4.) The answer to these cries, pulled from the soul of believing sons and daughters, is, "Thine afflictions shall be but a small moment." (D&C 121:7.) To a world waiting for her King to arrive and set all in order, John encourages, "Be patient for just an half an hour, the end is in sight."

THE HALF HOUR

The time period of half an hour should not be taken at face value. It represents a short period of time offered to man to repent before the final cleansing preparations begin. A Book of Mormon example might serve as an illustration. The new star and the day-night-day of light told the people without equivocation that Christ was coming; still, things went along as usual for the next thirty-four years. Then the destruction of the wicked occurred and Jesus appeared in glory to usher in a reign of peace. This can be viewed as a shadow for the Second Coming, as the chronology is similar. The half-hour corresponds to the thirty-four-year period. Samuel the Lamanite told the citizens of Zarahemla that the purpose of the signs was "to the intent that ye might believe on his name. And if ye believe on his name ye will repent of all your sins." (Helaman 14:12–13.)

The Lord has no desire to destroy his children. He wants them to enjoy the wonders of the millennial reign, just as he wanted Lehi's children to share in the glories of His visit and the following centuries of peace. He gave them every opportunity to believe, change, and prepare. If Samuel was right about the three days of light, surely he would be right about the three days of darkness that would follow closely thereafter.

Now, I am not suggesting that the half-hour will be thirty-four years. I have no such intention. Some draw upon the Lord's statement from 2 Peter that "one day is with the Lord as a thousand years." (2 Peter 3:8.) Neither do I feel comfortable with dividing a twenty-four-hour day into a thousand and coming up with twenty-one years as the equivalent to the half-hour. I shy away from such methods of pinpointing the Lord's timetable. Perhaps the half-hour will be fifteen, thirty-five, fifty, or seventy-eight years. The point is that it will be a relatively short time. Our attitude toward it should be one of gratitude that the Lord's mercy and longsuffering are so great. Righteous action is called for in the meantime. When the half-hour is over, the Lord's cup of indignation will be full. (See D&C 43:26.)

THE FIRE FROM THE ALTAR

At the conclusion of the silence, trumpets are given to seven angels. An eighth angel is seen standing at the altar, offering to God the "prayers of all [the] saints." (Revelation 8:3.) Before the veil in the ancient temple stood a golden altar of incense. Incense symbolized the prayers of the Saints. The smoke could pass through the veil into the presence of God, just as do our prayers. It filled the whole temple with its sweet odor, thus making the temple a house of prayer. The incense and supplications rise to God, and he responds. Later in Revelation we read of the main theme of these petitions: "The Spirit and the bride say, Come." (Revelation 22:17.) Both heaven and the Church plead with God that Jesus may return and take his rightful crown as king of the earth. The Lord is now ready to respond. Even his immense patience can hold its peace no longer. But the earth must go through preliminary cleansing first. The final cleansing is to be done by the Lord himself when he appears.

There are three major cleansing agents in biblical ritual—water, fire, and blood. The Lord offers the world a choice. "You can be cleansed by the waters of baptism, the fire of the Holy Ghost, and the blood of the atonement," he says in effect, "or you can be cleansed by water, fire, and blood of a different hue—that of war and destruction." The earth was once cleansed by the waters of heaven that produced the Flood, but flood waters, fire, and blood are used extensively in the scriptures as symbols of war. It appears that war, therefore, will play a dominant role in the earth's cleansing and should be kept in mind as we study the images of chapter 8, but especially those of chapter 9, which continues the ideas introduced in chapter 8.

In response to the prayers of the Saints, an "angel took the censer, and filled it with fire of the altar, and cast it into the earth." (Revelation 8:5; see also Ezekiel 10:2 for the Old Testament background of this verse.) Fire will now become the chief cleansing medium, but blood will play an almost equal role. In war they are rarely inseparable. "Fire mingled with blood" (Revelation 8:7) is mentioned in connection with the first trumpet. "A great mountain burning with fire" (Revelation 8:8) is mentioned with the second trumpet. And with the third trumpet "there fell a great star from heaven, burning as it were a lamp." (Revelation 8:10.) The obscuring smoke of fire may be implied with the fourth trumpet's darkening of the sun, moon, and stars. (See Revelation 8:12.) The "smoke of a great furnace" (Revelation 9:2) gives birth to the locusts of the fifth trumpet. Finally, the horses of the sixth trumpet send "fire and smoke and brimstone" out of their mouths. (Revelation 9:17.) The seventh trumpet then announces that "the kingdoms of this world are become the kingdoms of our Lord, and of his Christ." (Revelation 11:15.)

Just as the seven descriptions of the sixth seal, seen as a whole, intimate instability, change, darkness, anger, removal, and insecurity, so do the above characterizations presage cleansing, purifying, purging, and refining. Much of it will undoubtedly be a self-purging as history and scripture demonstrate with manifold examples. As to their literal fulfillment, I hesitate to venture a theory, other than the forces of war coupled with those of nature, as in Doctrine and Covenants 87. The fifth and sixth trumpeting angels of the ninth chapter are almost surely intended as images of warfare, as are descriptions in chapter 16. With these limitations in mind, let us do our best in obtaining discernment and judgment.

THE SEVEN TRUMPETS

Even to this day, the sounding of a trumpet announces the arrival of something, often a person or event of importance. Christ is coming, but so is the earth's millennial day of rest. The Sabbath was so important to the Jews that as the sun set on the eve preceding the Sabbath, trumpets were blown to announce its arrival. We might want to keep this in mind while reflecting on the commencement of the seventh dispensation, for it will be the earth's Sabbath, its day of rest, when peace and righteousness abide upon its face.

There are, however, other, perhaps more compelling, levels of meaning for the sounding of the seven trumpets. An obvious story that comes to mind is the fall of Jericho. For each successive day of the week, Joshua was commanded to march around the wall blowing seven trumpets and then return to camp. On the seventh day, the circling armies led by the trumpeting priests were to make the circuit of the city seven times and shout. Then Jericho's defenses would tumble. Only Rahab (who helped the spies) and her family would be spared the destruction, protected by the sign of a scarlet cord that was placed before her house as a token of protection. (See Joshua 2, 6.)

I've often wondered about this strange way of fighting a battle. The sounding of the seven trumpets for seven days was the Lord's way of warning the people of Jericho that destruction was imminent. (See also Hosea 8:1 for a trumpet announcing coming destruction.) They still had time to repent, however. We will see that the Lord continues to offer the world's inhabitants the opportunity to repent during the blowing of the trumpets of Revelation, but as the citizens of Jericho refused to heed the warning, so too will the wicked of the seventh seal. The idea of rejected repentance is the controlling factor throughout much of Revelation and should be kept constantly in the mind. The closer humanity comes to destruction, the more the warnings increase—hence the seven trips around the city on the very last day. When the day of reckoning arrives, there is no wall strong enough to hold back the justice of God. Mercy was refused, and justice will now have its way. We will explore the false security of manmade walls or defenses and how they relate to Revelation in a later chapter.

In Leviticus the Lord listed the problems his people would have if they rebelled against his laws. He repeatedly used phrases that would apply to the seven trumpets as well as the seven vials filled with the wrath of God in chapter 26: "I will punish you seven times more for your sins. . . . I will bring seven times more plagues upon you according to your sins. . . . I, even I, will chastise you seven times for your sins." (Leviticus 26:18, 21, 28.) Each of these phrases suggests a total judgment. The world is now ready for a complete cleansing.

THE PLAGUES OF EGYPT

The other major Old Testament story that we should contemplate while reading chapters 8, 9, and 16 is the plagues of Egypt. John repeats many of these plagues, such as water to blood, hail and fire, darkened sun, locusts, sores, and frogs. If we cross-referenced section 29 of the Doctrine and Covenants to this period, we could also add the plague of flies. (See D&C 29:18.)

Two ideas immediately become apparent when connecting John's plagues with those of Egypt. Though the plagues were unbearable for the Egyptians, most of them did not fall upon the children of Israel. The Lord specifically said, "I will put a division between my people and thy people: tomorrow shall this sign be." (Exodus 8:23.) More than once Exodus mentions that the Lord was not sending the plagues upon his own people. (See Exodus 9:4, 26; 10:23; 11:7.) We can take comfort in that thought. Revelation was not unfolded to our view to cause distress and anxiety but to give us confidence and reassurance. These are often imparted, however, with allusions to stories

114

John expects us to know thoroughly. What is not said is as critical as what is overtly stated by the Revelator. Though not spared entirely, the Saints will receive the same division if they will be worthy.

The second thought that comes to mind centers on the role of Pharaoh. We are specifically told that each new plague was designed to convince Pharaoh and the Egyptians that Jehovah was God. (See Exodus 5:2; 7:5, 17; 8:10, 22; 9:14, 29; 10:2.) Again and again Pharaoh asked Moses to have the Lord remove the plagues, and each time the Lord responded only to have Pharaoh "harden his heart." "I have sinned against the Lord," Pharaoh once said. "Now therefore forgive, I pray thee, my sin only this once, and intreat the Lord your God, that he may take away from me this death only." (Exodus 10:16–17.) The long-suffering, forgiving nature of God is seen so perfectly throughout this story. But Pharaoh's repentance was never sincere.

The reference to the Egyptian plagues throughout Revelation suggests a similar response from the world in general. Regardless of what happens as the warning trumpets blow, mankind will repent Pharaoh-like but not deeply, not permanently, if at all. Perhaps the most important verses for understanding the applications we should receive when reading about the plagues unleashed during the blowing of the trumpets is at the end of chapter 9 and repeated in chapter 16 (which is, in many ways, a twin—though not an identical one—to chapters 8 and 9). Here we read of "the rest of the men which were not killed by these plagues *yet repented not* of the works of their hands, that they should not worship devils, and idols of gold, and silver, and brass, and stone, and of wood: which neither can see, nor hear, nor walk: *neither repented they* of their murders, nor

of their sorceries, nor of their fornication, nor of their thefts."
(Revelation 9:20–21; italics added.)

The direct meaning of the four plagues found in chapter 8
is not nearly as critical as the above understanding. We sense
that their fulfillment will center in war and its accompanying
miseries, but other interpretations have been offered. Aware of
our limitations, let us take a closer look at some of the details
of the first four angels with their sounding trumpets.

THE THIRD PART

Once again we are confronted with a fraction, the "third
part," which may mean a limitation of destruction. The expression has also been used as a figure of speech suggesting a great
amount. An illustration is found, for example, in Shakespeare's
play *The Tempest*. When Prospero gives his beloved child,
Miranda, to her future husband, he remarks, "I have given you
here a third of mine own life, or that for which I live, whom
once again I tender to thy hand." (Act IV, Scene I, lines 4–7.)
A third part when used as a figure of speech means a large part.
This reading of the fraction seems to command more credence.

Old Testament roots for the third part are found in Ezekiel
chapter 5, where it represents those who are destined for
destruction, meaning the wicked. This understanding fits well
with Revelation 8. As Ezekiel's third part is critical in understanding part of the language of Revelation 16, we will examine it more fully when arriving at that chapter. Zechariah 13
also speaks of dividing the people into thirds, two of which are
to be destroyed, while the last third becomes the remnant of
Israel. Generally speaking, the third part can allude to those
who will be destroyed because of their rebellion and refusal to
repent.

In Revelation 12 we are shown a red dragon, representing Satan, whose "tail drew the third part of the stars of heaven." (Revelation 12:4.) This we recognize as a reference to the war in heaven and the expulsion of Lucifer and his legions. These souls are lost, suffering spiritual death, once again linking destruction to the fraction of "a third part." In this context, the third part may portray those who follow the adversary. Cautiously, we might entertain the idea that the third part intimates the telestial as separate from the terrestrial or the celestial. At the Second Coming, it is those who have lived a telestial life who will be cleansed from the earth. (See D&C 76:102.)

TREES, SEA, RIVERS, AND STARS

The earlier interpretation of the "third part" raises new questions. The fire and destruction accompanying the sounding angels fall on elements of nature, but how can nature be wicked, rebellious, or unrepentant? How can trees, fountains, and stars be set aside for destruction? Certainly these kinds of disasters would make life difficult for people, but let us search in another direction and see if the pieces fit on another level. Earlier we spoke of a figure of speech called synecdoche in which a part stands for the whole. Since all the things mentioned in chapter 8, as recipients of the cleansing fires, are part of the creation story in Genesis, the imagery may simply suggest the totality of the earth. There is no safe place, for destruction is everywhere. Remember, the angels were holding back the winds from blowing on "the earth, . . . the sea, . . . [or] any tree." (Revelation 7:1.) It is more obvious that the usage in that instance refers to mankind. Now that the winds are blowing in chapter 8, we need not change the meaning applied in the earlier chapter.

Another closely related figure of speech is known as metonymy, which is when a closely associated object stands for something else. The Old Testament speaks, for instance, of the cedars of Lebanon. The cedar tree was so closely associated with the nation of Lebanon that it could stand for the nation in the language of the day. Another illustration would be our use of "the crown," meaning the ruler of a nation or its government. Since the earth and mankind are so intricately interwoven, in biblical language it is possible to read these cleansing events as relating to man.

Even in the details, mankind can be implied. Trees are used as symbols of armies and the pride of nations in Isaiah, Ezekiel, Daniel, and Zechariah. Speaking of the armies and multitudes of Assyria, the Lord revealed, "The light of Israel shall be for a fire . . . and shall consume the glory of his *forest*, and of his fruitful field, both soul and body: and they shall be as when a standardbearer fainteth. And the *rest of the trees of his forest* shall be few. . . . The Lord of hosts, shall *lop the bough* with terror: and the high ones of stature shall be *hewn down*, and the haughty shall be humbled. And he shall cut down the *thickets of the forest* with iron, and *Lebanon shall fall* by a mighty one." (Isaiah 10:17–19, 33–34; italics added.)

The whole of Ezekiel 31 compares mighty nations to "trees by the waters [that] exalt themselves for their height." (Ezekiel 31:14.) Daniel interprets another dream of Nebuchadnezzar in which the king is depicted as "a tree in the midst of the earth, and the height thereof was great." The angels who are given charge over the earth, "the watchers," decree the cutting down of the tree, that "the living may know that the most High ruleth in the kingdom of men." (Daniel 4:10, 17.) A major symbol for Israel itself was that of an olive tree.

Zechariah's message includes a number of trees that were used in biblical times to denote the pride of nations: "Open thy doors, O Lebanon, that the fire may devour thy cedars. Howl, fir tree; for the cedar is fallen; because the mighty are spoiled: howl, O ye oaks of Bashan; for the forest of the vintage is come down." (Zechariah 11:1–2.) The book of Zechariah is particularly relevant, for it mentions fire as the element used to humble the trees, just as fire is used in Revelation. Even Nahum states that the "fir trees shall be terribly shaken" in his descriptive version of falling armies of men. (Nahum 2:3.)

The sea is also used to represent mankind. This is plainly explained to John himself in Revelation: "The waters which thou sawest, where the whore sitteth, are peoples, and multitudes, and nations, and tongues." (Revelation 17:15; see also 1 Nephi 14:11.) Many people massed together look like the movement of water from a distance. Even in our sports arenas we mimic moving water when people stand in a circling motion around the stadium in imitation of a wave. Further use of the sea, as representative of mankind, will be explored in chapter 13.

Rivers as a symbol for nations, cities, or empires is also used extensively in the Old Testament. A few examples will serve as illustrations. "The Lord bringeth up upon them the waters of the river, strong and many, even the king of Assyria, and all his glory: and he shall come up over all his channels, and go over all his banks." (Isaiah 8:7.) Here the rising empire is compared to a flood, with the banks depicting the borders of the country. In verses hauntingly similar to Revelation 8, Habakkuk speaks of the Lord sending his "burning coals" before him. He then measures (or judges) the earth, driving "asunder the nations" and scattering the mountains. The rivers and the sea are then mentioned: "Was the Lord displeased against the rivers? was

119

thine anger against the rivers? was thy wrath against the sea, that thou didst ride upon thine horses and thy chariots of salvation? . . . Thou didst march through the land in indignation, thou didst thresh the heathen in anger." (Habakkuk 3:5–8, 12.) These verses are particularly significant since Habakkuk asks the Lord the same question posed by the martyrs in Revelation 6: "How long shall I cry, and thou wilt not hear! even cry out unto thee of violence, and thou wilt not save!" (Habakkuk 1:2.)

Both the Psalms and Zechariah speak of a future day when Jesus "shall have dominion also from sea to sea, and from the river unto the ends of the earth." (Psalms 72:8; see also Zechariah 9:10.) "River" here can mean the borders of a nation out to the farthest limits of human habitation, or it can mean the heavily populated centers to the tiniest hamlet. Since major empires and cities were located on rivers (the Nile, the Tiber, the Euphrates, the Thames, the Tigris, the Seine, the Rhine, and so on), the association of rivers with nations was natural.

The heavens have also suggested, from time to time, mankind, especially the stars. This we have already seen in Revelation. In Joseph's dream, his eleven brothers and his parents were portrayed as the sun, moon, and stars. (See Genesis 37:9.) God's children are stars in Job. (Job 38:7.) More fitting to the topic is Daniel's vision of the rising empires of Persia and Greece, which are compared to a goat and ram: "And it waxed great, even to the host of heaven; and it cast down some of the host and of the stars to the ground, and stamped upon them." (Daniel 8:10.)

We need not be dogmatic about these ideas, but they may help us remove some of the mystery and sensationalism of this chapter. This is equally true of interpreting the reference to the falling star "called Wormwood" (Revelation 8:11), which turns the waters bitter. Jeremiah offers explanatory help in two passages. Because of the wickedness of Israel, the Lord told Jeremiah, "I will feed them, even this people, with wormwood, and give them water of gall to drink." (Jeremiah 9:15; see also 23:15.) Today we have the expression "That's a bitter pill to swallow," meaning an experience is painful or distasteful. With the opening of the seventh seal, there will be bitter consequences to face. The best interpretation of the falling star, therefore, appears to be Satan. In chapter 9 he is definitely depicted as a falling star, and Wormwood is a perfectly logical name to give the arch deceiver, whose influences upon the earth will cause mankind to drink some very bitter water. But then, they have rejected the living water offered by Christ.

OUT FROM THE BOTTOMLESS PIT

he fifth and sixth angels sound their trumpets in chapter 9. More focus is paid to these two soundings than the first four. At the note of the fifth trumpet, John sees "a star fall from heaven unto the earth: and to him was given the key of the bottomless pit." (Revelation 9:1.) Jesus once told his disciples, "I beheld Satan as lightning fall from heaven." (Luke 10:18.) We are on pretty safe ground to identify the star with the adversary.

Consistent with the parallel imaging of Revelation, Lucifer, as did Jesus, holds a key to hell. However, when he turns it, "there arose a smoke out of the pit, as the smoke of a great furnace; and the sun and the air were darkened by reason of the smoke of the pit." (Revelation 9:2.) Lucifer always tries to obscure our vision. He "veil[s] the whole face of the earth with darkness" (Moses 7:26), seeks to "deceive and to blind men" (Moses 4:4), and obscures their path with "an exceedingly great mist" (1 Nephi 8:23).

Smoke shuts out light, and if a furnace door was opened and billows of black smoke belched forth, it would not only cloak our surroundings but also sting our eyes. It was revealed to Nephi that the purpose of the mists in his father's dream was twofold; in addition to blinding the eyes, they would also "[harden] the hearts of the children of men." (1 Nephi 12:17.) This explanation was given in the context of the Nephite-Lamanite centuries of animosity. The smoke of Revelation and the mists of Lehi's dream both depict similar attributes of the adversary's tactics. The mists of 1 Nephi were designed to shroud three other symbols of the dream—the tree, or the love of God; the iron rod, or the words and truths of God; and the river, the misery into which the wicked fall, which is the eventual consequence of being lost in the mists of darkness. If there is no love, no absolute truth, and no eternal consequences for sin, the heart naturally hardens. The smoke of Revelation 9 accomplishes the same objectives.

The smoke from the furnace of the bottomless pit, therefore, can be identified by listing those things that tend to blind men in such a way that their hearts harden, resulting in contention and bloodshed. "Contention," Jesus told the Nephites, ". . . is of the devil, who is the father of contention, and he stirreth up the hearts of men to contend with anger, one with another." (3 Nephi 11:29.) Hate is, perhaps, the thickest smoke of hell, but fear, anger, bigotry, greed, tradition, intolerance, suspicion, selfishness, religious prejudice, and revenge provide some blinding billows also. We need not look far for evidence of the blinding, hardening rage that rises from the smoke of hell. From these choking fumes the locusts of war are born, and like locusts they devour every living thing in their path, men, women, children, infants, and animals. The forces of war that are locked in

123

the blackness of Satan's hell have been released and arise in fury.

"And there came out of the smoke locusts upon the earth." (Revelation 9:3.) Lest there be any doubt that we are dealing with the forces of human destruction not that of insects, John specifically says, "It was commanded them that they should not hurt the grass of the earth, neither any green thing, neither any tree; but only those men which have not the seal of God in their foreheads." (Revelation 9:4.)

The locusts are sent to torment men for "five months." (Revelation 9:5, 10.) This undoubtedly means "for a season." Locust season lasts about five months, usually covering from late spring to early fall when fields are growing, ripening, and harvested. Changes in the temperature eventually solve the problem, but the next season sees the marching hordes moving again. Ancient armies found it difficult to fight during the winter months. Forage was needed for animals. Many lived off the land as they conquered, and rains turned roads to mud, making progress difficult. The season to fight was often late spring to early fall. I hesitate to read the armies of locusts as a one-time phenomenon; rather, it is a yearly cycle of war. Each new season sees fresh swarms arising from the ever-present smoke that pours from the mouth of the pit. Every new year finds the devouring face of conflict in different areas, but the results are always the same.

Somewhat puzzling is the command not to kill men but only to sting them as does a scorpion. The next verse says, "In those days shall men seek death, and shall not find it; and shall desire to die, and death shall flee from them." (Revelation 9:6.) Light on this information can be obtained from some of Mormon's comments about his people during their last ruinous wars:

"Their sorrowing was not unto repentance . . . but . . . rather the sorrowing of the damned, because the Lord would not always suffer them to take happiness in sin. And they did not come unto Jesus with broken hearts and contrite spirits, but *they did curse God, and wish to die*. Nevertheless they would struggle with the sword for their lives. . . . And I saw that the day of grace was passed with them, both temporally and spiritually; for I saw thousands of them hewn down in open rebellion against their God, and heaped up as dung upon the face of the land." (Mormon 2:13–15; italics added.) The sting of war burns with such fury in the bloodstream of society that the peace of the grave becomes the only one possible, and the only one sought.

The physical depiction of the locusts is calculated to instill fear and exhibit their power. They also have a certain unnatural quality, for the viciousness of the warrior is an unnatural condition for the child of God. They are part human and part animal. They are both male and female. Their shapes are "like unto horses prepared unto battle; and on their heads were as it were crowns like gold, and their faces were as the faces of men. And they had hair as the hair of women, and their teeth were as the teeth of lions. And they had breastplates, as it were breastplates of iron; and the sound of their wings was as the sound of chariots of many horses running to battle. And they had tails like unto scorpions . . . and their power was to hurt men five months." (Revelation 9:7–10.)

Their horse bodies emphasize their size, strength, and speed. Crowns may suggest helmets and past conquests, or that they are all kingly warriors. In a normal battle, the king was one of the most powerful fighters. Enemies inevitably sought to kill the king, but what terror would be instilled in the minds of an opposing force if the entire army came wearing crowns? Their intelligence is indicated by their having the faces of men. This is not a mindless mass following instinct but a thinking enemy, alert, cunning, and resourceful. Long hair is a sign of strength, in the legacy of Samson, Absalom, the barbarian Germanic tribes, and so on. To this day long hair on a man imparts a sense of brute power, earthiness, endurance, and prowess. Lion's teeth signify ferocity, savageness, aggression, and violence. Their breastplates make them invulnerable, invincible. The sound of their chariot wheels and horse's hooves create fear before they are even seen. They are rapid, unstoppable, indomitable, unyielding, crushing, surging. Their tails send the message that they are intent on inflicting pain. Though they have power for only five months, as indicated above, they will be back, year after succeeding year. Could John have been shown a better depiction of the forces and souls of the many nations, states, and organizations of today?

THE COUNSELS OF JOEL

The locust army's king is the "angel of the bottomless pit," Lucifer himself. At the head of this battalion he is called Abaddon and Apollyon, both of which mean "destruction" or "destroyer." His purpose is clear, and all who stand in his way will be swept aside. Much of this imagery, and that which will follow with the sounding of the sixth angel, has its foundation in the Book of Joel. Joel centered his message of the Lord's vengeance on wickedness with a vivid description of armies marching year after year like hordes of locusts. What is spared one year is devoured the next. (See Joel 1:4.)

"A fire devoureth before them," he wrote, "and behind them a flame burneth: the land is as the garden of Eden before them, and behind them a desolate wilderness; yea, and nothing shall escape them. . . . They shall run like mighty men; they shall climb the wall like men of war; and they shall march every one on his ways, and they shall not break their ranks: neither shall one thrust another; they shall walk every one in his path: and when they fall upon the sword, they shall not be wounded. They shall run to and fro in the city; they shall run upon the wall, they shall climb up upon the houses; they shall enter in at the windows like a thief." (Joel 2:3, 7–9.)

Joel's words are so visual that we can picture thousands of insects swarming everywhere. So too does a marauding army when it loots and despoils. No wonder Joel tells us that the "face [of] the people" who confront them "shall be much pained: all faces shall gather blackness." (Joel 2:6.)

It is extremely important that we realize the army of hell's locusts in Revelation comes from the pages of Joel's long-silenced voice. Revelation 9 may be more important for what it leaves out than what it includes. Those who have ears to hear will understand and receive the comfort that is not written by John but is offered by him just the same. The images are horrific, terrifying, which is the intention of both writers. We will therefore be prepared to receive the counsel that Joel offers, but Revelation leaves us to remember that it was given centuries and centuries ago. Those who know that the roots of Revelation 9 come from Joel will turn to his prophetic words and heed the counsels offered against such legions. As John did in chapter 6 of Revelation, Joel asks, "The day of the Lord is great and very terrible; and *who can abide it?*" (Joel 2:11; italics added.) This question follows immediately after the advance of Joel's locusts. Notice how he then counsels the generation that must live with such recurring plagues:

"Therefore also now, saith the Lord, turn ye even to me with all your heart, and with fasting, and with weeping, and with mourning: And rend your heart, and not your garments, and turn unto the Lord your God: for he is gracious and merciful, slow to anger, and of great kindness. . . . Sanctify a fast, call a solemn assembly: Gather the people, sanctify the congregation, assemble the elders, gather the children. . . . Let the priests, the ministers of the Lord, weep between the porch and the altar, and let them say, Spare thy people, O, Lord." (Joel 2:12–17.)

The results of this repenting, fasting, gathering, sanctifying effort will be the Lord's protection. In spite of the roar of wings that sound like chariots running to battle, we will hear the quiet whispers of the Lord saying, "Fear not, O land; be glad and rejoice: for the Lord will do great things. . . . Be glad then, ye children of Zion, and rejoice in the Lord your God." (Joel 2:21, 23.) It is in this context that Joel speaks of the Lord "pour[ing] out [his] spirit upon all flesh. . . . And it shall come to pass, that whosoever shall call on the name of the Lord shall be delivered: for in mount Zion and in Jerusalem shall be deliverance, as the Lord hath said." (Joel 2:28, 32.)

The Restoration is the answer. Though war is poured out, so too will be the Spirit. We will gather and sanctify the Saints, whose broken hearts and contrite spirits will touch the Lord's mercy. The priesthood will put on their strength, plead for the people, and magnify their callings. In Zion the righteous will find deliverance while the rest of the world moves to the final climax of Armageddon for refusing to repent—as we shall see.

THEY REPENTED NOT

The trumpet of the sixth angel is similar to those of its predecessor. Instead of battalions of locusts, an army of horses is loosed from the "bottomless pit." (Revelation 9:14, JST.) Four angels appear to loose the horsemen, who are described in language echoing that applied to the locusts, suggesting similar traits and purposes. (See Revelation 9:17–19.) Undoubtedly the number four indicates that they are heading to the four corners of the earth. Though they, too, bring death upon only a third of mankind, the implication seems clear that they will go forth in every direction. The four chariots of Zechariah 6 presents a likely backdrop for the angel's work. These chariots "walk to and fro through the earth," causing the Lord to say they have "quieted [his] spirit," or executed his sentence upon the wicked. (Zechariah 6:7–8.)

We are told they "were prepared for an hour, and a day, and a month, and a year, for to slay the third part of men." (Revelation 9:15.) This sounds like a rather mysterious description on our first reading, but it is probably not as enigmatic as it appears. We divide time into different units in order to designate a precise moment in history. We have minutes, hours, days, months, years, centuries, and so on. The most basic date consists of a day, a month, and a year; hence we circle a number on the calendar to mark a future appointment. Then we record the hour of the engagement, obligation, or activity. The reference in Revelation means that the angels, with their cavalry of fiery horses, were prepared for that moment in time. They are not late for their appointment with mankind. They have arrived right on schedule.

GODS WITHOUT EYES OR EARS

Far more critical for our understanding are the last two verses of chapter 9. These were mentioned earlier when we studied Pharaoh's hardened heart in chapter 8. The purpose for all of chapters 8 and 9 falls under the shadow of these last verses. It would be well to repeat them again:

"And the rest of the men which were not killed by these plagues yet repented not of the works of their hands, that they should not worship devils, and idols of gold, and silver, and brass, and stone, and of wood: which neither can see, nor hear, nor walk: Neither repented they of their murders, nor of their sorceries, nor of their fornication, nor of their thefts." (Revelation 9:20–21.) The repeated use of the conjunction "nor" is a figure of speech called paradiastole, which is designed to emphasize each of the words in the list. It also shows the exasperation of the writer. Each sin alone is serious. Taken as a whole, they are worthy of destruction.

In the summer of 1976, when we celebrated this nation's bicentennial, President Spencer W. Kimball offered the nation some advice in an article titled "The False Gods We Worship." (See *Ensign*, June 1976.) He identified the two major false gods of the world as materialism and military might. Materialism will be spoken of in a later chapter, for Revelation has much to say of this perpetual weakness. Most interesting for the present are his remarks about the weapons of the day:

"We are a warlike people. . . . When enemies rise up, we commit vast resources to the fabrication of gods of stone and steel—ships, planes, missiles, fortifications—and depend on them for safety and deliverance." On another occasion he used language hauntingly similar to the last verses of Revelation 9: "We look to foreign programs, summit conferences, land bases. We depend on fortifications, or gods of stone; upon ships and planes and projectiles, our gods of iron—gods which have no ears, no eyes, no hearts. We pray to them for deliverance and

depend upon them for protection . . . like the gods of Baal."
(Kimball, *Teachings of Spencer W. Kimball*, 416–17.)

There is a certain convenience in worshiping gods without eyes or ears. We don't have to answer to them. They will not judge us or hold us accountable for violating commandments. They can neither punish for sins nor reward for virtues. They care nothing about repentance. On the other hand, they are equally indifferent to our happiness. The true God of heaven and earth knows keenly the difference between good and evil and responds accordingly. He gives commandments and laws. When mankind does not recognize the God of law—the seeing, hearing God of reality—choosing instead the gods of stone and metal, the law of the jungle becomes the replacement. It is kill or be killed, devour or be devoured. In such a world, power replaces principle and brute strength supersedes morality and ethics. God is "a being who never has been seen or known, who never was nor ever will be," asserted Korihor. Therefore, "every man conquered according to his strength; and whatsoever a man did was no crime." (Alma 30:17, 28.) The association of the two ideas is a foregone conclusion. An unseeing god does not care if one continues in "murders . . . sorceries . . . fornication . . . thefts." (Revelation 9:21.) Such gods will not condemn us, but they cannot save us, either.

Prophets, past and present, rarely address a problem without offering answers and counsel. As did Joel, President Kimball suggested that the right defense against the ravages of scorpion-tailed locusts and lion-headed horses was righteousness. "Experience is a dear teacher," he said, "but fools will learn by no other. But we continue on in our godlessness. . . . While armies are marshalled and march and drill, and officers teach men how to kill, . . . we continue in idolatry and adultery.

131

While corridors are threatened and concessions made, we live riotously and divorce and marry in cycles like the seasons. While leaders quarrel, and editors write, and authorities analyze and prognosticate, we break the Sabbath as though no command had ever been given. While enemies filter into our nation to subvert us and intimidate us and soften us, we continue with our destructive thinking: 'It can't happen here.' Will we ever turn wholly to God? Fear envelops the world which could be at ease and peace. In God is protection, safety, peace. He has said, 'I will fight your battles.' But his commitment is on condition of our faithfulness." (Kimball, *Teachings of Spencer W. Kimball*, 415–16.)

In light of recent world events, these powerfully prophetic words, given decades ago, invite the mind to solemn thought. We know what we must do, both as individuals and as nations. May we have the moral courage and spiritual fortitude to stand strong when Lucifer's smoke curls threateningly out of the pit, blinding the world with hatred and rage. May prophetic wisdom guide us when we hear the sound of horses' hooves and locusts' wings gathering in the distance.

THE SEVEN THUNDERS

Since the visions of the first six trumpets are so intense, it is time to ease the emotions and let the mind rest. There are forces greater than those just described. John is therefore shown "another mighty angel," who descends from heaven. The smoke, darkness, and fire of the four angels from hell is sharply contrasted with the cloud, rainbow, and radiance of the newly introduced angel. He has in his hand a "little book," which is open, "and he [sets] his right foot upon the sea, and his left foot on the earth." (Revelation 10:1–2.) The adjective "mighty" and the placing of his feet on both land and sea seal the impression that this angel is stronger and more powerful than the previous angels from the pit. Placing one's foot on something represents the idea of conquest. (See Joshua 10:24 as an example.)

The angel cries "with a loud voice" and is answered by "seven thunders." He then lifts up his hand "and [swears] by him that liveth for ever and ever . . . that there should be time no longer." (Revelation 10:3, 6.) The expression "time no longer" does not indicate the abolition of time; rather, it means there will be no more delay. The earth will wait no longer for her king. Thunder in Revelation often accompanies voices from heaven and is therefore almost exclusively interchangeable with the idea of communications from God. John is told to "seal up those things which the seven thunders uttered, and write them not." (Revelation 10:4.) Other prophets who had a similar experience, such as Nephi and the brother of Jared, were told to seal up their visions, but this is the only time in John's account that he is not permitted to reveal what he was shown. However, we can, without much doubt, learn what the seven thunders said, for they were disclosed to the Prophet Joseph Smith, and he was allowed to write them in section 88 of the Doctrine and Covenants. In this same section we also learn the identity of the mighty angel as Michael.

We obtain this knowledge by noticing that the same events that dominate this part of Revelation are paralleled in section 88. We have already seen that the cosmic signs in the earth, in the sun, in the moon, and in the stars, and the half hour of silence, are included in this section. Joseph Smith describes an angel who "shall stand forth upon the land and upon the sea, and swear in the name of him who sitteth upon the throne, that there shall be time no longer." (D&C 88:110.) Just before this announcement, however, seven trumpets each sound twice. It is reasonable to conclude that the seven thunders and the seven trumpets are one and the same. They represent the final announcements of God's will.

The first four trumpets announce the resurrection of the celestial, terrestrial, telestial, and sons of perdition in their proper order, the first two commencing at the beginning of the millennium and the last two at its conclusion. (See D&C 88:96–102.) At the sound of the fifth trumpet, "every ear shall hear it, and every knee shall bow, and every tongue shall confess . . . saying: Fear God, and give glory to him who sitteth upon the throne, forever and ever; for the hour of his judgement is come." (D&C 88:103–4.) The sixth trumpet declares that the apostasy's grip on mankind is broken: "She is fallen who made all nations drink of the wine of the wrath of her fornication; she is fallen, is fallen!" (D&C 88:105.) Lastly the seventh trumpet proclaims, "It is finished; it is finished! The Lamb of God hath overcome and trodden the wine-press alone. . . . And then shall the angels be crowned with the glory of his might, and the saints shall be filled with his glory, and receive their inheritance and be made equal with him." (D&C 88:106–7.)

Immediately the same angels sound a second time; each will "reveal the secret acts of men, and the thoughts and intents of their hearts, and the mighty works of God" in each dispensation or thousand-year period of time. (D&C 88:108–9.) Joseph Smith then identifies for us the mighty angel whose voice declares "there shall be time no longer." He is "Michael, the seventh angel." (D&C 88:110–12.)

This review of the past gives us the opportunity to understand the wisdom of God in his dealings with his children over the ages. When I was young, I recall a teacher likening the earth's history to a great tapestry that God weaves. We see the back of it, which consists of hanging threads and blotches of color that seem to have no sense, order, or meaning. But God sees the front of the tapestry, and when the seven thunders utter their voices in the grand parade of earthly events, he will turn it around so we can see his master skills at the loom of history. All of our questions, criticisms, misunderstandings, and puzzlings will then be over, and we will acclaim with reverence the Father's genius and artistry.

CALL YOUR SOLEMN ASSEMBLY

Once again it is important that we read Revelation in light of other passages of scripture. As Joel's words of counsel gave direction for those who faced the locusts and horsemen of fire, so too does section 88 give counsel about the seven thunders of chapter 10. Joel spoke of calling a solemn assembly. (See Joel 2:15.) Likewise, the Lord counsels in section 88, "Call your solemn assembly, as I have commanded you." However, this time the work of the Saints' assemblies is outlined in detail. We are to seek and to "teach one another words of wisdom . . . out of the best books." We are to "establish a house, even a house of prayer, a house of fasting, a house of faith, a house of learning, a house of glory, a house of order, a house of God." All "light speeches . . . lustful desires . . . pride and light-mindedness" must be ceased. All are to edify all, sharing both spiritual and temporal blessings. Idleness, uncleanliness, fault-finding, and sloth must be controlled and in time eliminated. "And above all things, clothe yourselves with the bond of charity, as with a mantle, which is the bond of perfectness and peace." Lastly, we are to "pray always," that we may not faint until the Lord comes. (D&C 88:117–26.)

As is so true throughout Revelation, that which is not stated directly by John is equally critical to what he recorded. We must not read Revelation without the added instructions given elsewhere. It is easy to see how these counsels dovetail perfectly with past areas of Revelation already studied. They will also conform to the future visions of John.

The sounding of the seven trumpets in the Doctrine and

Covenants ends with millennial peace, the subsequent release of Satan, and the last great battle of Michael and the devil. In Revelation we do not encounter these events until chapter 20. Nine more chapters of imagery await us. Except in its faintest outlines, we should beware of searching Revelation for a detailed chronology. We are being shown a great mosaic of action. John calls our attention to different-colored stones or regions, but the mosaic presents a vast landscape. Directed by John, our eyes shift from segment to segment, from the foreground to distant horizons, until we can comprehend the great whole of truth presented for our understanding.

THE LITTLE BOOK

A personal touch is offered to John in the second half of the tenth chapter. Perhaps he pondered his own role in the unfolding of God's will in this period. He is instructed to take the little book from the hands of Michael: "Take it, and eat it up; and it shall make thy belly bitter, but it shall be in thy mouth sweet as honey." (Revelation 10:9.) When Joseph Smith explained the meaning of the little book, he said, "It was a mission, and an ordinance, for him [John] to gather the tribes of Israel; behold, this is Elias, who, as it is written, must come and restore all things." (D&C 77:14.)

The title and role of an Elias was discussed earlier. John's personal responsibility would center on the gathering of Israel in the last days. That work would be both sweet and wonderful as well as bitter and frustrating. The Second Coming itself is a paradox of this type, for it is called "the great and dreadful day of the Lord," a "day of vengeance" as well as "the acceptable year of the Lord." (Malachi 4:5; Isaiah 61:2.) It is great and acceptable for the righteous but dreadful and filled with vengeance for the wicked. John's message is similar. It is sweet to be involved in God's work, to speak his words and offer his counsels, especially when they are received. Yet the resistance we encounter, the apathy, antagonism, and eventual outcome are sometimes painful to experience and watch. Every missionary who has labored to share the marvelous doctrines of eternity with the families of the world understands the dual nature of sweet to the mouth and bitter to the belly; so too do those who labor with less-active families, belligerent youth, or their own straying child.

This metaphor was originally given to Ezekiel in describing his commission with the house of Israel in his generation: "Thou shalt speak my words unto them, *whether they will hear, or whether they will forbear:* for they are most rebellious. But thou, son of man, hear what I say unto thee; Be not thou rebellious like that rebellious house: open thy mouth, and eat that I give thee. And when I looked, behold, an hand was sent unto me; and, lo, a roll of a book was therein; and he spread it before me; and it was written within and without: and there was written therein *lamentations, and mourning, and woe.* . . . So I opened my mouth, and he caused me to eat that roll. And he said unto me, Son of man, cause they belly to eat, and *fill thy bowels with this roll* that I give thee. Then did I eat it; and it was in my mouth as honey for sweetness." (Ezekiel 2:7–3:3; italics added.)

Numerous elements of Ezekiel's vision comment on those of Revelation. John's message was also filled with lamentations and woe. It would be offered to a rebellious generation living in the last days, some of whom would listen, but the majority would not. The idea of eating the Lord's words is common in scripture. Ezekiel and John were to make the Lord's message, his

ordination for them, a part of their very being. (We say of callings, material, or assignments today that we must internalize
them, or digest a message or instruction.) This would be especially important because of the nature of their call.

Perhaps the experiences of Jeremiah offer the best study for
understanding the paradox of eating the little book with its
sweet-bitter combination. In a moving prayer, Jeremiah poured
out his anguish to the Lord at the refusal of the people to heed
his words: "O Lord, thou knowest: remember me, and visit me
. . . take me not away in thy longsuffering: know that for thy
sake I have suffered rebuke. *Thy words were found, and I did
eat them; and thy word was unto me the joy and rejoicing of mine
heart:* for I am called by thy name. . . . Why is my pain perpetual, and my wound incurable, which refuseth to be healed?"
(Jeremiah 15:15–18; italics added.) The sweetness of an assignment from the Lord is seen in these words, as is the bitterness
that may accompany it.

In spite of massive opposition from all quarters, Jeremiah
continued his message, loving the very people who mocked
him. (See Jeremiah 18:18–20.) When placed "in the stocks"
(Jeremiah 20:2) for public display, Jeremiah called to the Lord,
again revealing the power of eating the Lord's words until they
become a part of one's innermost soul. Prophets called to work
in such troubled times must eat God's message to enable them
to stand strong against the currents that flow against them: "I
am in derision daily, every one mocketh me. For since I spake,
I cried out, I cried violence and spoil; because the word of the
Lord was made a reproach unto me, and a derision, daily."
(Jeremiah 20:7–8.) The bitterness of eating the little book is
readily seen in this passage. Yet, in spite of the bitterness, the
sweetness lingers in the mouth and overcomes the bitter: "Then

I said, I will not make mention of him, nor speak any more in his name. *But his word was in mine heart as a burning fire shut up in my bones, and I was weary with forebearing, and I could not stay.*" (Jeremiah 20:9; italics added.) Once ingested, the Lord's words light the inner fires that not only fortify the messenger but purify his very being.

❦

MEASURING THE TEMPLE OF GOD

Chapter 11 is for me one of the most difficult to understand. Perhaps for that reason I have pondered it more than the rest. My comfort level in talking about it is not as high as with others, especially if pushed into too much detail. This chapter is well known, for it contains the prophecy about the two witnesses. Joseph Smith attaches a fairly literal meaning to this section.

It is somewhat helpful to look at chapter 11 in the context of what precedes it and what follows it, both immediately and further out. Chapter 9 contains the commanding images of the smoke-born locusts and the cavalry of fire. Chapter 13 describes a beast that arises from the sea to dominate the world of men. These chapters center on the power of the opposition. Sandwiched between them are three chapters that seem, when taken together, to suggest that John himself (chapter 10); prophets, apostles, and the house of Israel (chapter 11); and the Christian church (chapter 12) will yet have an important role to play. The contenders will not win complete victories, nor will they go unchallenged.

Though banished to Patmos, John in chapter 10 was assured he would yet "prophesy again before many people." (Revelation 10:10.) Though the Church is driven into a state of apostasy, John is comforted in chapter 12 by the knowledge that she will not be completely overcome with apostasy and thereby destroyed. Her survival is assured. She will yet rise out of the darkness of infidelity to challenge the authority of the dragon in the latter days. Chapter 11, then, can be understood in the spirit of these hopes. Israel and her prophets will also reappear; a gathering, both spiritual and literal, will take place; both Old and New Jerusalem will be rebuilt; temples will yet be constructed.

John is given "a reed like unto a rod: and the angel stood, saying, Rise, and measure the temple of God, and the altar, and them that worship therein. But the court which is without the temple leave out, and measure it not; for it is given unto the Gentiles: and the holy city shall they tread under foot forty and two months." (Revelation 11:1–2.)

The first question we must ask ourselves centers on the meaning of "measure" as used in these verses. Two ideas come to mind. Measuring can suggest the placing of a protective line around the area to be shielded. This has been suggested in numerous commentaries and has some Old Testament justification. (See Zechariah 1:16; 2:1–5.) In this reading, the Saints are within the protective line while the Gentiles outside are subject to the traumas and destructions of the day.

Measuring is also often equated with judgment in the scriptures. In the Sermon on the Mount Jesus said, "With what measure ye mete, it shall be measured to you again." (Matthew

142

7:2, see also Luke 6:38.) The idea is similar to that of weighing a people, as the writing on the wall indicated would happen to Babylon: "Thou art weighed in the balances, and art found wanting." (Daniel 5:27.) Speaking of an earlier destruction of Jerusalem, the Lord said, "I will stretch over Jerusalem the line of Samaria [who had already been destroyed], and the plummet of the house of Ahab: and I will wipe Jerusalem as a man wipeth a dish, wiping it, and turning it upside down." (2 Kings 21:13.) Referring to the same destruction of Jerusalem, Jeremiah lamented, "The Lord hath purposed to destroy the wall of the daughter of Zion: he hath stretched out a line, he hath not withdrawn his hand from destroying: therefore he made the rampart and the wall to lament." (Lamentations 2:8.) Amos also saw the Lord standing "upon a wall made by a plumbline, with a plumbline in his hand." (Amos 7:7.) Here, too, the measuring was a judgment foreboding destruction. In a chapter deeply connected to the last days, Isaiah indicated that God would "stretch out upon [the world] the line of confusion, and the stones of emptiness." (Isaiah 34:11.) I favor this second usage of measuring the temple, altar, and worshipers. Though both meanings may have value, the idea of judgment rather than protection seems more likely.

THE TIMES OF THE GENTILES

If you look in the map section of your Bible, you will find a depiction of Jerusalem in the time of Jesus Christ. The temple mount is drawn with its various courts. In the center is the temple, with a tiny square in front of it representing the altar. A smaller court surrounds the temple, delineating the sacred area where offerings were made, and in front of it is another courtyard where the women were allowed and the treasury was located. An enclosure wall was built around this whole area, separating the sacred quarters, where no Gentile could go upon pain of death, from the rest of the temple mount. The large outer area was called the Court of the Gentiles.

Since John is asked to measure or judge the temple, the altar, and the worshipers, the house of Israel is implied. John is to judge his own people. However, he is not to judge the Gentiles. They had not been given the same light and truth as Israel. The preaching of the gospel among the Gentiles had just begun. In fact, they would be the very means of executing the Lord's verdict upon rebellious Israel. In A.D. 70 the Romans destroyed the temple, thus fulfilling the Savior's prophecy that not one stone would be left upon another. (See Matthew 24:1–2.) The holy city was completely trampled underfoot. In the Gospel of Luke, Jesus spoke of this event in language that closely parallels that of Revelation 11:

"And they (the Jews) shall fall by the edge of the sword, and shall be led away captive into all nations: *and Jerusalem shall be trodden down of the Gentiles, until the times of the Gentiles be ful-fillled.*" (Luke 21:24; italics added) From Abraham to Jesus, the house of Israel held custodianship of the gospel. They were to share it with the world and be examples of the joy and stability it brought to those who obeyed its precepts. But because of their delinquency in fulfilling its responsibilities, and their own rebellion against its truths, the Lord granted stewardship of the gospel to the Gentiles beginning with the apostolic era and continuing into the latter days. This period is called the Times of the Gentiles in scripture.

The Doctrine and Covenants gives a fuller account of Jesus' words as quoted above, and a clearer picture of the times of the Gentiles: "Desolation shall come upon this generation [his own] as a thief in the night, and this people shall be destroyed and scattered among all nations. And this temple which ye now see shall be thrown down. . . . And this I have told you concerning Jerusalem; and when that day shall come, shall a remnant be scattered among all nations; but they shall be gathered again; but they shall remain until the times of the Gentiles be fulfilled. . . . And when the times of the Gentiles is come in, a light shall break forth among them that sit in darkness, and it shall be the fulness of my gospel; but they receive it not; for they perceive not the light, and they turn their hearts from me because of the precepts of men. And in that generation shall the times of the Gentiles be fulfilled." (D&C 45:19–20, 24–30.)

The gospel has been restored; the light has broken forth. The times of the Gentiles is being fulfilled in our own generation. The gospel must be turned back to the children of Israel again. But during the time allotted to the Gentiles, Israel's descendants would be subjected to the heel of their treading feet. This is the time of the great apostasy, for the Gentiles showed no better ownership of the gospel than did ancient Israel—which brings us to the phrase "forty and two months."

FORTY AND TWO MONTHS

Forty-two months are three and a half years. Divided into days, they equal one thousand two hundred and sixty. All three of these numerical expressions are seen in Revelation. The phrase "a time, and times, and half a time" is also used. (Revelation 12:14, see also Daniel 7:25; 12:7.) Time = 1 year, times = 2 years, half a time = 1/2 year, totaling three and a half years. All are interchangeable and suggest the same thing. Many explanations are given for these time equivalents—some from Jewish historical events and others from numerical symbolism. I

145

will offer only one, with its basis in the Old Testament, as I feel it is the easiest to understand and remember; all others teach basically the same thing.

When Ahab married Jezebel, she introduced the worship of Baal into Israel's religious practices, at the same time persecuting and killing the worshipers of Jehovah. This was a dark time for the righteous; many fled, and others were hidden for their protection. But there was one bright spot of hope. Elijah was Israel's prophet, and though he too went into hiding, he called a famine upon the land in the expectation that the people would repent and turn again to Jehovah. There was no rain, and the famine lasted three and a half years. Jesus referred to this time when he said, "Many widows were in Israel in the days of Elias, when the heaven *was shut up three years and six months, when great famine was throughout all the land.*" (Luke 4:25; italics added.) The importance of this story in a New Testament context is further attested to by James, who also wrote, "Elias was a man subject to like passions as we are, and he prayed earnestly that it might not rain: and it rained not on the earth by the space of three years and six months." (James 5:17.)

Three and a half years, or its equivalent in months or days, embodies a time of persecution, dissent, and apostasy—in short, a time of spiritual famine. We can date the beginning of the great apostasy roughly from the destruction of Jerusalem and the scattering of the Jews. Amos described this period of renunciation and abnegation of spiritual truth as a famine: "Behold, the days come, saith the Lord God, that I will send a famine in the land, not a famine of bread, nor a thirst for water, but of hearing the words of the Lord: and they shall wander from sea to sea, and from the north even to the east, they shall run to and fro to seek the word of the Lord, and shall not find it. In that day shall the fair virgins and young men faint for thirst." (Amos 8:11–13.) This is one of the best passages to think about when confronting three and a half years; forty-two months; a time, times, and half a time; or one thousand two hundred sixty days.

Putting all these elements together, the first two verses of chapter 11 tell us that John's measuring of Israel finds them wanting. They will be scattered by the Gentiles, who will then take stewardship over the gospel truths. Their failure in that trust will result in the great apostasy, which will endure for many years of spiritual famine and persecution. But John does not despair; there is hope in the lessons of history.

THE TWO OLIVE TREES

The next few verses are replete with allusions to the Old Testament. As is often the case in Revelation, what is not said is as important as what is: "I will give power unto my two witnesses, and they shall prophesy a thousand two hundred and threescore days, clothed in sackcloth. These are the two olive trees, and the two candlesticks standing before the God of the earth." (Revelation 11:3–4.)

The allusion to the two olive trees and candlesticks takes us back to the post-Babylonian return of the Jews to Jerusalem and into the world of Zechariah and provides one of the main clues for our edification. The destruction of Jerusalem, her temple, and the taking of her citizens into captivity had occurred before. The Roman dominion is a repetition of an earlier Babylonian one. When their vassalage was completed and their hearts turned again to Jehovah, they returned to their homeland to rebuild the city, dedicate a new temple, and gather their scattered people. In Zechariah's prophetic record, two men were responsible for their return—Joshua, the high priest, and

Zerubbabel, a descendant of David and heir to his throne. A king and a priest were both necessary. Both were callings that required an anointing, symbolizing that they were filled with the Holy Spirit, for without the Spirit one was not fit to rule God's inheritance either spiritually or politically.

Zechariah calls these men the "two olive branches . . . the two anointed ones, that stand by the Lord of the whole earth." (Zechariah 4:12, 14.) He also is shown a candlestick that receives "golden oil" from the two olive trees so it may give light. It is the role of prophets, priests, and kings of the Lord's realm (all anointed positions) to instill the Spirit into the Church, which provides light for the world. Why John changes the image of Zechariah from one candlestick to two and associates both with the two witnesses is difficult to ascertain. Perhaps he wanted the best of both worlds. The witnesses, whose very name suggests they are apostles, would yield the oil of the Spirit as well as being the actual light of a candlestick. They are examples of living truth themselves and provide revelatory verities that the whole body of God's people may shine brightly in a darkened world. (It is also possible we have a problem with translation.)

Both men face strong opposition to the accomplishment of their tasks: "And he shewed me Joshua the high priest standing before the angel of the Lord, and Satan standing at his right hand to resist him." But Lucifer is rebuked, for "the Lord hath chosen Jerusalem." (Zechariah 3:1–2.) Since Joshua is "clothed with filthy garments," he is cleansed and given a "change of raiment." He is then given instructions: "If thou wilt walk in my ways, and if thou wilt keep my charge, then thou shalt also judge my house, and shalt also keep my courts, and I will give thee places to walk among these that stand by. Hear now, O

Joshua the high priest, thou, and thy fellows that sit before thee: for they are men wondered at: for, behold, I will bring forth my servant the BRANCH." (Zechariah 3:4–8.)

Those who hold the priesthood and officiate in its ordinances, especially those of the Lord's house, must be clean. Joshua is not alone in his work; he has "fellows" to assist him. They prepare the way for the coming of the greatest high priest, Jesus Christ, who in Zechariah's terminology is called the BRANCH. Every descendant of Abraham is a branch on the family tree, but only one child holds that appellation in capitals. The righteousness of these men causes them to be "wondered at." Malachi also prophesied concerning the cleansing of the priesthood that they might officiate in the temples of the Lord: "He shall purify the sons of Levi, and purge them as gold and silver, that they may offer unto the Lord an offering in righteousness." (Malachi 3:3.) This prophecy is strongly emphasized in the unfolding of the Restoration.

Zerubbabel is the focus of the next chapter in Zechariah. He is confronted by a mountain: "Who art thou, O great mountain? before Zerubbabel thou shalt become a plain: and he shall bring forth the headstone [of the temple] thereof with shoutings, crying, Grace, grace unto it. . . . The hands of Zerubbabel have laid the foundation of this house; his hands shall also finish it." (Zechariah 4:7, 9.) Nothing will stand in the way of rebuilding the temple. God will watch over it from the laying of the headstone with shouts of "grace" to the capstone with the great Hosanna shout.

God instructs Zerubbabel as he did Joshua. He must not believe that kingly power will accomplish the Lord's gathering work. "Not by might, nor by power, but by my spirit, saith the Lord of hosts. . . . For who hath despised the day of small things?" (Zechariah 4:6, 10.) The Lord's work moves forward through the influence of the Holy Ghost. In the Doctrine and Covenants he frequently speaks of the weak and the simple who will move forward his kingdom because they are directed by his Spirit: "I call upon the weak things of the world, those who are unlearned and despised, to thrash the nations by the power of my Spirit; and their arm shall be my arm, and I will be their shield and their buckler; and I will gird up their loins, and they shall fight manfully for me; and their enemies shall be under their feet; and I will let fall the sword in their behalf, and by the fire of mine indignation will I preserve them." (D&C 35:13–14; see also 1:23.) In another passage, the Lord encourages the early Saints with these comforting words, which echo the sentiments of Zechariah: "Be not weary in well-doing, for ye are laying the foundation of a great work. *And out of small things proceedeth that which is great."* (D&C 64:33; italics added.)

Interwoven through Zechariah's imagery is that of "seven eyes. . . . They are the eyes of the Lord, which run to and fro through the whole earth." (Zechariah 3:9; 4:10.) These eyes are upon a stone and are associated with the work of Zerubbabel in building the temple. Christ is often referred to as the Rock in scripture, as well as the cornerstone. In the fifth chapter of Revelation, John sees the Lamb with seven eyes, which we are informed represents those "sent forth into all the earth" (Revelation 5:6), wording almost identical to that of Zechariah. Joseph Smith changes the number from seven to twelve. It is a fair assumption that we can change it to twelve in Zechariah also.

Kings, high priests, a cleansed priesthood, the twelve eyes of the Lord (his apostles and Seers), gathering scattered Israel, being released from Babylon's captivity, rebuilding the city of

Jerusalem, constructing the temple at its center, preparing the way for the BRANCH, overcoming Satan's challenges, surmounting every mountain, accomplishing all things through the weak and simple endowed with heaven's Holy Spirit—every element of Zechariah's visions is repeated in the great latter-day work.

All of this richness of detail John is granted by the simple allusion to the olive trees. "You will have your future Joshuas and Zerubbabels!" the Lord seems to say through the images of Revelation. They will face opposition from the adversary, and the priesthood must be purged, but the way of the Lord's return will be accomplished again, just as it was after the Babylonian captivity that preceded his first coming. History repeats itself. Types are established for future contemplation and instruction. God's work moves through its cyclical patterns. Though Jerusalem is destroyed, her children scattered, her temple thrown down, do not despair, for this all happened once before. Yet we know what the Lord did at that time. He will do it again! In the latter days, however, its accomplishment is both literal and spiritual.

If we read Revelation with the poetic frame of mind, paying strict attention to the allusions to Zechariah and searching for the spiritual meaning, we will see the fulfillment of the two olive trees in every prophet from Joseph Smith to Gordon B. Hinckley. We will see the whole thrust of the Restoration and our own personal role within that marvelous work and wonder. But we will miss all this if we do not pay strict attention to what John leaves out but anticipates we already know, or have the wisdom to search out in the words of Zechariah. Nephi told his questioning brothers, who asked if the words of Isaiah he had quoted were to be taken temporally or spiritually, that they must be read with both realities in mind. I believe we must do this with chapter 11. I have focused on the spiritual applications rather than the literal, because the literal is almost always stressed, often to the exclusion of insight that is both powerful and personal.

THE POWER OF ELIJAH AND MOSES

The description of the two witnesses continues in verses 5 and 6. Now the allusions shift to the "authority held by Elijah and Moses." "And if any man will hurt them, fire proceedeth out of their mouth, and devoureth their enemies. . . . These have power to shut heaven, that it rain not in the days of their prophecy: and have power over waters to turn them to blood, and to smite the earth with all plagues, as often as they will." (Revelation 11:5–6.)

The first reference above takes us to the first chapter of 2 Kings. Here, Elijah was accosted twice by captains and their fifty soldiers, who were sent by the king Ahaziah. Each time, Elijah called down fire from heaven to consume his adversaries. The third captain pleaded with Elijah with great deference, thus saving his life and the lives of his men. Elijah accompanied this man to the king. (See 2 Kings 1:1–15.) The second story referred to is the famine called by Elijah for three and a half years. This was discussed earlier.

The mention of plagues brings to mind Moses and his confrontation with Pharaoh. These stories suggest that the witnesses of the last day will be stronger than any earthly force they confront. This goes hand in hand with the opposition faced by Joshua and Zerubbabel and imparts the same message. There is a particular implication that they are stronger than the false gods of their enemies. The three and a half years of drought ended in the battle between the Canaanite god Baal and

152

Jehovah. Elijah's God broke the drought after the confrontation upon Mt. Carmel. In Exodus we are specifically told that God would execute judgment against all the gods of Egypt. (See Exodus 12:12.)

Perhaps the strongest message we are to receive from these verses centers on the Melchizedek Priesthood. In the Joseph Smith Translation, this priesthood is described by delineating what wonders it can perform when necessary. The ministries of both Elijah and Moses are remarkably contained in this review: "Every one being ordained after this order and calling should have power, by faith, to break mountains, to *divide the seas, to dry up waters* . . . *to put at defiance the armies of nations* . . . to do all things according to his will, according to his command, subdue principalities and powers; and this by the will of the Son of God. . . . And men having this faith, coming up unto this order of God, *were translated and taken up into heaven*. (Genesis 14:30–32, JST; italics added.)

It is interesting to note that both Moses and Elijah were translated. The witnesses of the last days will hold the Melchizedek Priesthood and with it do all that is necessary to further the work of God on the earth. We should also not forget that both Moses and Elijah returned to earth in 1836 in the Kirtland Temple to bestow upon Joseph Smith their priesthood keys. Moses conferred that of "the gathering of Israel from the four parts of the earth, and the leading of the ten tribes from the land of the north." Elijah returned "to turn the hearts of the fathers to their children, and the children to the fathers." (D&C 110:11, 15.) These are called the "keys of this dispensation." (D&C 110:16.)

The Elijahs, Moseses, Joshuas, and Zerubbabels of our own time will, with the priesthood of Melchizedek, and in spite of all opposition, succeed in gathering scattered Israel and freeing them from spiritual Babylon, building the New Jerusalem, and restoring temples with their redeeming work.

THE LITERAL VIEW

I have accentuated the figurative reading of the first verses of chapter 11, but the comments of Joseph Smith place the fulfillment also fairly solidly in the literal. Since this has been discussed many times, by many leaders and teachers, it does not seem necessary to add many more observations. "What is to be understood by the two witnesses, in the eleventh chapter of Revelation?" Joseph Smith asked. "They are two prophets that are to be raised up to the Jewish nation in the last days, at the time of the restoration, and to prophesy to the Jews after they are gathered and have built the city of Jerusalem in the land of their fathers." (D&C 77:15.)

Three things need to happen before the two witnesses can literally fulfill John's words: (1) The restoration must be accomplished. (2) The Jews must gather to the land of their forefathers. (3) The Jews must rebuild Jerusalem. The expression "time of the restoration" is a bit puzzling to me. What do we consider to be the time of the restoration? Most of us would attach that phrase to the period of Joseph Smith's ministry. Here it apparently has a broader meaning, taking in the whole generation of the last days. "Restoration" is used not only of the gospel truths but also of the tribes of Israel as stated in the tenth Article of Faith. The Jewish nation was established in 1947–48 when they were given their own state by United Nations vote and then won their war of independence against the combined armies of their Arab neighbors. In 1967 the Jewish nation fought another war that resulted in their control of the entire city of Jerusalem. The Jewish Quarter of the Old City was rebuilt as were many other neighborhoods. One of the major obstacles that will need to be settled in the Middle East today concerns the fate of Jerusalem and how it will be shared between Palestinians and Israelis.

We could conclude that recent events in several past decades have placed into position all the factors mentioned by Joseph Smith as preparatory to the literal fulfillment of the death and resurrection of the two prophets. They are opposed by the beast, which arises from the bottomless pit. (This beast has not yet been mentioned by John, but it will be given full coverage when we discuss Revelation 13.) Their ministry is widely known, for "[all] that dwell upon the earth shall rejoice over them." (Revelation 11:10.) It is not too strange that the wicked make merry when the righteous are removed, as nothing is quite so disturbing to those who are not obedient as those who are, for they are a reminder of all that the wicked could and should be.

At the time of their ascension comes a great earthquake, which results in the fall of the tenth part of the city and the death of seven thousand men. I must admit I don't know quite what to do with this verse. It is a field I have tried numerous times to plow, but I can't get around the stumps. I am familiar with other interpretations of it but have not been totally convinced. We have already spoken about John's use of earthquakes and will speak of it again in chapter 16. For the sake of redundancy, we will leave it alone here. Some suggest that the tenth is the Lord's part, much as we give tithing. "Seven thousand" is a little easier to work with. When Elijah told the Lord, "I, even I only, am left" in his despair over Jezebel's murderous purging of the believers in Israel, he was answered, "Yet I have left me seven thousand in Israel, all the knees which have not bowed unto Baal." (1 Kings 19:14, 18.) I doubt that the Lord had taken a census of the believers; he was assuring his discouraged prophet that *many* were left who were still worthy. The slaying of the seven thousand, therefore, is used as an expression to suggest numerous, multiple, abundant.

This section of Revelation ends with the announcement that "the second woe is past; and, behold, the third woe cometh quickly." (Revelation 11:14.) The three woes were introduced in chapter 9. The first was the locust plague. The second consisted of the horses of fire. John includes the ministry of the two witnesses in the period of the second woe, a period when men would not repent. There is light, however, in the midst of darkness, for the earthquake and the witness of the two prophets does result in "the remnant" being frightened enough to give "glory to the God of heaven." (Revelation 11:13.)

INTRODUCING THE THIRD WOE

The last of the seven angels now sounds his trumpet. His message is a brief introduction, a table of contents so to speak, of the rest of Revelation. In the last chapters, "the kingdoms of this world . . . become the kingdoms of our Lord, and of his Christ." In anticipation, the four and twenty elders offer thanks and praise to the "Lord God Almighty" because he will take his "great power" and reign on the earth. (Revelation 11:15–17.)

Before Christ can govern, the present regime of wickedness must meet its demise. As we shall see, it will self-destruct in its own anger, so there is deep irony in John's next words: "And the nations were angry, and thy wrath is come." (Revelation 11:18.) Chapters 13–18 and part of 19 deal largely with the wrath of God, which consists of the withdrawal of his Spirit, thus allowing the minions of the adversary to bring about their own collapse. Nephi spoke of the natural consequence of the Lord's Spirit withdrawing. He had seen in vision the downfall of his own people, and we know from the records of Mormon that the Nephites, in their hatred, anger, love of war, and lust for power and wealth, doomed their own civilization. "I know that it shall come to pass," Nephi testified, "and they sell themselves for naught; for, for the reward of their pride and their foolishness they shall reap destruction; for because they yield unto the devil and choose works of darkness rather than light, therefore they must go down to hell. For the Spirit of the Lord will not always strive with man. And *when the Spirit ceaseth to strive with man then cometh speedy destruction*, and this grieveth my soul." (2 Nephi 26:10–11; italics added) God will, therefore, in his own ironic, paradoxical manner, "destroy them which destroy the earth." (Revelation 11:18.) But we are getting ahead of our story.

The last chapters of Revelation, 19 through 22, detail the judgment when God will "give reward unto [his] servants the prophets, and to the saints, and them that fear [his] name, small and great." (Revelation 11:18.) That reward will consist of a wedding, a feast, a magnificent city, healing fountains, and fruit-laden trees of life, and the comforting peace of the Master's gentle touch. Each side receives its reward, one from the Lord directly as a result of their goodness, and the other from themselves in a manifestation of what we call poetic justice.

THE HEAVENLY TEMPLE

Chapter 11 ends with a vision of the heavenly temple. The earthly temple that had been destroyed was but a type of the heavenly one that cannot be removed. "The temple of God was opened in heaven, and there was seen in his temple the ark of his testament: and there were lightnings, and voices, and thunderings, and an earthquake, and great hail." (Revelation 11:19.) Though the ark, which represented the covenant between God and his people, was destroyed on earth, the heavenly ark still rests in its accustomed place. The covenant is not broken; its promises remain. Future witnesses, latter-day Joshuas, Zerubbabels, Elijahs, and Moseses, will arise and see that covenant Israel is not forgotten nor her promises given to another nation. As candlesticks they will bring light. As olive trees they will bring peace. No obstacle will stand in their way.

The temple is open in preparation for its chief occupant to leave its sanctity and descend to the earth. As we will see, all of the images mentioned in this last verse are repeated in the ensuing chapters. We will discuss them point for point when we arrive at their place in the final unfolding of events. A table of contents is interesting to study, but only within the pages of the book will the details be revealed. The brief introduction of the seventh angel's voice of triumph now gives way to a key player in the drama he has just announced—that of a radiant woman whom Christ loves and will not allow to be completely overcome of the dragon.

A WOMAN CLOTHED
WITH THE SUN

Chapter 12 portrays the age-old battle between good and evil, between the church of God and the kingdom of the adversary. It is best to read this chapter in the Joseph Smith Translation at the back of your Bible, where the entire chapter is presented. All the words in italics are the changes made by the Prophet. The first representation seen is of a woman, which we are told in verse 7 represents the "church of God." Four main ideas make up her description: "There appeared a great sign in heaven, in the likeness of things on the earth; a woman clothed with the sun, and the moon under her feet, and upon her head a crown of twelve stars. And the woman being with child, cried, travailing in birth, and pained to be delivered." (Revelation 12:1–2, JST.)

It seems obvious that the crown of twelve stars represents the twelve apostles. The significance of this image we explored in an earlier chapter. A verse in the Song of Solomon that is repeated several times in the Doctrine and Covenants can deepen our understanding of the sun and the moon as part of the light associated with the church of God.

The Song of Solomon is love poetry between a husband and his wife or a bride and her bridegroom. We will apply it in the manner the Lord suggests in the Doctrine and Covenants, to th relationship of Jesus and his church. Christ as the bridegroom and the Church as his bride are dominant symbols throughout both Old and New Testaments as well as modern scripture. Since Revelation speaks of the bride of Christ in later chapters, it might be worth our while to become familiar with the Song of Solomon, as it will illuminate the beauty of that relationship.

Throughout the Song of Solomon, both bride and bride-groom speak. Each is convinced that no other is like their beloved. A good example is found in chapter 2: "As the lily among thorns, so is my love among the daughters," the husband asserts. Returning his praise, the bride says, "As the apple tree among the trees of the wood, so is my beloved among the sons. I sat down under his shadow with great delight, and his fruit was sweet to my taste." (Song of Solomon 2:2–3.) Later when asked by other women, "What is thy beloved more than another beloved, O thou fairest among women?" she answers, "My beloved is . . . the chiefest among ten thousand." (Song of Solomon 5:9–10.) Such conversation, mutual devotion, and delight continue in varying degrees and settings throughout the book.

The verse that is central for us to understand contains the acclaiming words of the husband: "Who is she that looketh forth as the morning, *fair as the moon, clear as the sun,* and terrible as an army with banners?" (Song of Solomon 6:10; italics added.) The first three lines of this compliment would please any woman. All three speak of light in its most beautiful manifestations—that of the sunrise, the softness of moonlight, and the brightness of noonday. If we think of the Church as the light of the world as Christ desires, that light is welcoming as the sunrise, gentle and soft as moonlight, and bright and warming as the sun. The sun gives life with its rays and chases darkness away so we can see all things clearly. There really are no vital issues on which we as Latter-day Saints are not given light and understanding.

There are few women, however, who want to be called "terrible as an army with banners." *Terrible* in this instance means stirring, lifting, awe-inspiring. In the Doctrine and Covenants the Lord uses this same phrase to depict his growing church in the latter days. Section 5 speaks of the "beginning of the rising up and the coming forth of my church out of the wilderness— clear as the moon, and fair as the sun, and terrible as an army with banners." (D&C 5:14.) It is repeated as encouragement to the Saints after their expulsion from Jackson County. (See D&C 105:31.) It is last used in the dedicatory prayer of the Kirtland Temple in conjunction with other Old Testament prophecies: "Remember all thy church, O Lord, with all their families, and all their immediate connections . . . that thy church may come forth out of the wilderness of darkness, and shine forth fair as the moon, clear as the sun, and terrible as an army with banners; and be adorned as a bride for that day when thou shalt unveil the heavens . . . that thy glory may fill the earth." (D&C 109:72–74.)

The allusion to the wilderness is important in the verse above, for the wilderness will play an important role in Revelation 12. In section 109, it is the wilderness of apostasy or darkness (not necessarily, but not excluding, the more literal reading that the Church arose from frontier America). There is one more verse in the Song of Solomon that has to do with the wilderness: "Who is this that cometh up from the wilderness," we are asked, "leaning upon her beloved?" (Song of Solomon 8:5.) When applied to the relationship of the Savior with his church that is struggling to rise up from the wilderness, this verse is wonderfully comforting. It presents a beautiful and touching picture of the help that has been given in the past and that we might anticipate will continue to be offered. Leaning on the strength of the Savior, the Church cannot fail to come forth from the dark wilderness of apostasy.

The importance of this description is seen in such places as temple architecture. The Nauvoo temple had starstones, moonstones, and sunstones. These were repeated in the Salt Lake Temple and even in more recent temples, such as the one in Palmyra. In descending order from top to bottom the stones are placed—stars, sun, moon. The stars encircle the top of the temple, resting above the sunstones. The moonstones lie at the foot of the pillars. Thus, when seen together, they duplicate the description of the woman in Revelation 12. Within the walls of the temple, the covenants and ordinances necessary to give birth to a Zion people are entered into.

She Brought Forth a Man Child

The woman is with child and "travailing in birth. . . . And she brought forth a man child, who was to rule all nations with a rod of iron; and her child was caught up unto God and his throne." (Revelation 12:2–3, JST.) If the woman is the Church, then the child cannot be the Savior, for he occupied the role of husband in the analogy. Besides, the Church does not give birth to Christ. He is the parent, not the child. In verse 7, Joseph Smith reveals the identity of the "man child." The Church is to bring "forth the kingdom of our God and his Christ." The name of the child is Zion. It has been the purpose of the Church in every age to establish a Zion community on the earth. From the earliest beginnings of the Restoration, this was the guiding goal of Joseph Smith and his followers. Even a cursory reading of the Doctrine and Covenants teaches this.

Our knowledge of Lehi's dream tells us that the rod of iron with which the man child will rule all nations is the word of God. Christ promised the righteous Saints of Thyatira that they would rule "over the nations . . . with a rod of iron," which Joseph Smith changed to read "with the word of God." (Revelation 2:26–27, JST.) Being caught up to God and his throne may refer to the final translation of the City of Enoch, but in the general context of Revelation, it more likely refers to the ultimate destiny of God's kingdom at the end of the earth.

Isaiah concludes his prophetic mission by speaking of the future birth of the man child, emphasizing how quickly it will be established in the latter days: "Before she travailed, she brought forth; before her pain came, she was delivered of a man child. Who hath heard such a thing? Who hath seen such things? Shall the earth be made to bring forth in one day? or shall a nation be born at once? for as soon as Zion travailed, she brought forth her children." (Isaiah 66:7–8.) This is followed by a description of the nourishment that will be found in the new nation. All her children will be "delighted with the abundance of her glory." Her "peace" will be "extend[ed] . . . like a river, and the glory of the Gentiles like a flowing stream" will augment her prosperity. (Isaiah 66:11–12.)

Brigham Young once spoke of the speed with which the Latter-day Saints would progress toward the perfection of a Zion people, comparing them with the City of Enoch: "I believe with all my heart that the people who gathered around Enoch, and lived with him and built up his city, when they had traveled the same length of time in their experience as this people have, were not as far advanced in the things of the kingdom of God. Make your own comparison between the two people, think of the tradition of the two. How many nations were there in the days of Enoch? The very men who were associated with him had been with Adam; they knew him and his children, and had the privilege of talking with God. Just think of it." (*Journal of Discourses*, 26 vols. [London: Latter-day Saints' Book Depot, 1854–86], 3:319.)

THE RED DRAGON

The kingdom of God on earth does not grow unopposed. Another claims the earth as his private domain, which he rules with the sword of the fist rather than the sword of the mouth, with an iron rod that oppresses rather than guides. Isaiah described Lucifer as one "who smote the people in wrath with a continual stroke, he that ruled the nations in anger." (Isaiah 14:6.) Obviously if the Church gives birth to the man child of Zion and it grows to adulthood, Satan's rule over the nations will be replaced by a gentler scepter and a more commanding sword. Hence, John sees "a great red dragon, having seven heads and ten horns, and seven crowns upon his heads. . . . And the dragon stood before the woman which was delivered, ready to devour her child after it was born." (Revelation 12:4, JST.)

A number of ideas are suggested by the seven heads and ten horns. This image is repeated in chapter 13 with the description of the beast. We discussed the meaning of horns in chapter 5, where the slain lamb was portrayed with twelve horns representing the apostles. The horn as an extension of power suggests that those rulers, nations, or forces are under the influence of the adversary. Crowns denote kingdoms, dominions, possessions, and sovereignties. Lucifer has always claimed authority on the earth. Did he not once offer its kingdoms to Jesus if He would fall down and worship him?

The seven heads can imply different things, many of which have been detailed before. For me, however, the image primarily advances the idea that evil has many faces. If I were an artist and assigned to paint the dragon, I would make each head different. The heart of evil, however, would be the same. One of the most dangerous things one could do when fighting a seven-headed dragon would be to single out one head, label it the enemy, and focus all attention on its destruction. The single focus would allow the other heads to attack. The kingdom of God has faced many different faces of opposition, but the heart of evil remains ever the same. The idea of multiple facets of Lucifer's kingdom will be explored more fully in a later chapter.

As in the stories of Moses and Jesus (but on a larger scale), a promised child, destined to replace the ruling dynasty, is sought for while in infancy that he might be killed. The rightful ruler must be eliminated so that the illegal one may remain in power. Such thinking led to the casting into the Nile of the infants of Israel and the slaughter of the babes of Bethlehem. The Lord is not to be thwarted, however, for he hid Moses in the inner circle of Pharaoh's court, and Jesus was taken to Egypt by Joseph and Mary, then hidden in the obscurity of a tiny village called Nazareth until he reached adulthood.

THE WOMAN IN THE WILDERNESS

The man child of Revelation is not mentioned again. Did the dragon devour it, or was it taken into the wilderness with its mother? However we answer that question, the emphasis is placed on the woman, for the dragon seeks her destruction with equal ferocity. Though a Zion society was established by Enoch and for a time also by the Nephites and Lamanites after the appearance of Christ, neither one ruled over the earth. The man child of Revelation, however, must replace the dragon's dominion worldwide. For the time being, the attack moves to the mother of the child: "The woman fled into the wilderness, where she hath a place prepared of God, that they should feed her there a thousand two hundred and threescore days." (Revelation 12:6.) The Joseph Smith Translation changes days to years.

In chapter 11 we discussed the meaning of 1,260 as a time of trial, apostasy, turmoil, and spiritual famine. The wilderness into which the woman was chased by the dragon is that of apostasy and darkness. John the Baptist was a voice crying in the wilderness of Judea, but he was also a voice of prophetic warning in an apostate world—a wild, uncultivated, undomesticated, disobedient world. Hints of Zenos' allegory of the wild and tame olive tree are seen in this rendering of the idea of wilderness. The association of wilderness with apostasy is also found in section 86 of the Doctrine and Covenants, where "the great persecutor of the church, the apostate . . . drive[s] the church into the wilderness." (D&C 86:3.)

Verses 6 through 13 of Revelation 12 can be read as an interlude, interjected into the narrative. We could put parentheses around these verses to set them off, a common literary and scriptural technique. Verse 14 is a repetition of verse 5, albeit using different wording: "Therefore, to the woman were given two wings of a great eagle, that she might flee into the wilderness, into her place, where she is nourished for a time, and times, and half a time, from the face of the serpent." (Revelation 12:14, JST.) The expression "time, times, and half a time" originates in Daniel. (See Daniel 7:25.) There the time delineated meant a period of apostasy and trial, as even a cursory reading will reveal. The phrase is akin to forty-two months, three and a half years, and one thousand two hundred and sixty days.

The time in the wilderness seems to best represent the great apostasy, the time of Lucifer's most total power. He now claimed what the Old Testament accords only to Jesus, the right to rule "from the river unto the ends of the earth." (Psalms 72:8; see also Zechariah 9:10.) In the New World, the lights went out completely with the last great battles of the Nephites and Lamanites at the time of Mormon and Moroni. The sacred plates were buried, and within a few centuries almost all remnants of Christian belief were eclipsed in the mystery religions of the Maya, Aztec, and other groups on this continent. Only fleeting shadows of a white god who promised to return, along with some distorted rituals, remained as witness of the American gospel. Using John's imagery, we might say that the woman died in the wilderness jungles of the Americas. Yet even here, the buried plates with their precious messages would not perish.

However, in the Old World, in spite of the apostasy, Christianity survived. Though changed in many of its doctrines, ordinances, and priesthood, many essential truths remained. Most remarkable, the scriptures survived. Some "plain and precious truths" were removed, but what endured still carried a rich fullness. The belief in resurrection, baptism, sacrament, atonement, priesthood, and scripture, though all distorted, continued to exist. The story of Christianity's survival in Europe is a fascinating tale, and one we cannot undertake in the context of this book. We owe a deep debt of gratitude to hundreds of individuals who preserved, copied, debated, lived, displayed in art, and passed on the tenets of Christ's teachings. The great cathedrals of Europe have always filled me with thanksgiving, in spite of their more somber elements, for they represent the triumph of the woman over the dragon. This is not to deny the condemnation of the apostate church that will be discussed in chapter 17 but to give credit where credit is due and validate the Lord's wisdom in keeping the woman from annihilation. She fled into a gentile wilderness and lived. The reason the Restoration had to come through the Gentiles and not the house of Israel is that they were the only ones who believed in Christ and still read and studied his teachings. (See 3 Nephi 16:6–7.) God prepared a place for the woman in the monasteries, kingdoms, artworks, cathedrals, and writings of Europe. She was nourished and passed through a Reformation, and enough was left to send a fourteen-year-old boy into a grove of trees in response to a verse of scripture still surviving after nearly two thousand years of apostasy. When coupled with the surviving remnant of the New World buried in a hill by the Smith farm, the woman would arise out of the wilderness to shine clear as the sun and fair as the moon.

These same ideas are validated in the allegory of the tame and wild olive trees found in Jacob chapter 5. The allegory presents a history of the house of Israel from Abraham's time to the end of the Millennium. During the early Christian era, apostles like Paul and Peter grafted the Gentiles into the spiritual legacy of the house of Israel. At first the early Christian Gentiles drew nourishment from the roots, but in time the branches overcame the roots. "Is it not the loftiness of thy vineyard—have not the

168

branches thereof overcome the roots which are good? And because the branches have overcome the roots thereof, behold they grew faster than the strength of the roots, *taking strength unto themselves.*" (Jacob 5:48; italics added.) The rudiments of the apostasy are contained in these words.

Because of this, the Lord of the vineyard finds "all sorts of fruit" that "cumber the tree." Tasting each one, he discovers that "none of it . . . is good." (Jacob 5:30–32.) However, notice the positive comment the servant of the Lord makes about the survival of the roots: "Behold, because thou didst graft in the branches of the wild olive-tree they have *nourished the roots, that they are alive and they have not perished;* wherefore thou beholdest that they are yet good." (Jacob 5:34; italics added.) Both Zenos and John use the word *nourished* when describing what will happen to the woman while in the wilderness.

THE SERPENT'S FLOOD

Lucifer, ever wary of the fruitful possibilities of the woman and her ability and desire to bring forth the destined man child who will end his rule on the earth, seeks to destroy the woman while she is in the wilderness: "And the serpent cast out of his mouth water as a flood after the woman, that he might cause her to be carried away of the flood." (Revelation 12:15, JST.) Earlier we spoke of the sword of truth that comes from the mouth of the Savior. Here we are given the parallel image. The flood betokens lies, falsehoods, and apostate doctrines. The history of Christianity is replete with examples of that flood. "And the earth helpeth the woman, and the earth openeth her mouth, and swalloweth up the flood which the dragon casteth out of his mouth." (Revelation 12:16, JST.)

Swallowing up something means its death. This reminds us

of the story of Korah and his supporters in the book of Numbers. These men challenged the leadership of Moses, threatening a general apostasy in the camp. "And Moses said. . . . If the Lord make a new thing, and the earth open her mouth, and swallow them up, with all that appertain unto them, and they go down quick into the pit; then ye shall understand that these men have provoked the Lord." Whereupon "the earth opened her mouth, and swallowed them up." (Numbers 16:28, 30, 32; see also Numbers 26:10; Deuteronomy 11:6.) The story of Korah had importance in New Testament times, for it is alluded to in Jude verse 11. Other scriptures also speak of the open mouth of the earth swallowing up evil. Nephi spoke of the wicked who "kill the prophets, and the saints, the depths of the earth shall swallow them up." (2 Nephi 26:5.)

Foiled in his attempts to destroy the Church completely, the adversary continues to fight her children. The children of the Church are the Saints in whatever dispensation they live. He may not completely destroy the gospel or the Church, but he can win some victories over individual members. Until the final victory of the Lamb, the Saints will combat the forces of evil: "And the dragon was wroth with the woman, and went to make war with the remnant of her seed, which keep the commandments of God, and have the testimony of Jesus Christ." (Revelation 12:17.) Joseph Smith viewed "that old serpent, even the devil, who rebelled against God, and sought to take the kingdom of our God and his Christ—Wherefore, he maketh war with the saints of God, and encompasseth them round about." (D&C 76:28–29.) This war was waged before the earth was created, and we should not find it surprising that it continues here. That we may know of the broader implications of that war and obtain a wonderful degree of hope, John is shown the foundations of the war in the premortal existence. He is also shown the key to winning its battles in any generation. This is the purpose of the interlude, the parenthesis, placed in the middle of chapter 12.

THERE WAS WAR IN HEAVEN

"And there was war in heaven: Michael and his angels fought against the dragon; and the dragon fought and his angels, and prevailed not; neither was their place found any more in heaven. And the great dragon was cast out, that old serpent, called the Devil, and Satan, which deceiveth the whole world: he was cast out into the earth, and his angels were cast out with him."(Revelation 12:7–9.)

These verses are well known among Church members and need little commentary. We may suppose that as the forces of evil were expelled from heaven, so too will they be removed from the earth: "Woe to the inhabiters of the earth . . . for the devil is come down unto you, having great wrath, *because he knoweth that he hath but a short time.*" (Revelation 12:12; italics added.) Though he may "rage in the hearts of the children of men" (2 Nephi 28:20), in the context of eternity it will be but a small moment. Even Satan himself knows this. His objective, therefore, is to spread as much misery as he can in the time allotted.

In the meantime, we must deal with him here. He can be overcome, we are told, "by the blood of the Lamb, and by the word of . . . testimony." (Revelation 12:11.) Having lost the battle in heaven, he continues to persecute the woman who will one day bring "forth the man child." (Revelation 12:13.) When the forces of darkness seem to prevail, we must remind ourselves that this is but a small battle in a much larger war. Great victories have been won in the past; both forces know the ultimate outcome. Besides, the generals who were triumphant in the earlier battles of our premortal existence still lead the armies of righteousness.

Satan is called "the accuser of our brethren . . . which accused them before our God day and night." (Revelation 12:10.) A good example of Lucifer in this role is found in the book of Job. Presenting himself before the Lord, he accuses Job of worshiping God for purely selfish motives. "Doth Job fear God for nought?" he tauntingly addresses the Lord. "Hast not thou made an hedge about him, and about his house, and about all that he hath on every side? thou hast blessed the work of his hands, and his substance is increased in the land. But put forth thine hand now, and touch all that he hath, and he will curse thee to thy face." (Job 1:9–11.)

When Job passes the first test thrown at him by Satan, another accusation is leveled against him: "Skin for skin, yea, all that a man hath will he give for his life. But put forth thine hand now, and touch his bone and his flesh, and he will curse thee to thy face." (Job 2:4–5.) Though deprived of all he has (including his children), broken in health, covered with boils, and sitting on an ash heap, Job maintains his testimony. Remember that John identifies testimony, knowledge of the Savior's final victory over the adversary, as the power that enables the brethren to overcome the "accuser." "Though he slay me," Job proclaims, "yet will I trust in him. . . . He also shall be my salvation." (Job 13:15–16.) Those accused in Revelation also "loved not their lives unto the death." (Revelation 12:11.) Notice how Job's stirring testimony of Christ incorporates the elements of Revelation 12: "I know that my redeemer liveth, and that he shall stand at the latter day upon the earth: and though after my skin worms destroy this body, yet in my flesh shall I see God." (Job 19:25–26.) Even death, the last weapon in the accuser's arsenal, will finally be vanquished. God's answer to the devil's accusation is the confidence He has in His children: "They will love, worship, and trust me no matter what happens to them," he seems to reply. "You may bring whatever trials you wish upon them, but they will not abandon their faith in me. You have falsely accused them."

How many hope-filled truths are contained in Revelation 12! Though the war once commenced in a world we no longer remember, the enemy was defeated. With the help of the atoning blood of the Lamb, the power of our own testimonies, the radiant woman with her crown of apostles, and the growth to manhood of the man child, what have we to fear? We must trust Christ in spite of life and Lucifer's proving tests, thus denying him of his greatest accusation. This knowledge must sustain us as we encounter the realm of the beast, the whore, and the great merchant city of Babylon that next pass before the wondering eyes of John.

THE BEAST
AND ITS IMAGE

Beginning in chapter 13, and largely ending in chapter 18, we are shown the three major influences through which Satan wields power over mankind. These are his weapons for fighting the woman and her children. Knowing the weaknesses of humanity, he exercises these weapons with great skill. These three factors are (1) political power of various kinds, (2) religious falsehoods contained in apostate doctrines, and (3) economic temptation and seduction. Lucifer essentially boasts that he will use the treasures of the earth to create mighty armies, empower oppressive forms of priestcraft, support destructive tyrants, and thus rule the earth with cruelty, blood, and terror. A cursory glance at the world in any generation is sufficient to realize that he has made good his boast.

Obviously power, apostasy, and money are so deeply inter-twined that it is difficult at times to separate them. So it will be in the next chapters of Revelation. The three factors are symbolically introduced in the images of a beast (political), a harlot (religious), and a great merchant city (economic). The woman rides the beast, and later she becomes the great city. Buying and selling are to a certain degree controlled by the beast, and the kings mourn the downfall of the city as the merchants wail. It is sometimes challenging to think of these images as shifting, merging, melting, and blending into each other, but using the less-logical, poetic part of our minds will help us understand why they do so.

A BEAST OUT OF THE SEA

It is important that we realize that the bulk of Revelation 13 arises from the book of Daniel. If we miss this fact, we are likely to stumble greatly in our efforts to understand.

John is first shown a "sign, in the likeness of the kingdoms of the earth; a beast rise up out of the sea, and he stood upon the sand of the sea, having seven heads and ten horns; and upon his horns ten crowns; and upon his heads the name of blasphemy." (Revelation 13:1, JST.)

In Daniel's vision, "the four winds of the heaven strove upon the great sea. And four great beasts came up from the sea, diverse one from another." (Daniel 7:2–3.) Here we have the added detail of the four winds. A troubled sea, driven by wind, was often used anciently as a symbol of chaos. But Daniel's and John's sea is not the chaos of nature but that of men. In Revelation the sea represents "peoples, and multitudes, and nations, and tongues." (Revelation 17:15.) Driven by unholy winds, human history, like waves in conflict, gives rise to various empires. Often a nation will rise to sovereignty because other nations are fighting each other. The beasts of Daniel and the beast of Revelation arise from the clash and divisions of nations.

Later in Daniel the beasts are described as four kingdoms "which shall arise out of the earth." (Daniel 7:17.) "Earth" in this instance also means from the multitudes of mankind.

The beast then plants its feet on the sand of the sea. The sands of the sea have also been used to portray the teeming millions of the earth. Abraham, for example, was promised seed like the sands of the sea. Lifting themselves out of the troubled tribes of mankind, nations and kingdoms form empires and then dominate the masses of mankind who come under their feet.

THE BEASTS OF DANIEL'S VISION

Daniel saw four beasts. The first was "like a lion." The second was "like to a bear" who was allowed to "devour much flesh." The third was "like a leopard . . . and dominion was given to it." The fourth was "dreadful and terrible, and strong exceedingly; and it had great iron teeth: it devoured and brake in pieces, and stamped the residue with the feet of it: and it was diverse from all the beasts that were before it; and it had ten horns." (Daniel 7:4–7.)

It is easy to see that the image of John's beast comes from these four: "The beast which I saw was like unto a leopard, and his feet were as the feet of a bear, and his mouth as the mouth of a lion: and the dragon gave him his power, and his seat, and great authority." (Revelation 13:2.) Did not Lucifer offer Jesus "all the kingdoms of the world"? When doing so, he claimed, "All this power will I give thee, and the glory of them: for that is delivered unto me; and to whomsoever I will I give it." (Luke 4:5–6.) Satan's claim is not completely true, for Daniel was taught that "the most High ruleth in the kingdom of men, and giveth it to whomsoever he will." (Daniel 4:17.) But for the sake of argument, let us grant Satan the glory he claims. He is certainly behind the cruelty of despotic nations.

Daniel's beasts represented four empires of the eastern and Mediterranean world: Babylon, the lion; Persia, the bear; Greece, the leopard; and Rome, the "dreadful and terrible" beast. They were all predatory, devouring by strength the weaker nations, just as leopards, bears, and lions prey upon more defenseless animals. In short, mankind is the most aggressive proponent of the law of the jungle; again, as Korihor put it, "every man conquered according to his strength; and whatsoever a man did was no crime." (Alma 30:17.) That is just the way things are, Korihor argued; as there is no sin in a wolf killing a lamb, there is no sin in one nation dominating, enslaving, and destroying a smaller one, for "every man prospered according to his genius" and "fared in life according to the management of the creature." (Alma 30:17.)

John's beast incorporates all the qualities of past conquering nations. In this sense, the beast is not some future creation but a continuation of something that has lived since Cain killed Abel. It chooses different faces and forms, but the heart is the same, just as there are seven heads but only one heart. If I were an artist, I would paint each head different from its fellows and have them all snapping and hissing at one another: communism, fascism, Nazism, militant Islam, monarchy, dictatorship, imperialism, and terrorism are all different forms of political repression, but they share the same methods of threat, tyranny, force, brutality, fear, and intimidation.

When one of the beast's heads dies or is wounded, it is soon replaced by a new one. Amos described this succession of dangers: "As if a man did flee from a lion, and a bear met him; or went into the house, and leaned his hand on the wall, and a serpent bit him." (Amos 5:19.) In our dog-eat-dog world, escape from one enemy merely leads to a new, sometimes more deadly foe. We emerged from the dangers of World War II only to enter the Cold War. Emerging from that, we now face international terrorism.

HORNS OF POWER

The scriptures use numerous images to portray this succession. In Daniel's vision, the fourth beast (Rome) grows ten horns, each representing different kingdoms that arose after the fall of Rome. Three of these horns are replaced by "another little horn." (Daniel 7:8.) In Revelation, the beast from the sea also has "ten horns," each capped with a crown.

In a later vision, Daniel is shown a goat with a "notable horn between his eyes." (Daniel 8:5.) This represents Alexander the Great, who would conquer Persia. However, "the great horn was broken; and for it came up four notable ones toward the four winds of heaven. And out of one of them came forth a little horn, which waxed exceeding great." (Daniel 8:8–10.) Alexander's empire was broken into four kingdoms by his succeeding generals. Horns represent power, as discussed earlier. When an animal loses its horns, new ones grow. Power follows power, nation follows nation, empire follows empire, tyranny follows tyranny, despot follows despot. In these images the nations crash into each other like rams, goats, or other horned animals fighting for dominance over the herd.

When I lived in Canada, I used to go into the Rockies to watch the bighorn sheep butt heads during the mating season. I could hear the impact of their contests echoing from the rocks. Daniel uses this image as well as the image of predatory animals to depict the wars and battles of contentious nations. They devour the defenseless; they slam into each other until the weaker turn away in defeat, if not death. New horns grow as old ones are broken, cast away, and ground into the dust.

With this understanding, we can grasp the idea in verse 3 of Revelation 13: "I saw one of his heads as it were wounded to death; and his deadly wound was healed: and all the world wondered after the beast." (Revelation 13:3.) We can destroy one form of evil, one repressive entity, but, Phoenix-like, another will rise from its ashes. Hercules was given the task of killing the Hydra, a swamp animal of many heads. When one head was cut off, two heads sprouted from the wound. Evil follows a similar pattern. It is the heart of dominating power and brutality that must be defeated; if we kill only the heads, they will grow again and again, and we will see "the deadly wound healed." This verse also shows an ironic mockery of Christ's resurrection: He was wounded unto death but came back to life.

At certain times, the oppression of government has been wounded. Classic Athens, Republican Rome, and Renaissance Florence all gave promise of an enlightened rule that would deny the laws of tyranny. The American Constitution dealt a heavy blow to the predatory nature of government, spreading its liberating freedoms to many other nations. Yet still we see the ugly heads of the beast constantly challenging "the spirit of freedom," which, as the book of Mormon teaches, is in reality "the Spirit of God." (Alma 61:15.)

THE GOD OF FORCES

"And they worshipped the dragon which gave power unto the beast: and they worshipped the beast, saying, Who is like unto the beast? who is able to make war with him?" (Revelation 13:4.) Each new empire or dictator attempts to overawe all opposition. These words of Revelation arise from those of

Daniel: "I saw the ram pushing westward, and northward, and southward; so that no beasts might stand before him, neither was there any that could deliver out of his hand; but he did according to his will, and became great." (Daniel 8:4.) Whether the phalanx of Greece, the cavalry and elephants of Persia, the legions of Rome, the long bowmen of the Normans, the tanks of Hitler, or the missiles of the modern world—each instills the fear that nothing can stand before it. Each, however, is eventually replaced. No sooner did the ram reach its full strength than the "he goat came from the west on the face of the whole earth, and touched not the ground." (Daniel 8:5.) Like the "lightning war," the blitzkrieg of Germany, the conquering goat "ran unto him in the fury of his power." (Daniel 8:6.)

The worshiping of Revelation's beast is the worship of brute force, which is the prime motivator of Satan's dominions. Worship is imitation; it is obedience to the laws of the being or entity one venerates. Imitating or obeying the laws of the jungle constitutes the worship of the beast and places its mark or brand upon the devotee. Even the description of the beast is given in a cadence that is almost hypnotic, creating a sense of awe. Each new detail is set off by the word "and." We spoke of this literary device earlier. Daniel clearly identifies this worship in the following quotation, where he speaks of yet another rising power that will dominate a section of the earth: "The king shall do according to his will; and he shall exalt himself, and magnify himself above every god, and shall speak marvelous things against the God of gods, and shall prosper till the indignation be accomplished: for that that is determined shall be done. Neither shall he regard the God of his fathers, nor the desire of women, nor regard any god: for he shall magnify himself above all. *But in his estate shall he honour the God of forces.*" (Daniel 11:36–38; italics added.) The god of forces, the god of power, the god of military might, the god of domination has been worshiped long on this earth. Remember we quoted earlier the words of President Spencer W. Kimball, who pointed out that the major gods of the modern world, those we look to for security and safety, are the gods of steel, ships, missiles, and planes. In reality, there is little in the seventh seal that has not already burdened man in each preceding one.

Speaking Great Things

The mockery of the Savior is also inherent in the claim that nothing is like the beast. The Lord spoke identical words in Isaiah: "To whom will ye liken me, and make me equal, and compare me, that we may be like?" (Isaiah 46:5.) The obvious answer to the people's question "Who is like unto the beast?" is "Christ!" The power of the Savior's gospel is more than a match for the desperate struggles of men to stay on top. Not only *can* Jesus make war with the beast, but he *will*, and Revelation details his victory.

The seven-headed beast of Revelation draws upon more imagery from the book of Daniel: "There was given unto him a mouth speaking great things and blasphemies; and power was given unto him to continue forty and two months. And he opened his mouth in blasphemy against God, to blaspheme his name, and his tabernacle, and them that dwell in heaven." (Revelation 13:5–6.)

This description parallels the actions of the "little horn" of Daniel's vision. (See Daniel 7:8, 20.) The blasphemy is apparent in light of what we discussed above. The Lord is anxious for us to repent, and his longsuffering will give us every opportunity

181

to do so. Thus, as we saw earlier, to blaspheme God's name, his tabernacle, and the heavens is to utter the final, defiant cry of the deeply wicked: "Curse God and die." (See Mormon 2:14 for an example. We might note that the footnote to this verse refers to the topic of "Blasphemy" in the Topical Guide.)

What greater blasphemy is there than to reject the mercy of the Lord when he offers it right up to the last defiant cry of rejection? "How could ye have rejected that Jesus, who stood with open arms to receive you!" Mormon laments. (Mormon 6:17.) What greater blasphemy than to worship the god of war and force rather than the inviting God of peace and gentleness? What greater blasphemy than to believe that a bullet or a missile offers more convincing protection than the righteousness demanded of the Lord? To which God will we turn—the gods that men create or the Creator of man? Whose laws will we live? Which God will we imitate?

OVERCOMING THE SAINTS

In both Daniel and John, the little horn or the beast "make war with the saints, and . . . overcome them: and power was given him over all kindreds, and tongues, and nations. And all that dwell upon the earth shall worship him, whose names are not written in the book of life of the Lamb slain from the foundation of the world." (Revelation 13:7–8; see also Daniel 7:21.) Daniel uses the word "prevail" rather than "overcome." At the beginning of the Restoration, be it remembered, God himself told Joseph Smith that "the powers of darkness prevail upon the earth, among the children of men." (D&C 38:11.)

If we view the history of the earth as a long, prolonged battle between the forces of good and evil, between the Saints of the Most High and those who wield the destructive forces of

Lucifer, between freedom and tyranny, between forgiveness and vengeance, between charity and hatred—then in truth, the horns and beasts of man have been dominant. They have prevailed. They have ruled the world, not the Saints. Even the City of Enoch was removed from a violent world so the waters of the Flood could cleanse the bloodstained surface of the earth.

Nephi spoke of the battle for mastery of the world in terms much plainer for us to understand. In his imagery, the great and spacious building represents the forces of Lucifer's kingdom, or those that fight the influence of the Saints: "I beheld the church of the Lamb of God, and its numbers were few, because of the wickedness and abominations of the whore who sat upon many waters; nevertheless, I beheld that the church of the Lamb, who were the saints of God, were also upon all the face of the earth; and their dominions upon the face of the earth were small. . . . And it came to pass that I beheld that the great mother of abominations did gather together multitudes upon the face of all the earth, among all the nations of the Gentiles, to fight against the Lamb of God." (1 Nephi 14:12–13.)

Clearly, the three-pronged attack of the beast, the whore, and the great city have dominated this earth and will continue to dominate it into the seventh seal. To the objective observer, they have overcome and prevailed against the Saints, both in the establishment of war as the common denominator among men and also in the power of apostasy, falsehood, and love of wealth. It is a battle for dominion among the hearts of God's children—the woman constantly trying to give birth to the destined man child, and the dragon waiting to destroy it and to chase the woman into the wilderness. Satan has had the great day of his power and will hold on to the end. But we are not to fear, all will be well, and John takes the necessary steps to assure us if we have an ear to hear.

THE PATIENCE AND FAITH OF THE SAINTS

In the middle of Revelation 13 we find the most crucial verses: "If any man have an ear, let him hear. He that leadeth into captivity shall go into captivity: he that killeth with the sword must be killed with the sword. *Here is the patience and the faith of the saints.*" (Revelation 13:9–10; italics added.) I believe this is John's way of saying, "I hope you have read Daniel carefully and paid attention to the parts I left out!" As seen earlier, often what John does not say is more important than what he records. If we catch the allusions to Daniel, then turn to Daniel and read the full account, we will understand what happens to all predatory beasts, horns, heads, and crowns.

These are some of the verses we should ponder deeply before drawing conclusions about the latest beast we see rising from the storm-wracked sea of humanity. "I beheld till the thrones were cast down. . . . I beheld even till the beast was slain, and his body destroyed, and given to the burning flame. As concerning the rest of the beasts, they had their dominion taken away: yet their lives were prolonged for a season and time." (Daniel 7:9, 11–12.)

Those who live by the law of the jungle will also die by it. "The day of the Lord is near," Obadiah wrote, "upon all the heathen: as thou hast done, it shall be done unto thee: thy reward shall return upon thine own head." (Obadiah 1:15; see also Habakkuk 2:8 and Ezekiel 32.) In time, those who worship the god of forces will self-destruct. Knowing this truth, John urged the Saints to be patient and have faith. "When you see Nazi tanks rumbling across the hills of Europe," John seems to say, "attempting to establish a Third Reich to endure a thousand years, or Soviet missiles threatening to spread communism in every developing country, be patient and have faith, for they will not stand."

While the sword descends in vengeance and captivity moves into captivity, a small kingdom will begin to grow. Daniel saw it all, and John believed his words: "The Ancient of days did sit. . . . I saw in the night visions, and, behold, one like the Son of man came with the clouds of heaven, and came to the Ancient of days, and they brought him near before him. And there was given him dominion, and glory, and a kingdom, that all people, nations, and languages, should serve him: his dominion is an everlasting dominion, which shall not pass away, and his kingdom that which shall not be destroyed. . . . The saints of the most High shall take the kingdom, and possess the kingdom for ever, even for ever and ever." (Daniel 7:9, 13–14, 18.)

THE INHERITANCE OF THE ANCIENT OF DAYS

John had already seen that Michael, Adam, the Ancient of Days, won a glorious victory in the premortal world. Our past victorious general will return. As our first father, he has the right to bestow rulership over the earth, for the power over which men have fought in every one of the seven seals belongs to him. He was initially promised "dominion over the fishes of the sea, and over the fowl of the air, and over the cattle, and over all the earth, and over every creeping thing that creepeth upon the earth." (Moses 2:26.) It is his legacy, his inheritance, his dominion, his kingdom to pass on to his children. To which of his many children will he grant the ultimate birthright, the right and responsibility to guide and rule? Even to the One who first bestowed it upon him in the Garden of Eden. There is no descendant of Adam more able, more worthy, to inherit the birthright of kingship than Christ, for "the spirit of the Lord shall rest upon him, the spirit of wisdom and understanding, the spirit of counsel and might, the spirit of knowledge and of the fear [reverence] of the Lord." (Isaiah 11:2.) The issue is settled, the feuding family can rest, for he whose right it is to rule will return. Adam himself will turn the keys of all dispensations over to Christ.

Ever gracious and willing to share all that he has with those who love and trust his name, Christ in turn will bestow his inheritance among his righteous brothers and sisters: "And the kingdom and dominion, and the greatness of the kingdom under the whole heaven, shall be given to the people of the saints of the most High, whose kingdom is an everlasting kingdom, and all dominions shall serve and obey him. Hitherto is the end of the matter." (Daniel 7:27–28.)

All other kingdoms that have raised themselves to prominence have eventually tumbled to the dust. I think of this often when walking the ruins of Greece or Rome. But the Savior's kingdom, the kingdom of which we are already a part, will eventually prevail. Those who have ears to hear let them hear, so they can resist the fear that says, "Who is like unto the beast? Who is able to make war with him?" One is coming who *will* make war with him and triumph. The first salvos of that great battle have already been fired.

AND A LITTLE CHILD SHALL LEAD THEM

Now Isaiah's famous words begin to take on new power. In the Savior's kingdom, eternal principles will replace the law of beasts: "The wolf also shall dwell with the lamb, and the leopard shall lie down with the kid; and the calf and the young lion

186

and the fatling together; and a little child shall lead them. And the cow and the bear shall feed; their young ones shall lie down together. . . . They shall not hurt nor destroy in all my holy mountain: for the earth shall be full of the knowledge of the Lord, as the waters cover the sea." (Isaiah 11:6–9.)

Though this passage may have literal fulfillment in the animal kingdom, its figurative meaning is much more beautiful. No longer will the great powers prey upon the defenseless ones—no more invasions, attacks, and conquests. The great nations will live in peace with the smaller ones. The harmless innocence of children will lead, and not the brutality of warriors, generals, and champions. The children will no longer learn war from the hatred of their parents, as we see in the Middle East and numerous other battlefields of the nations. The children will be at peace.

What will bring about this greatest of all victories? The answer is given: the knowledge of the Lord, which will cover the earth "as the waters cover the sea." The testimony of Jesus, preached by missionaries throughout the world, will in time turn the key. Lucifer will be expelled "in the name of Jesus Christ." The missionaries of this church are striking at the heart of the beast. With each proselytizing success, the claws and teeth and horns grow weaker. The king of this new, never-ending dominion will not be called "the Great" or "the Terrible," as have other conquering rulers. His titles will include "Wonderful, Counsellor, The mighty God, The everlasting Father, The Prince of Peace." (Isaiah 9:6.)

Recorded in the Book of Life

John stated that everyone would worship the beast except those whose names were written in the book of life. (See

187

Revelation 13:8.) This also is an allusion to Daniel, and John anticipates that we will read his words in that context, for it is magnificent and filled with hope: "At that time shall Michael stand up, the great prince which standeth for the children of thy people: and there shall be a time of trouble, such as never was since there was a nation even to that same time: and at that time thy people shall be delivered, every one that shall be found *written in the book*. And many of them that sleep in the dust of the earth shall awake, some to everlasting life, and some to shame and everlasting contempt. And they that be wise shall shine as the brightness of the firmament; and they that turn many to righteousness as the stars for ever and ever." (Daniel 12:1–3; italics added.)

What must we do to have our names written in that protective book of life that brings security on earth and glorious resurrection? Daniel supplied the answer. We must be wise, as were the five virgins of Jesus' parable of preparation, and above all, we must turn others to righteousness. Here is the great work of the Saints in the seventh seal, just as it is in our own.

John is shown other details concerning the beast in the remaining half of chapter 13, but the focus now shifts from the beast to a great image. By now, however, we know to look to Daniel for understanding about the mystery of the image. With that comprehension, we will discover the reasons that we must not, and need not, fear or worship it.

THE IMAGE OF THE BEAST

After assuring the Saints that patience and faith are needed when confronting the distressing injustices of worldly empires, John is ready to move into round two of his emphasis on Lucifer's political, religious, and economic kingdoms. Another beast lifts itself from the earth, "and he had two horns like a lamb, and he spake as a dragon. And he exerciseth all the power of the first beast before him, and causeth the earth and them which dwell therein to worship the first beast, whose deadly wound was healed." (Revelation 13:11–12.)

Appearing as if power were not important to it (what harm can a lamb do?), this second beast nevertheless still desires power and can obtain it surreptitiously through the first beast. The lamb is called the false prophet in three other places in Revelation. (Revelation 16:13; 19:20; 20:10.) This steers our thinking toward the religious arm of the dragon's dominion, which is inextricably linked to the political and economic. The religious can always claim they are thinking only of the salvation of mankind, with no other motive for their actions. They are accomplishing God's will, and how can anyone question the desires of God? Their words and teachings emerge from the mouth of a lamb, but the tuned ear will hear the dragon's voice underneath. As simply and plainly as we can put it, the dragon-voiced lamb is apostasy in all its multiplicity of forms and voices.

Since the religious imagery of Revelation is more strongly portrayed in chapter 17, we will wait to examine it with greater care when we arrive at that chapter. It is sufficient to say at this point that as there are nations, peoples, and areas of the world dominated by various political systems, so too are some under the sway of controlling religious systems, either linked to the political or exercising power independent of it. We might also note that the temptation ever exists to compromise eternal truth, moral rectitude, prophetic positions, and ethical stability with a political correctness that corresponds in a more pleasing and acceptable manner with the temperament of the times.

Who do we really worship in such cases? Jesus said the way to heaven is strait and narrow; unfortunately, both political and religious entities constantly try to broaden the way until every exception becomes the new rule. This is particularly evident in such areas as those addressed in the Proclamation on the Family.

We can take warning from the two-horned lamb. The wicked never have doubts about whom they are to oppose; they always seem to know their foes. Unfortunately, this is not always true of those who would do well. The devil and his doctrines appear from time to time as angels of light. Sometimes the righteous are deceived by appearances, and with the best of intentions they support what appears to them an innocent lamb. We must learn to listen carefully to the voice, for it is in the message that we will perceive the rasp of the dragon's breath.

THE GREAT IMAGE AND THE ROLLING STONE

The false prophet convinces men to "make an image to the beast. . . . And he had power to give life unto the image of the beast, that the image of the beast should both speak, and cause that as many as would not worship the image of the beast should be killed." (Revelation 13:14–15.) We should not read this too literally. To give life to something means to make it real, to bring about its existence, to endow it with influence and power. We might say the Founding Fathers gave life to the American nation, its institutions, and its way of life. Similarly, Henry Ford gave life to the automobile, and Bill Gates to Microsoft. Each one brought something into existence. The image has a message to communicate; therefore, it is portrayed as speaking. It can do great "wonders" or works.

There is something in us that seeks to worship. If faith in the living God dwindles, faith in something else arises. We turn to something we think can answer our desires, supply our wants, and protect our interests, whether it be a person, a state, a financial institution, a false religion, or any combination of these. We look to the powerful, to that which we perceive as greater than ourselves, and align ourselves with it. The deference to power runs deep in the souls of men. But it must be trained to worship heavenly authority, not the transitory might of the world.

The book of Daniel includes two stories that deal with great images or idols. These provide the backdrop for Revelation's living, speaking image. Both of these stories are so well known that we recognize them immediately. Nebuchadnezzar had a dream of a great image, and Daniel explained, "This great image, whose brightness was excellent, stood before thee; and the form thereof was terrible. This image's head was of fine gold, his breast and his arms of silver, his belly and his thighs of brass, his legs of iron, his feet part of iron and part of clay." (Daniel 2:31–33.)

Daniel told the marveling king that each of the metals represented a new kingdom that would triumph and win empires. Babylon was the head of gold; Persia, the silver; Greece, the brass; and Rome, the iron. The breaking up of the Roman Empire would create dozens of smaller kingdoms that would never again unite. These are the nations of Europe, which constitute the iron-clay mix of the toes.

If this sounds familiar to us, it should. Nebuchadnezzar's dream and Daniel's vision of the beasts discussed earlier are essentially the same. The lion, bear, leopard, and beast with ten horns correspond perfectly to the different metals and the ten clay toes. As each beast was different but of the same disposition, so too are the various metals different but part of the same idol. When the gold head fails, the silver breast and arms follow. They have different qualities, appearances, and degrees of hardness, but the shape of the image never changes. What we have in the Old Testament and in Revelation is the same message delivered with different symbols. Crashing rams and goats, devouring beasts of prey, different colors and hardnesses of metals, horns breaking only to be replaced by newly grown ones, many heads, and healed wounds—all testify to the same truth. John unites them in one marvelous whole in Revelation. But it is essential that we understand what happens to all these powers.

Daniel's beasts were replaced by the sitting of the Ancient of days, who delivered the keys of earth's kingdoms to Christ. It was then promised that the Saints would possess the earth. In Nebuchadnezzar's dream, this role is played by the "stone . . . cut out without hands, which smote the image upon his feet that were of iron and clay, and brake them to pieces. Then was the iron, the clay, the brass, the silver, and the gold, broken to pieces together, and became like the chaff of the summer threshingfloors; and the wind carried them away, that no place was found for them: and the stone that smote the image became a great mountain, and filled the whole earth." (Daniel 2:34–35.)

This stone is The Church of Jesus Christ of Latter-day Saints. It is "cut out without hands," suggesting that it was not made or fashioned as the image was. It is created and set in motion by God. That it is made of stone also emphasizes this natural quality, as opposed to the metals, which were usually molten from ore and then shaped by the artificer.

Daniel's interpretation stresses the replacement of the statue with the stone: "In the days of these kings [the clay toes] shall the God of heaven set up a kingdom, which shall never be destroyed: and the kingdom shall not be left to other people [no one will replace it as were the others], but it shall break in pieces and consume all these kingdoms, and it shall stand for ever." (Daniel 2:44.)

When we read of the great image of Revelation 13, we must realize that it will fall. We belong to the very stone that will depose it. We need not fear it! We must not worship it! Whether it is dictatorial, monarchial, totalitarian, imperialistic, republican, democratic, aristocratic, or oligarchic, if it does not defend and incorporate the principles of eternal truth, with moral agency at its base, it cannot stand. Brigham Young taught, "Should any legislature sit without the Lord? If it do, sooner or later it will fall to pieces. No nation ever did live that counseled and transacted its national affairs without the Lord, but what sooner or later went to pieces and came to naught. The same is true of all nations that now live or ever will live." (*Journal of Discourses*, 13:60.)

WITH THE SON OF GOD IN THE FURNACE

Over the years of conversing with people about this chapter, I have found many distressed and worried about the threat the image levels: Worship me or "be killed." Since every aspect of Revelation 13 so far has arisen out of Daniel, we might search Daniel for our response to this apparent danger. There is in Daniel another "image" constructed by Nebuchadnezzar: "The king made an image of gold, whose height was threescore cubits. . . . He set it up in the plain of Dura, in the province of Babylon." (Daniel 3:1.) The king gathered all the leaders of his realm for the dedication. There it was announced, "To you it is commanded, O people, nations, and languages, that at what time ye hear the sound of . . . all kinds of musick, ye fall down and worship the golden image that Nebuchadnezzar the king hath set up: and whoso falleth not down and worshippeth shall the same hour be cast into the midst of a burning fiery furnace." (Daniel 3:4–5.)

We all know the rest of the story. Three young men, Shadrach, Meshach, and Abed-nego, refused to bow when the music played. Given another chance by the king—who threatened them with "Who is that God that shall deliver you out of my hands?"—they affirmed their unwillingness to bow to the images of Babylon. God can save us, they testified, "but if not, be it known unto thee, O king, that we will not serve thy gods, nor worship the golden image which thou hast set up." (Daniel 3:15–18.)

Thrown into the furnace, they were joined by a fourth individual. Staring in amazement, the king spoke: "Lo, I see four men loose, walking in the midst of the fire, and they have no hurt; and the form of the fourth is like the Son of God." (Daniel 3:25.) If we refuse to bow to the gods of Babylon, we may anticipate that the Savior will walk with us even in our most fiery trials. The answer of these young men must be our answer when confronted with the images and gods of Babylon today. We have nothing to fear from the beast, his image, his false prophet, or his threats. John does not overtly give any of these assurances, but he expects us to know our Old Testament, catch the allusions, and read the rest of his message there. "If any man have an ear, let him hear." (Revelation 13:9.)

BUYING AND SELLING

Identifying applications of the image in the modern world should not be too difficult. First we must remember that Babylon figures prominently in both the dream and the image of Nebuchadnezzar. We ask ourselves, "What are the gods of Babylon in our own generation to which so many nations, peoples, and tongues bow when the music sounds? Do these gods ascribe to the law of power: the strong over the weak, eat or be eaten? The Lord himself supplies an answer in the very first section of the Doctrine and Covenants. After speaking of the great apostasy that caused people to stray from the ordinances and break the covenants of the gospel, the Lord said, "They seek not the Lord to establish his righteousness, but every man walketh in his own way, and after the image of his own god, whose image is in the likeness of the world, and whose substance is that of an idol, which waxeth old and shall perish in Babylon, even Babylon the great, which shall fall." (D&C 1:16.)

The images of the world shift and change from generation to generation, though they tend to revolve around repeating and familiar themes. In an article entitled "The False Gods We Worship," President Spencer W. Kimball gave a powerful example of just such an image. Unfortunately, when the music sounds, far too many of us bow. He said, "The Lord has blessed us as a people with a prosperity unequaled in times past. The resources that have been placed in our power are good, and necessary to our work here on the earth. But I am afraid that many of us have been surfeited with flocks and herds and acres and barns and wealth and have begun to worship them as false gods, and they have power over us. Do we have more of these good

195

things than our faith can stand? Many people spend most of their time working in the service of a *self-image* that includes sufficient money, stocks, bonds, investment portfolios, property, credit cards, furnishings, automobiles, and the like to guarantee carnal security throughout, it is hoped, a long and happy life." (Kimball, *Teachings of Spencer W. Kimball,* 357; italics added.) A few sentences later President Kimball quoted the above warning from section 1 of the Doctrine and Covenants, thus tying his comments to the revealed words of the Lord.

This is not the only image of modern Babylon of which we need be aware, but it is surely one of its most influential ones. (President Kimball also indicated that military might is a powerful false god of the modern world.) It is not surprising, therefore, that in the next verses dealing with the image of the beast, John recorded, "No man might buy or sell, save he that had the mark, or the name of the beast, or the number of his name." (Revelation 13:17.) In this verse, the third element of Lucifer's captivating power (economic) enters a partnership with the first two (political and religious). To achieve commercial success often requires an almost complete devotion of time, talent, and resources. If I don't sell, and sell high, how can I possibly buy all the things that are constantly arrayed before my eyes? And everything is for sale in Babylon, including the souls of men. This we shall see when we reach chapter 18.

The astute person must make moral compromises, the world insists, in order to achieve success. The law of the jungle, the beast's corollary, operates in the world of finance also. Even here the rule is often "devour or be devoured." Survival of the fittest controls the tactics of a buying and selling world: "Every man fared in this life according to the management of the creature; therefore every man prospered according to his genius . . . and whatsoever a man did was no crime." (Alma 30:17.) Korihor's words echo in the halls of wealth also.

THE MARK OF THE BEAST

In contrast to the seal set in the foreheads of the righteous, the beast also has a mark: "He causeth all, both small and great, rich and poor, free and bond, to receive a mark in their right hand, or in their foreheads." (Revelation 13:16.) So many strange ideas about this mark have been offered that it would take pages just to mention them. Partial understanding, at least, can be obtained if we remember the verse we examined when seeking insight about the seal of God. Deuteronomy may offer the best help for personal application.

The children of Israel were told to have only one God, whom they were to love and serve with all of their hearts, souls, and might. This commitment and consecration was to be the guiding light of their lives. The Lord commanded, "Thou shalt teach [my words] diligently unto thy children, and shalt talk of them when thou sittest in thine house, and when thou walkest by the way, and when thou liest down, and when thou risest up." He also commanded, "Thou shalt bind them for a sign upon thine hand, and they shall be as frontlets between thine eyes." (Deuteronomy 6:7–8.)

A full reading of Deuteronomy reveals that greed, selfishness, and the constant search for the world's luxuries were the major things against which Moses warned the children of Israel. If the things of the world—wealth, possessions, and power—become the central focus of our lives; if we transfer these ambitions to our children; if we think of positions, influence, riches, investments, and owning more and more constantly; if we find ourselves talking about them during the day; if the last thoughts

197

of our minds before retiring and the first thoughts upon rising gravitate toward all that Babylon has to offer; if our hands reach to grasp more and more while our eyes wander and roam through the stocked shelves of material gain and domination; if we fear that we cannot survive without acquiring the qualities of the predatory beast—then we may be assured that the mark is beginning to burn its way into our foreheads and hands. The beast with his false prophet and his image is receiving our worship. They may one day claim us as their own. We may be numbered among their sheep as a rancher numbers his livestock. To give loyalty to the guiding principle of Lucifer's kingdom marks us, for the Lord's law teaches the opposite of "might makes right." In his realm, the Lord encourages us with these words: "Let every man esteem his brother as himself, and practise virtue and holiness before me." (D&C 38:24.)

John reveals that the number of the beast is "the number of a man; and his number is Six hundred threescore and six." (Revelation 13:18.) In many ancient languages, letters had numerical equivalents. (Our occasional use of Roman numerals is all that is left in English to illustrate this former practice.) Therefore, a person's name could be read as varying combinations of numbers. These could be listed or added, depending on the purpose of the individual.

As in other areas of this chapter, so many speculations have been given that they make the head spin. Since the name of the Father was the seal of the righteous, it makes some sense to suppose that the name of the beast has to do with Lucifer and his many titles. As the "number of a man," it represents a man-made title or office. Those for whom wealth was so desirable that they would conquer, rob, murder, and enslave were given the title "Master Mahan." (Moses 5:31.) If I had to offer an opinion about this number's meaning, my best answer would be this title. The footnote to Moses 5:31 states, "'Mind,' 'destroyer,' and 'great one' are possible meanings of the roots evident in 'Mahan.'" I can't help but notice the similarities indicated here with Korihor's assertion of prospering according to "genius" and "conquer[ing] according to . . . strength." Lucifer is a destroyer, whether he is destroying truth through the apostasy, or life and property through the application of jungle law.

In the temple, where the seal of the living God is placed upon the righteous, we learn that our role in life is just the opposite. So many of the sacred truths, symbols, covenants, and order shown in the temple compel us to be edifiers and builders. We must build Zion, thus overturning the destroying paradigms of the world. May the seal, name, and stamp of the builders ever rest upon us; may we wield these tools and never allow their destructive counterparts to find access to our time, talents, or resources.

The Old Testament includes only one verse where this number is used; interestingly, it deals with a king who had great wealth: "Now the weight of gold that came to Solomon in one year was six hundred threescore and six talents of gold." (1 Kings 10:14.) I am not sure what to make of this entry. It may have nothing to do with Revelation, but it is curious that Solomon, he who built and dedicated God's first temple at Jerusalem, the wisest man of his generation, was eventually turned (through the influence of his political marriages, entered into to secure his position among the nations) to the construction of shrines for the worship of every false god of the nations that surrounded him.

Though chapter 13 is often read as a dark portion of Revelation, I find it one of the most inspiring. But its power to lift and its application for our day-to-day lives are found in the Book of Daniel. To read it alone is to miss the message, and it is critical that we do not miss it. I find nothing to fear in John's description of the beast. I marvel not that a deadly wound can heal and the head rise up again. I sense no brooding mystery in the image that is raised by the false prophet. I do not tremble that the sentence of death may be passed if I fail to bow when Babylon's plains fill with the sound of the idol's music. I am not anxious that buying and selling may be denied me, for commercial offerings cannot satisfy. I do not want the mark that promises protection from earth's newly risen wonder. Protection of another kind can be found in the Father's seal, in the Father's name. If that mark is on us and we remain true to it, then with faith and patience we will watch the empires rise and fall, devour each other, worship every newly formed image, and buy and sell their temporal merchandise, and we will remain unstained by the whole beastly mess. Intent on our assignment as builders, we will watch the kingdom of God arise to end destruction's iron grip upon God's children.

❦

THE HARVEST

Since a major purpose of Revelation is to profile two opposing forces (that we might choose wisely which to follow), it is proper that Revelation 14 should return us to those who have received the name of the Father in their foreheads. The immediate contrast with the beast's mark in the previous chapter is clearly evident. Now the Lamb stands with his followers as the "new song," the song of victory, is sung again. Because so many of the visions of Revelation are deeply sobering, images of victory, glory, love, song, praise, and judgment are interposed to turn our minds constantly forward to the future hour of triumph. John wants us to keep that ever in our consciousness lest the temporary prevailing forces of evil leave us in despair and we are tempted to abandon the fight, lay down our tools, and pick up those of the destroyer. Even in the dawn of history, the Lord made it clear to all generations that the serpent would be crushed.

When evil appears to prevail, we may be tempted to think

we are alone in trying to resist it. We look around, and the mark of the beast appears to be on everyone's head, "small and great, rich and poor, free and bond." (Revelation 13:16.) Discouragement may set in, as it did with Elijah. "I, even I only, am left," he said. But the Lord comforted him, saying, "I have left me seven thousand in Israel, all the knees which have not bowed unto Baal, and every mouth which hath not kissed him." (1 Kings 19:14, 18.) There is reassurance in knowing that 144,000, accompanied by a great multitude, have not bowed the knee or received the mark but are standing with Christ, having the Father's name instead of the beast's evil mark. We are not alone, and we must never allow that temptation to weaken our resolve to reject the laws of the beast. We must not receive his brand, even if it appears that everyone else has done so.

THE SINGERS OF THE NEW SONG

We all want to be part of the ultimate triumph of goodness. We all wish to stand with Christ on "mount Sion." We all want to sing the new song. Now John gives specific instructions about the lifestyle that will allow our energies to be consistent with our future desires: "These are they which were not defiled with women; for they are virgins. These are they which follow the Lamb whithersoever he goeth. These were redeemed from among men, being the firstfruits unto God and to the Lamb. And in their mouth was found no guile: for they are without fault before the throne of God." (Revelation 14:4–5.)

Though not a complete list, these qualities define the essential aspects of character the Lord expects of those who will stand with him. They have lived the law of chastity, keeping all their desires within the boundaries established by God. They have lived the law of obedience, as indicated by their willingness to follow the Lamb in all things, in all places, and in all circumstances. They are not without sin, for only One ever reached that height of perfection, but they applied the law of the gospel in their lives, thus appealing to the cleansing power of the Atonement and receiving its redeeming benefits. The last quality mentioned by John is that of honesty; there was no deceit in their communications or dealings with their fellowman.

Since the influence of the beast, the false prophet, and their image holds sway over all the earth, so too must the gospel. If it were otherwise, God's children would not be free to choose between the two offerings. John, therefore, "saw another angel fly in the midst of heaven, having the everlasting gospel to preach unto them that dwell on the earth, and to every nation, and kindred, and tongue, and people, saying with a loud voice, Fear God, and give glory to him; for the hour of his judgment is come: and worship him that made heaven, and earth, and the sea, and the fountains of waters." (Revelation 14:6–7.)

This prophecy is often attributed to Moroni and heralds the restoration of the gospel through Joseph Smith. We are presently bending our energies as a Church to spreading the truth to every nation. We need not worry about temporary barriers to the preaching of the gospel. We have seen them removed before, and we will continue to witness the Lord's power in opening the nations. In time, the inviting voice of the Spirit will search the souls for "inquirers after truth" (JS—H 1:1) in China and the Islamic nations, the last major portions of the earth yet untouched by the glories of the Restoration, or, for that matter, the liberating freedoms that inspired the Constitution.

On the day of Pentecost, the apostles spoke in the tongues

of many foreign nations, thus foreshadowing the manner in which the gospel message must be imparted. Each has the opportunity to hear and read the good news in his or her own language, that it might have the deepest power in the mind and heart.

Wisdom dictates that it is better to worship the God of creation than the gods we create for ourselves. John, as have other prophets, invites us to look around, study the creation, and find in its beauty the footprints of the Almighty. We learn a great deal about an author, an artist, a composer by what they create. In like manner, we can perceive much about the nature, attributes, and character of God by contemplating the order, variety, and wonder of creation. "Lift up your eyes on high," Isaiah wrote, "and behold who hath created these things, that bringeth out their host by number: he calleth them all by names by the greatness of his might." (Isaiah 40:26.)

THE HOUR OF HIS JUDGMENT

The counsel of the angel to reverence God and worship him is well advised. The judgment hour has arrived, and we are informed of some of the Lord's verdicts. "Babylon is fallen, is fallen" constitutes the first pronounced conclusion. Since the fall of Satan's chief city is detailed in chapter 18, we will look at it there. There is also a judgment for those who have received the adversary's mark and worshiped his beast: "The same shall drink of the wine of the wrath of God, which is poured out without mixture into the cup of his indignation." (Revelation 14:10.)

God's cup of wrath is filled only when there is no longer hope for repentance. The Psalmist wrote, "The Lord is merciful and gracious, slow to anger, and plenteous in mercy. . . . He hath not dealt with us after our sins; nor rewarded us according to our iniquities. For as the heaven is high above the earth, so great is his mercy toward them that fear him." (Psalms 103:8–11.)

Ever anxious to extend mercy, the Lord witholds the cup of wrath while trying everything in his power to turn the feet of the wicked from their calamitous path. After speaking of the many voices at his disposal, the Lord reveals in section 43 of the Doctrine and Covenants that "the day has come, when the cup of the wrath of mine indignation is full." (D&C 43:26.) C. S. Lewis once wrote, "I believe that if a million chances were likely to do good, they would be given. But a master often knows, when boys and parents do not, that it is really useless to send a boy in for a certain examination again. Finality must come sometime, and it does not require a very robust faith to believe that omniscience knows when." (C. S. Lewis, *The Problem of Pain* [Glasgow: Fountain Books], 112.) In its fullest extent, the wrath of God occurs when his Spirit ceases to strive with man and He leaves him to pursue his own destructive path. He does not need to punish, for the wicked will bring sufficient justice down upon their own heads. They will wield the whips of their own chastisement.

I used to be troubled by John's words that the wicked would "be tormented . . . *in the presence* of the holy angels, and *in the presence* of the Lamb." In their torments, "they have no rest day nor night, who worship the beast and his image, and whosoever receiveth the mark of his name." (Revelation 14:10–11; italics added.) Though the passage deals with God's justice, it did not seem consistent with his compassion. Why would this torment be "in the presence" of such holy beings? I found an answer in the Doctrine and Covenants and the Book of Mormon.

In section 76, after speaking of those who are overcome by

the adversary, the Lord says that "their torment, no man knows; neither was it revealed . . . unto man, except to them who are made partakers thereof; nevertheless, I, the Lord, show it by vision unto many, but *straightway shut it up again; wherefore . . .* the misery thereof, they understand not." (D&C 76:45–48; italics added.) In other words, it is so painful to behold, so distressing to those whose feelings are gentle, tender, and filled with compassion, that the sight must be shut up lest they are overcome by it. Was not the weeping of God in the vision of Enoch induced by his knowledge of the eventual suffering of the rebellious? When shown that misery, did not Enoch also weep and say, "I will refuse to be comforted"? (Moses 7:44.) Though the cup of wrath must and will be poured out, the heavens take no pleasure in it. Justice and judgment have come, but mercy weeps at the failed opportunity to grasp her outstretched hand.

Another thought may be helpful in understanding this verse. In the Book of Mormon, Moroni spoke of the feelings of those who have denied the Savior's gospel and his atoning mercy. He posed several questions, the answers to which shed light on the torment of those with the mark of the beast who find themselves in the presence of the Lamb and his holy angels: "Do ye suppose that ye shall dwell with him under a consciousness of your guilt? Do ye suppose that ye could be happy to dwell with that holy Being, when your souls are racked with a consciousness of guilt that ye have ever abused his laws? Behold, I say unto you that ye would be more miserable to dwell with a holy and just God, under a consciousness of your filthiness before him, than ye would to dwell with the damned souls in hell. For behold, when ye shall be brought to see your nakedness before God, and also the glory of God, and the holiness of Jesus Christ, it will kindle a flame of unquenchable fire upon you." (Mormon 9:3–5.) Thus, the torment is self-inflicted, born of guilt and shame. Verses 12 and 13 are offered as encouragement for the Saints in the same spirit as verse 10 of chapter 13. The Saints must patiently keep the commandments and have faith, for the final harvest will soon be consummated. Even if the turmoils and persecutions of the world lead to their death, they "die in the Lord" and "rest from their labors; and their works do follow them." (Revelation 14:12–13.)

THE FIRST HARVEST

The wheat and the tares are now fully grown together, and it is time for the harvest. On a white cloud, John sees "one . . . like unto the Son of man, having on his head a golden crown, and in his hand a sharp sickle." (Revelation 14:14.) The expression "like unto the Son of man" can be confusing. If this figure is Jesus, why not say so? The answer lies in the reverence due the great Creator and Savior of worlds. We show a similar respect in referring to the priesthood as that of Melchizedek, as explained in Doctrine and Covenants 107:2–4.

Jesus himself will lead in the harvest of the righteous. "Behold the field is white already to harvest," the Lord told Joseph Smith, "and lo, he that thrusteth in his sickle with his might, the same layeth up in store that he perisheth not." (D&C 4:4.) The first harvest has been going on since the earliest days of the Restoration. "The Lord of the vineyard labored also with them," we read in Jacob. (Jacob 5:72.) We can be certain that with the Lord working alongside his other faithful laborers, no soul will be missed in the corners of the field or dropped in gathering the sheaves.

To participate in this harvest is a great honor, for it is a "marvelous work. . . . Therefore, if ye have desires to serve God ye are called to the work." (D&C 4:1, 3.) Notice the attitude inherent in these words. The distinction of thrusting in the sickle is such that all who desire may be granted the opportunity to labor. Desire, along with the other virtues named in Doctrine and Covenants 4, is the paramount qualification. It is as if the Lord is saying, "This is such a magnificent work that I will let you help me in it!" Serving a mission is not a duty but a gift.

THE GRAPES OF WRATH

Upon the completion of the gathering of the righteous, "another angel came out of the temple which is in heaven, he also having a sharp sickle." An angel who has "power over fire" instructs the first angel, "Thrust in thy sharp sickle, and gather the clusters of the vine of the earth; for her grapes are fully ripe." (Revelation 14:17–18.) It is time to burn the unproductive fields, and the angel of fire takes command. These are the grapes of wrath. There are two ways in which the title fits. First, the grapes are about to suffer the wrath of God as his judgment is fulfilled. The fullest wrath of God consists in the withdrawal of his Spirit. John Taylor said, "Why is it that thrones will be cast down, empires dissolved, nations destroyed, and confusion and distress cover all people, as the prophets have spoken? Because the Spirit of the Lord will be withdrawn from the nations in consequence of their wickedness, *they will be left to their own folly.*" (*Journal of Discourses*, 6:24.) Second, the grapes are filled with wrath, ripe and bursting with it. They are consumed in the anger and hatred that, like a blinding smoke, gives birth to the locusts of war. The rancor that leads to Armageddon is their inheritance. The fury that gives the "beasts" of the earth their destructive natures has grown heavy on the vine. Since they are filled with wrath, God's justice gives them wrath in return. They have lived by the sword, and now they will die by it. Their anger and application of the jungle law of beasts lead them naturally to the winepress, to Armageddon.

Figuratively speaking, the angel who now begins to wield his sickle is the angel of death—the grim reaper, who will find an ample harvest in the clash of nations: "And the angel thrust in his sickle into the earth, and gathered the vine of the earth, and cast it into the great winepress of the wrath of God." (Revelation 14:19.)

A certain place in Israel comes to mind each time I read these words. At this site is an ancient winepress cut into the rock. The depression is about a foot deep, with a channel carved into one side so the juice of the grapes can flow out and be collected in a deep basin, also cut into the rock. Looking up, one can see many different vineyards on the hillsides and plains surrounding the city. Grapes from each vineyard are gathered at the winepress, where they are mixed together and crushed.

This is the picture John knew the early Church members would recognize. However, we are not talking about vintage in this harvest, but of men, tribes, and nations. The various fields now become countless countries and peoples. They gather together for war in their attempts to dominate each other. With the Spirit of the Lord withdrawn, they are left to their own willful devices. As they crush each other in the winepress of the battlefield, the liquid life begins to flow: "And the winepress was trodden without the city, and blood came out of the winepress, even unto the horse bridles, by the space of a thousand and six hundred furlongs." (Revelation 14:20.)

Allusions to war in this verse are inherent with the words

"blood" and "horse bridles." Anciently, the horse was used primarily for combat. The destruction is great as casualties rise, creating a river many miles long as it flows from the press. These images should not be taken too literally. The scene is horrific, designed to reflect the murderous nature and magnitude of the conflicts. We have seen such conflicts in our own day. Again we must note that the events of the seventh seal are not atypical in human history. Only the final outcome of the seventh seal will be unique. All of its other facets have been with the world since the four horsemen first began to ride.

Other Old Testament prophets described similar scenes using their own imagery. Isaiah spoke of discord in the last days that would produce great destruction: "Come near, ye nations, to hear; and hearken, ye people: let the earth hear . . . for the indignation of the Lord is upon *all nations, and his fury upon all their armies: he hath utterly destroyed them, he hath delivered them to the slaughter.* Their slain also shall be cast out, and their stink shall come up out of their carcasses, *and the mountains shall be melted with their blood.*" (Isaiah 34:1–3; italics added.) I have seen whole mountainsides in California slide because of heavy rains, so saturated that they melt in a flow of mud. This is the image of Isaiah, only the melting liquid is the life source of men.

Zephaniah wrote in equally graphic terms: "And I will bring distress upon men, that they shall walk like blind men, because they have sinned against the Lord: and *their blood shall be poured out as dust,* and their flesh as the dung. Neither their silver nor their gold shall be able to deliver them in the day of the Lord's wrath; but the whole land shall be devoured by the fire of his jealousy." (Zephaniah 1:17–18; italics added.)

THE VALLEY OF JEHOSHAPHAT

However, our greatest understanding of John's harvest of the grapes of wrath comes from Joel, who also gave us the picture of the marauding locusts of chapter 9. I believe that one additional background story will be helpful before we look at Joel's words. (We have traveled a distance from Revelation 14, but the journey will be helpful when we return to it.) It is the story of Jehoshaphat's encounter with a collection of nations that surrounded his kingdom of Judah. It is not a well-known story, but it may be vitally helpful in understanding Armageddon, for that is what the winepress is all about.

Word came to Jehoshaphat that there came "a great multitude" against him. The army consisted of warriors from a coalition composed chiefly of Ammon, Moab, and Edom. "And Jehoshaphat feared, and set himself to seek the Lord, and proclaimed a fast throughout all Judah." (2 Chronicles 20:1–3.) The people gathered at the temple, where their king offered a beautiful prayer beseeching the Lord to protect his own. "Be not afraid nor dismayed by reason of this great multitude," the Lord reassured them, "for the battle is not yours, but God's. . . . Ye shall not need to fight in this battle: set yourselves, stand ye still, and see the salvation of the Lord." (2 Chronicles 20:15, 17.) The Lord instructed Jehoshaphat to meet the invaders in a valley by Tekoa. Sending "singers" before his army, the king left the safety of Jerusalem's walls, marching to the spot designated by the Lord.

As they began singing praises to the Lord, "the Lord set ambushments against the children of Ammon, Moab, and mount Seir [Edom]. . . . For the children of Ammon and Moab stood up against the inhabitants of mount Seir, utterly to slay and destroy them: and when they had made an end of the inhabitants of Seir, *every one helped to destroy another.*" (2 Chronicles 20:22–23; italics added.) When Jehoshaphat arrived, there was no battle to fight. They collected the spoils, then gathered in the valley of Berachah to praise the Lord. "And the fear of God was on all the kingdoms of those countries, when they had heard that the Lord fought against the enemies of Israel." (2 Chronicles 20:29.)

Strictly speaking, the Lord did not really fight any battle. He knew that the dispositions of the allies would erupt in self-destructive war. Nevertheless, true to Middle Eastern philosophy, the Lord was the cause of the victory for Judah and was given full credit. Now we will return to Joel.

"I will . . . gather all nations, and will bring them down into the valley of Jehoshaphat, and will plead with them there for my people and for my heritage Israel, whom they have scattered among the nations." (Joel 3:2.) *Plead* is used ironically here. The nations by this time have refused every plea for repentance. When the pleading is done, the enemy will be destroyed. We may read, and many have, that the valley of Jehoshaphat refers to the Kidron Valley at Jerusalem. This is a literal reading. But nowhere in the Bible is the Kidron given this name. The association of the Kidron with the valley of Jehoshaphat is a post-biblical association, made many centuries after the Old and New Testaments close. Reading the above verse as an allusion to Jehoshaphat's greatest victory brings ironic richness. As the Second Coming draws near, the nations will repeat, on a grand scale, the episode of Jehoshaphat's valley victory. The imagery is enriched when we realize that *Jehoshaphat* means "Jehovah judges." The nations, ironically, will gather in the valley of God's judgment. The valley, therefore, need not necessarily be a specific geographic location but anywhere the Lord stands to judge the nations in the manner described in 2 Chronicles.

Zechariah's words give credence to this self-inflicted war of mutual enmity as applied to the last days: "In that day," he wrote, "a great tumult from the Lord shall be among them; and they shall lay hold *every one on the hand of his neighbour, and his hand shall rise up against the hand of his neighbour.*" (Zechariah 14:13; italics added.)

This is somewhat verified by Nephi's plain statement describing the events we are discussing here: "I beheld that the wrath of God was poured out upon that great and abominable church, insomuch that there were wars and rumors of wars among all the nations and kindreds of the earth. And as there began to be wars and rumors of wars among all the nations which belonged to the mother of abominations, the angel spake unto me, saying: Behold, the wrath of God is upon the mother of harlots." (1 Nephi 14:15–16.)

In a later passage, Nephi spoke with even greater clarity: "And the blood of that great and abominable church, which is the whore of all the earth, *shall turn upon their own heads; for they shall war among themselves, and the sword of their own hands shall fall upon their own heads, and they shall be drunken with their own blood. And every nation which shall war against thee, O house of Israel, shall be turned one against another.*" (1 Nephi: 22:13–14; italics added.) There is only one clearer description of Armageddon, which we will discuss when we reach Revelation 16. Nephi includes Satan's entire kingdom in the metaphor of the whore of all the earth. John grants us a more detailed portrait, stressing various aspects individually in descriptions of the beast, its image, the great merchant city of Babylon, and the apostate mother of harlots. However, the truths presented by both prophets are essentially the same.

In the Valley of Decision

We have circled around the harvest of the grapes of wrath completely now and are ready to look at the specific prophecy of Joel to which John alludes in the last verse of Revelation 14. When teaching, I always read this entry aloud with an ironic, nearly sarcastic tone, for then its full import sinks in: "Proclaim ye this among the Gentiles; Prepare war, wake up the mighty men, let all the men of war draw near; let them come up: beat your plowshares into swords, and your pruninghooks into spears: let the weak say, I am strong. Assemble yourselves, and come, all ye heathen, and gather yourselves together round about: thither cause thy mighty ones to come down, O Lord. Let the heathen be wakened, and come up to the valley of Jehoshaphat: for there will I sit to judge all the heathen round about." (Joel 3:9–12.)

The irony is apparent in this invitation of the Lord for all the warring nations to assemble at Jehoshaphat's valley. Since we know what once happened there, we are aware of how God will *judge* the "mighty ones" when they arrive. Irony is further seen in the reversal of Isaiah and Micah's words that also speak of a judgment and a rebuke of nations. (See Isaiah 2:4; Micah 4:3.) The Lord wants his children to beat swords into plowshares and spears into pruning hooks, but here it is just the opposite. When armed with their weapons, the "weak" consider themselves strong. There is nothing like a weapon to instill a false sense of prowess and superiority.

Now that the opposing Gentiles, the heathen, the mighty ones, the executors of war, and the lovers of conquest have gathered themselves together, the winepress is full, and the crushing weight of judgment may begin. The angel of death has been summoned, and a full yield waits for the cutting blade.

"Put ye in the sickle, for the harvest is ripe: come, get you down; for the press is full, the fats [vats] overflow; for their wickedness is great." (Joel 3:13.) As with the Nephites and Jaredites, every appeal to reason, repentance, common sense, humanity, compassion, fairness, and fear has been rejected. They are lost in the billowing smoke of the pit, or as Zephaniah indicated, "they shall walk like blind men." (Zephaniah 1:17.)

The haunting words of Joel continue: "Multitudes, multitudes in the valley of decision: for the day of the Lord is near in the valley of decision." (Joel 3:14.) The name of the valley is now "Decision." What choice have they been asked to make? That is not difficult to fathom. Will it be war or peace? Repentance or continued wickedness? Hatred or love? Vengeance or forgiveness? Zion or Babylon? Apostasy or Restoration? Destruction or salvation? The plowshare or the sword? Ultimately the decision is that to which John devotes the entire book of Revelation. Will it be the grasping dragon or the sacrificing Lamb? The devouring beast or the growing man child offering his gentle iron rod? The bride clothed in the sun or the whore appareled in her trappings? The harvest joy of the whitened fields or the despair of the grapes of wrath?

"Seek ye the Lord, all ye meek of the earth, which have wrought his judgment," Zephaniah pleaded, "seek righteousness, seek meekness: it may be ye shall be hid in the day of the Lord's anger. . . . Before the decree bring forth, before the day pass as the chaff, before the fierce anger of the Lord come upon you, before the day of the Lord's anger come upon you." (Zephaniah 2:2–3.) Repentance, meekness, and humility are always the answer, but once they have been crushed in the beast's world of "conquer or be conquered," the inevitable harvest is only a matter of time.

THE SONG OF MOSES
AND THE LAMB

T

he last scene of chapter 14, like those of chapters 9 and 13, is so intense that we need another breathing space to gather our emotions. John provides it in the eight verses comprising chapter 15. They are also important in preparing the heart for what will follow, as the tension, the drama, of Revelation mounts again in chapter 16.

For the moment, however, the soul may rest in the contemplation of the final destination to which the earth and the Saints are heading. As the last seven angels are preparing to pour out the last dregs of the wrath of God, John is shown the celestialized earth as "a sea of glass mingled with fire: and them that had gotten the victory over the beast, and over his image, and over his mark, and over the number of his name, stand on the sea of glass, having the harps of God." (Revelation 15:2.)

When I was young and had to face some unpleasant experience, like going to the dentist or taking end-of-semester exams, I would always pick a longed-for reward that I would receive after the trial was over. By focusing on my future happiness, the present pain was more sufferable and didn't seem to last as long.

In this spirit, John reminds us of what we have already learned, that the earth, though now steeped in blood, war, famine, plague, and smoke, will soon be purified and become the habitation of the faithful. It will be a place of light and truth, where all corruption has been burned away in the furnace of the premillennial cleansing.

Those who have endured to this end will sing the song of victory, just as Moses and the children of Israel sang a song of joy when the Egyptian host was destroyed in the Red Sea. The song of Moses is found in Exodus 15. The plagues are consummated, the pursuing chariots of Pharaoh have met their fate in the depths of the sea, and Israel "shall see them again no more for ever." (Exodus 14:13.)

The focus of Moses' song is the execution of God's judgment over the warring forces of Pharaoh contrasted with the mercy extended to His own people. "The Lord is a man of war," the song states, "Pharaoh's chariots and his host . . . his chosen captains also are drowned in the Red sea. . . . The enemy said, I will pursue, I will overtake, I will divide the spoil; my lust shall be satisfied upon them; I will draw my sword, my hand shall destroy them. . . . Who is like unto thee, O Lord, among the gods? who is like thee, glorious in holiness, fearful in praises, doing wonders? . . . Thou in thy mercy hast led forth the people which thou hast redeemed." (Exodus 15:3–13.)

As Pharaoh was defeated, so too has Christ overcome his enemies; hence the song of the Lamb is also mentioned. Both physical and spiritual death have been conquered. All effects of the Fall are reversed. God did not forget his oppressed and burdened people in the days of Moses; neither did he forget them

217

during his mortal ministry; neither will he fail to bring deliverance in the last days. All who share in the coming celebration of victory and deliverance praise the Lord, for his "judgments are made manifest." (Revelation 15:4.) John would have us sing the triumphant song of victory even before it is accomplished.

THE TABERNACLE OF THE TESTIMONY

Assured once again of this ultimate destiny of mankind and the earth, we are prepared for the last plagues. The "temple of the tabernacle of the testimony in heaven" is opened, and the final seven angels with their bowls of wrath exit. (Revelation 15:5.) The temple then fills with "smoke from the glory of God, and from his power; and no man was able to enter into the temple, till the seven plagues of the seven angels were fulfilled." (Revelation 15:8.)

The word "testimony" in verse 5 can be rendered "covenant" or "witness" for easier understanding. The coming judgments go forth from the Lord's own house, the repository of his covenant with his people, of which the earthly tabernacle with its Ark of the Covenant was a similitude. From the earliest ages, the temple has been associated with the idea of a covenant.

The Lord ever keeps his promises. He said he would come, and he will do so. He promised to cleanse the world and make it a fit abode for the redeemed. He will delay no longer. Looking into the very center of his temple, into the Holy of Holies beyond the veil at the Ark of the Covenant, is a sure reminder of his integrity. "Who am I, saith the Lord, that have promised and have not fulfilled?" (D&C 58:31.) No place and no object better assures us that God will fulfill his words than the temple with its sacred ark. Gazing at it fills the ears with the Savior's assurances: "I will make the earth a sea of glass. You will stand upon it. The song of victory will be sung." When Christ finally appears on the earth, the first thing we will hear are his confirming words relative to his promise: "I am he who spake in righteousness, mighty to save." (D&C 133:47.)

Numerous times in the Old Testament when the glory of the Lord was in his tabernacle, on Mt. Sinai, or in the temple, no one could enter. This suggests several ideas. First, neither man nor any force can stand before the Lord when his glory and power are manifested to their fullest degree. There will be no stopping the final execution of his will.

Secondly, when the Lord accepted the newly erected tabernacle of Moses and also at the dedication of Solomon's temple, his glory filled both to such a degree that no one could enter. (See Exodus 40:34–35; 1 Kings 8:10–11.) In both instances, the cloud of his divine presence suggested his approval. He had received his children's offered gift and would make their constructed dwelling his own house, into which no mortal could enter. The Lord approves of the missions of the final seven angels, whose bowls of wrath are about to be poured out; after all, they emerged from the smoke of his dwelling.

A third idea is also worthy of reflection. Anciently, the temple had strong associations with God's mercy. The covering of the Ark of the Covenant was called the mercy seat. In Solomon's dedicatory prayer, the idea that God will grant forgiveness when his people turn to his temple is the dominant theme. (See 1 Kings 8:23–53.) The rituals in the Holy of Holies on the Day of Atonement were centered on obtaining God's forgiveness for the nation.

The scriptures describe times when the people were so wicked that the Lord instructed his prophets to cease praying for them, as no forgiveness would be offered. This was not commanded because God's mercy ceased to be extended but because there was no chance that repentance would be sought. "Pray not thou for this people, neither lift up cry nor prayer for them, neither make intercession to me: for I will not hear thee," the Lord instructed Jeremiah. (Jeremiah 7:16; see also 11:14; 14:11.) "I cannot recommend them unto God lest he should smite me," Mormon told his son Moroni in a letter detailing the wickedness of the Nephites. (Moroni 9:21.) Abraham pleaded for Sodom and Gomorrah if he could find ten righteous souls. God's mercy would have extended even thus far, but the ten were wanting and judgment was required.

Now that the angels have gone forth, there will be no turning back. It is a time for judgment, as mercy has been rejected. Before the final destruction of the Nephites, the Lord explained to Mormon why "the day of grace was passed with them." (Mormon 2:15.) "Vengeance is mine, and I will repay; and *because this people repented not after I had delivered them, behold, they shall be cut off from the face of the earth.*" (Mormon 3:15; italics added.) As we shall see in chapter 16, the Lord knew the people well, for in the midst of the pouring bowls of the angels, no one desires to repent.

We may also contrast these angels emerging from the "smoke" of God's house with the four angels and the locusts of chapter 9 who came forth from the "smoke" of the bottomless pit.

A key word to which I am drawn in this last verse of chapter 15 is "till." Though for the present period of cleansing, the Lord's eternal temple is closed to man, the prohibition will not last forever. God's power and glory will be manifested in its most tender, gentle, and merciful rays again, and his righteous children will be admitted into his presence.

THE SEVEN GOLDEN VIALS

I n chapter 16 the angels introduced in chapter 15 pour out the judgments of God from the seven golden vials. Like the seven final circles around the walls of Jericho, these seven angels give the concluding sounds of warning. Is there no other Rahab in Jericho who wishes, even at this late date, to repent?

Chapter 16 is deeply akin to chapters 8 and 9. The plagues poured out are directed to various separate elements of creation but must be seen as standing for the whole. All creation, all mankind, is involved. Even the four elements of the ancient world can be traced in this chapter. People once believed that all things were composed of earth, air, fire, and water. These were the four basic elements of life. Each is present in chapter 16. Earth is in verse 2, water in verses 3–4, fire (the sun) in verse 8, and air in verse 17.

Earlier we discussed the interrelated forces of pestilence, war, and famine. It appears that in the first four vials these three destructive forces are spoken of again. The first vial, poured upon the earth, creates "a noisome and grievous sore upon the men which had the mark of the beast, and upon them which worshipped his image." (Revelation 16:2.) This is reminiscent of the boils that fell upon the Egyptians but not upon the Israelites. We are being reminded again that the plagues of the last days are directed to the wicked, not to the Lord's people, who are promised safety. (See D&C 45:65–71; 1 Nephi 22:16–25.) In this image, then, we have the scourge of pestilence, of disease. It is reminiscent of the pale horse seen at the time of the first opening of the seals in chapter 6.

WATER TO BLOOD

The second and third angel direct their vials to the element of water, one aimed at the sea and the other the rivers and fountains. In both cases the water is turned to blood. This too was a plague of Egypt. In this context it represents the power of the sword or war and is brother to the red horse of chapter 6. Commentary by the angels is given relative to these two vials: "Thou art righteous, O Lord . . . because thou hast judged thus . . . For they have shed the blood of saints and prophets, and *thou hast given them blood to drink; for they are worthy.*" (Revelation 16:5–6; italics added.)

The image of water being turned to blood is common in Revelation. Perhaps a prophecy of Joseph Smith will best help us understand the meaning behind this plague. Just before the martyrdom, Joseph was in conversation with some of the militia officers in Carthage.

"General Smith asked them if there was anything in his appearance that indicated he was the desperate character his enemies represented him to be; and he asked them to give him their honest opinion on the subject. The reply was, 'No, sir, your appearance would indicate the very contrary, General Smith; but we cannot see what is in your heart, neither can we tell what are your intentions.' To which Joseph replied, 'Very true, gentlemen, you cannot see what is in my heart, and you are therefore unable to judge me or my intentions; but I can see what is in your hearts, and will tell you what I see. I can see that you *thirst for blood,* and nothing but my blood will satisfy you. It is not for crime of any description that I and my brethren are thus continually persecuted and harassed by our enemies, but there are other motives, and some of them I have expressed, so far as relates to myself; and *inasmuch as you and the people thirst for blood, I prophesy, in the name of the Lord, that you shall witness scenes of blood and sorrow to your entire satisfaction. Your souls shall be perfectly satiated with blood,* and many of you who are now present shall have an opportunity to face the cannon's mouth from sources you think not of; and those people that desire this great evil upon me and my brethren, shall be filled with regret and sorrow because of the scenes of desolation and distress that await them. They shall seek for peace, and shall not be able to find it." (Joseph Smith, *History of The Church of Jesus Christ of Latter-day Saints,* 7 vols. 2d ed. rev., edited by B. H. Roberts [Salt Lake City: The Church of Jesus Christ of Latter-day Saints, 1932-51] 6:566; italics added.)

This prophecy was fulfilled during the Civil War. Water being turned to blood demonstrates the bloodthirsty nature of men and nations. "They have lost their love, one towards another," Mormon wrote, "and they thirst after blood and revenge continually." (Moroni 9:5.) God's justice is eventually shown in allowing them full rein in their desires. What they have practiced on others will come upon them. John asserted

this back in chapters 13 and 14 while speaking of the beast—
hence the counsel to have patience and faith. They have lived
by the sword and will soon die by it. (See Revelation 13:10,
14:12.)

A KINGDOM OF DARKNESS

The fourth angel pours his vial upon the sun, and "power
was given unto him to scorch men with fire. And men were
scorched with great heat." (Revelation 16:8–9.) The burning
heat of the sun has been used in scripture and other literature
to suggest trials, particularly those that offer no relief. (See
Matthew 13:6, 21 and Revelation 7:16 as examples.) Great heat
is commonly associated with barren, desert, wasted, unfruitful,
unproductive land. Heat and the drought that follows on its
heels is the most frequent cause of famine. Perhaps in this image
we see the return of the black horse, holding high his scales
once again. At any rate, ordeals of great magnitude are
intimated.

The plagues of Egypt are used in this chapter for the same
reason as discussed in chapters 8 and 9. Pharaoh-like, the people
will continue to harden their hearts. In spite of the sword, pestilence, famine, and scorching trials, they "blasphemed the name
of God, which hath power over these plagues: and they
repented not to give him glory." (Revelation 16:9.) History
repeats itself. John's use of the plagues indicates that man has
learned nothing from the past.

In the great storm and earthquake of 3 Nephi, the
Gadianton-robber city of Jacobugath was singled out for
destruction by fire "because of their sins and their wickedness,
which was above all the wickedness of the whole earth."
(3 Nephi 9:9.) As if to be even more obvious in his displeasure

at the sins of men, the fifth angel singles out "the seat of the beast" for his vial that results in darkness. The plague of darkness that covered Egypt is alluded to here. "And his kingdom was full of darkness; and they gnawed their tongues for pain, and blasphemed the God of heaven because of their pains and their sores, and repented not of their deeds." (Revelation 16:10–11.) I sense that this darkness is that of evil deeds and desires.

Speaking of a time of great evil, desolation, and despair, Isaiah wrote, "They shall pass through it, hardly bestead and hungry: and it shall come to pass, that when they shall be hungry, they shall fret themselves, and curse their king and their God, and look upward. And they shall look unto the earth; and behold trouble and darkness, dimness of anguish; and they shall be driven to darkness." (Isaiah 8:21–22.) They have reached the point when "the Lord would not always suffer them to take happiness in sin." (Mormon 2:13.) "The whole face of this land is one continual round of murder and bloodshed; and no one knoweth the end of the war." (Mormon 8:8.)

Chewing one's own tongue for pain intensifies the portrait of human anguish, but it can also suggest another idea that arises from Isaiah. Notice in the following passage how a darkened land, excluded from God's light, increases its own suffering: "Through the wrath of the Lord of hosts is the land darkened, and the people shall be as the fuel of the fire: no man shall spare his brother. And he shall snatch on the right hand, and be hungry; and he shall eat on the left hand, and they shall not be satisfied: *they shall eat every man the flesh of his own arm.*" (Isaiah 9:19–20; italics added.) A perfect example of the pain of a kingdom full of darkness is detailed in Mormon's letter to his son in Moroni chapter 9.

When the wicked find themselves on the eve of disaster, the scriptures seem to offer them three choices: (1) They can curse God and die, as they do in Revelation. (2) They can eat, drink, and be merry; since they will be destroyed anyway, why not have one more round of revelry. (3) They can take the choice urged by God and his prophets: "Look to God and live." (Alma 37:47.) But there is no hope of repentance. Accustomed to evil deeds, they have created an evil character. We become what we do, and then the hope of repentance is gone. No amount of pain, no trumpet blast echoing in the ear, can awake the sleeping conscience. The merciful thing is to let finality have its way and bring on the end.

THE KINGS OF THE EAST

"And the sixth angel poured out his vial upon the great river Euphrates; and the water thereof was dried up, that the way of the kings of the east might be prepared." (Revelation 16:12.) The sixth vial prepares the way for the final fall of Lucifer's kingdom, particularly that part best represented by the predatory beast. Several ideas come to mind about the drying up of the river. The most obvious is the Red Sea and the Jordan River, which were parted by Moses and Joshua, respectively. These partings allowed the escape of God's children or their entrance into a new homeland. There is irony that the drying up of the waters in this case prepares the way for an invasion instead.

However, I believe something else is going on with the drying up of the river. Babylon was located on the Euphrates River. Herodotus, a Greek historian who lived in the fifth century before Christ, tells the story of its fall.

Cyrus, a Persian king, besieged the city for some time. Great walls surrounded it, and the river ran through its middle. Along both sides of the river were brick walls and gates that led to docks and a bridge connecting the two halves. An earlier monarch of Babylon had dug a great lake further upstream during a time of building and beautifying the city. Cyrus had his armies divert the flow of the Euphrates into the lake. As the water level in the river dropped, his troops could walk down the streambed into the city. So confident were the Babylonians of their security that they had left open the gates along the river into the city. Babylon thus fell to the Persian kings. (See Herodotus, *History*, 190–91.)

Daniel tells us of the revelry that was taking place in the palace on the night Babylon fell when a hand wrote on the wall, predicting the demise of Babylonian power. (See Daniel 5.) Persia was east of Babylon. In fact, one of the principal cities of the Persians, Susa, lies on a line almost directly east. With the river Euphrates dried up, the way was prepared for the advance of the kings of the east.

THE PLAGUE OF FROGS

For anyone who knew the story of the fall of Babylon, John's meaning would be clear. The sixth angel is preparing spiritual Babylon for its fall. That fall will be accomplished with the help of another plague of Egypt, that of frogs: "And I saw three unclean spirits like frogs come out of the mouth of the dragon, and out of the mouth of the beast, and out of the mouth of the false prophet. For they are the spirits of devils, working miracles, which go forth unto the kings of the earth and of the whole world, to gather them to the battle of that great day of God Almighty." (Revelation 16:13–14.)

Remember that the sword of truth came out of the mouth

227

of the Savior. By contrast, therefore, the frogs represent lies, falsehoods, apostasy, and deceptions. A plague of lies coming from both the political and religious arms of Satan's arsenal will prepare the way for Babylon's fall. A close reading of a story in the Old Testament might reveal to us exactly what the frogs are saying to the kings of the world that will cause them to gather to the last battle.

There is a wonderful account of the demise of King Ahab in the last chapter of 1 Kings that sheds light on these verses. Ahab, who married the wicked Jezebel, told his servants, "Know ye that Ramoth in Gilead is ours, and we be still, and take it not out of the hand of the king of Syria?" (1 Kings 22:3.) Ahab forged an alliance with Jehoshaphat, the king of Judah. Before going to war, however, Jehoshaphat wanted the word of the Lord concerning the endeavor. Willing to humor his ally, Ahab "gathered the prophets together, about four hundred men, and said unto them, Shall I go against Ramoth-gilead to battle, or shall I forbear? And they said, Go up; for the Lord shall deliver it into the hand of the king." (1 Kings 22:6.)

That was exactly what Ahab wanted to hear from his religious counselors. Jehoshaphat, however, being a righteous man, wanted a true prophet of Jehovah to speak. Reluctantly, Ahab sent for Micaiah, saying, "I hate him; for he doth not prophesy good concerning me, but evil." (1 Kings 22:8.) Micaiah is sent for with a warning from the messenger: "Behold now, the words of the prophets declare good unto the king with one mouth: let thy word, I pray thee, be like the word of one of them, and speak that which is good." (1 Kings 22:13.) In other words, tell the king what he wants to hear.

Micaiah's message, however, was not one of victory for the king but the prediction of his defeat and death. He then added

228

the following ironic story, which gives insight about the frogs of Revelation 16: "I saw the Lord sitting on his throne, and all the host of heaven standing by him. . . . And the Lord said, Who shall persuade Ahab, that he may go up and fall at Ramoth-gilead? And one said on this manner, and another said on that manner. And there came forth a spirit, and stood before the Lord, and said, I will persuade him. And the Lord said unto him, Wherewith? And he said . . . *I will be a lying spirit in the mouth of all his prophets. And he said, Thou shalt persuade him, and prevail also: go forth, and do so. Now therefore, behold, the Lord hath put a lying spirit in the mouth of all these thy prophets, and the Lord hath spoken evil concerning thee.*" (1 Kings 22:19–23; italics added.)

Eager for conquest, Ahab willingly rejected Micaiah's voice, trusting instead to the flattering prophets who urged him on to war. True to Micaiah's prophecy and the Lord's desires, Ahab was slain in battle, and his forces were scattered. In like manner, the nations of the world listen to the lying spirits that promise they will be victorious. They will not be defeated but will win glory, power, lands, treasures, and spoil. Their strength is mightier than that of their enemy. We must conquer or be conquered. The end justifies the means. These thoughts encourage them to marshal their forces and come up to the winepress spoken of in chapter 14. In Revelation 16 the winepress is given a name: "And he gathered them together into a place called in the Hebrew tongue Armageddon." (Revelation 16:16.)

It is also interesting to contemplate how often in the affairs of men the political entity seeks the sanction and justification of the religious. All want to believe that God is on their side. The beast demands and deserves the approbation of the dragon-voiced lamb, the false prophet. Part of the lies spread by the frogs centers on that justification. Combining the voices, the dragon commands, "Conquer"; the beast asserts, "I am strong and powerful and my enemy is weak"; and the false prophet whispers, "Your cause is just and carries the approval of God."

ARMAGEDDON

This battle has been spoken of in literal terms so many times that it is difficult to view it any other way. As I mentioned before, I do not wish to challenge or deny any literal interpretation of the writings in Revelation. In time we will know their fulfillment both literal and figurative. For the present, let us look at the figurative, seeking to understand the allusion John employs by using this name.

Har in Hebrew means hill or mountain. Megiddo was a fortress city that guarded an important pass in the Carmel mountain range of northern Israel. God will gather all the Ahab-like deceived of the world to the Hill of Megiddo. Since many important battles were fought there, its very name was associated with conflict. Here many a warrior and many a conquering general met his fate. Its name has the same connotations as Waterloo and Little Big Horn in more recent history. Considering the forms of modern warfare, a profoundly significant battle in a valley of the Holy Land raises numerous questions.

Metaphorically speaking, Armageddon is a place where armies meet and deal out mutual destruction. This can take place in any number of places. The Hebrew name *Megiddo* suggests a gathering, a "rendezvous," for the purposes of war. The root word means "to crowd; also to gash (as if by pressing into): assemble (selves by troops), gather (selves together, self in troops), cut selves)." (James Strong, "Hebrew and Chaldee

Dictionary," in *The New Strong's Exhaustive Concordance of the Bible* [Nashville: Thomas Nelson Publishers, 1984], 25.) In our own time, perhaps, the Lord might say, "I will gather them together at Waterloo." We would, in all likelihood, not interpret that to mean that God would draw all nations to a field in Europe. We would understand that those gathered would meet their total defeat, as did Napoleon in the nineteenth century.

On Christmas day, 1832, Joseph Smith received his "Prophecy on War," recorded now as section 87 of the Doctrine and Covenants. This was an interesting day for the Lord to reveal truth about the conflicts of man, since it is the one day of the year most associated with "peace on earth, good will to men." (See Luke 2:14.) The message seems conspicuous: There will be no peace on earth from this time forth. The only peace men will find is that offered in the next revelation, section 88, known as "The Olive Leaf."

I can think of no better place to find a description of Armageddon in its broader, more comprehensive, fulfillment than in this revelation. It speaks of various types of wars that will "terminate in the death and misery of many souls; and the time will come that war will be poured out upon all nations." (D&C 87:1–2.) These include, civil wars, world wars or wars of alliances, and revolutions, as all are described in the revelation. (See D&C 87:3–4.) We have seen these types of conflicts since that Christmas day in 1832 and will, I am afraid, continue to see them. The prophecy concludes by combining many elements we read of in Revelation: "Thus, with the sword and by bloodshed the inhabitants of the earth shall mourn; and with famine, and plague, and earthquake, and the thunder of heaven, and the fierce and vivid lightning also, shall the inhabitants of the earth be made to feel the wrath, and indignation, and chastening hand of an Almighty God, *until the consumption decreed hath made a full end of all nations.*" (D&C 87:6; italics added.) It is the combination of all these forces and hostilities that bring the downfall of earthly kingdoms to make way for a heavenly one. The last line of this verse comes from Isaiah 28 and will be very helpful in understanding the results of the seventh angel's vial.

As we have seen many times throughout the book of Revelation, the inhabitants of the world are given a choice. Now the choice is between two mountains. We may choose to gather to Mount Zion, where we will be of "one heart and one mind," or we may gather to the Hill of Megiddo, where the exact opposite occurs. "If ye are not one ye are not mine," Jesus told the Saints. (D&C 38:27.) The two mountains are established, and we already begin to see both of them pull at the souls and loyalties of mankind like giant magnets. Ultimately man gravitates to one or the other of the two hills. It is in light of this choice that counsel, as usual, is given in Revelation: "Behold, I come as a thief. Blessed is he that watcheth, and keepeth his garments." (Revelation 16:15.) When the Lord comes, let him find us standing on the right hilltop, being true to our covenants. It is also with these challenges in mind that we should carefully read section 88, for it contains the Lord's guidance on finding peace in a world of discord. That section is beyond the scope of this book, but I would strongly recommend searching it for a safe pattern of life in an Armageddon world.

THE GREAT EARTHQUAKE

Heeding the frog voices of the dragon, the beast, and the false prophet, all are gathered now at Armageddon, and the wine press is full. "And the seventh angel poured out his vial into the air. . . . And there were voices, and thunders, and lightnings; and there was a great earthquake, such as was not since men were upon the earth, so mighty an earthquake, and so great. And the great city was divided into three parts, and the cities of the nations fell: and great Babylon came in remembrance before God, to give unto her the cup of the wine of the fierceness of his wrath. And every island fled away, and the mountains were not found." (Revelation 16:17–20.)

This verse is strongly reminiscent of the description of the sixth seal, which portrayed our own time. I repeat, there is nothing really new in the seventh seal that was not given birth and flourished in every other seal; it is in the final outcome where the difference lies. The purpose of earthquakes in most prophetic writing is to knock down temporal things. This is the only way some will recognize the eternal things: the city and kingdom that cannot fall, the one built on a firm foundation— that of the fullness of the gospel of Jesus Christ. This great earthquake levels the cities of the nations who have heralded the image of the beast and lived by his laws and principles, but there is one in particular that must fall. It will take the greatest of all earthquakes to level Babylon, which is spiritual wickedness. (See D&C 133:14.) That great earthquake now comes to bring down "the great Babylon." Babylon has stood since the Fall in one form or another. It holds sway over all the earth. It is now divided into three parts.

To graphically demonstrate to his people what Babylon would do to them because of their rebellions, Ezekiel shaved his beard and head, then took a balance and divided his hair into three piles, all at the Lord's command: "Thou shalt burn with fire a third part in the midst of the city . . . and thou shalt take a third part, and smite about it with a knife: and a third part thou shalt scatter in the wind; and I will draw out a sword after them." (Ezekiel 5:2.) What was once done by Babylon to Israel, the Lord will now do to Babylon. "With what measure ye mete, it shall be measured to you again." (Matthew 7:2.) Some will be destroyed by fire, some by the sword; some will flee but will be pursued wherever they run. Since the mountains and islands are also fleeing, there will be no place to hide, to regroup, to rebuild, and to fight again. Babylon's defeat will be total.

She once said to the world, "Bow down, that we may go over; and thou hast laid thy body as the ground, and as the street, to them that went over." (Isaiah 51:23.) That bitter cup, however, offered so often to the peoples of the world, is now pressed to Babylon's own lips.

A GREAT HAIL OUT OF HEAVEN

The culminating plague, which falls on the fleeing remnants of tumbling Babylon, is that of hail. This, too, was one of the plagues of Egypt, but there is much more in this image, making it rich in symbolic meaning. There are many places in the Old Testament to which we can turn for an awareness of the hailstorm in its metaphorical fulfillment. When Joshua fought a coalition of kings and defeated them at a city called Gibeon, the remnants of their forces began to flee. "And it came to pass, as they fled from before Israel, and were in the going down to Beth-horon, that *the Lord cast down great stones from heaven upon them . . . and they died: they were more which died with hailstones than they whom the children of Israel slew with the sword.*" (Joshua 10:11; italics added.) When the time of judgment comes, there will be no escaping, Revelation seems to say. Yet there is still more to discover in the pages of the Old Testament.

Joseph Smith's prophecy on war spoke of the consumption

234

decreed upon all nations that will make a full end of them. This comes from Isaiah 28, which also contains a reference to the defeat of the Canaanites by the hailstones at Gibeon but expands the image to a much greater degree. This is the same chapter that speaks of the apostasy and restoration that will be accomplished by the Lord, revealing to "them that are weaned from the milk. . . . precept upon precept . . . line upon line; here a little, and there a little." (Isaiah 28:9–10.) The doctrine that will thus be revealed will allow those who accept it to build upon a solid foundation in preparation for a mighty storm and flood. "Wherefore, I the Lord, knowing the calamity which should come upon the inhabitants of the earth, called upon my servant Joseph Smith, Jun. . . . and gave him commandments." (D&C 1:17.)

The commandments revealed in the Restoration will create a place of safety: "I lay in Zion for a foundation a stone, a tried stone, a precious corner stone, a sure foundation: he that believeth shall not make haste. Judgment also will I lay to the line, and righteousness to the plummet." (Isaiah 28:16.) The stone spoken of is that of the Savior. When the cornerstone is positioned, the rest of the building can be constructed. Other measurements are taken from the cornerstone—hence the importance of its being perfectly square. Such was the life, character, and teaching of the Lord Jesus Christ. With such a building for a refuge, there will be no need to rush to and fro, searching vainly for a place of safety.

Yet there are others in Isaiah's description who will not build upon the cornerstone, nor will they use righteousness and judgment for their measuring devices. "We have made a covenant with death," they say, "and with hell are we at agreement; when the overflowing scourge shall pass through, it shall not come unto us: for we have made lies our refuge, and under falsehood have we hid ourselves." Yet when the scourge comes, says the Lord, "the *hail shall sweep away the refuge of lies*, and the waters shall overflow the hiding place. And your covenant with death shall be disannulled, and your agreement with hell shall not stand; when the overflowing scourge shall pass through, then ye shall be trodden down by it. From the time that it goeth forth it shall take you: for morning by morning shall it pass over, by day and by night: and it shall be a vexation only to understand the report." (Isaiah 28:15, 17–19; italics added.)

It is evident from the Doctrine and Covenants that the scourge spoken of is war, with all its accompanying complications, which Isaiah compares to a great hailstorm and ancillary flood that sweeps away every hiding place. (See D&C 5:19–20; 87; 45:31–33; 97:23–26.) The association of the hail with the lies of mankind is also taught. In the dedicatory prayer of the Kirtland Temple, Joseph Smith asked the Lord to "confound, and astonish, and to bring to shame and confusion, all those who have spread lying reports abroad, over the world, against thy servant or servants . . . and that all their works may be brought to naught, *and be swept away by the hail, and by the judgments which thou wilt send upon them in thine anger, that there may be an end to lyings and slanders against thy people.*" (D&C 109:29–30; italics added.)

Daniel also compared war to a flood in describing the downfall of Jerusalem and the temple: "And the end thereof shall be with a *flood*, and unto the end of the *war* desolations are determined." (Daniel 9:26; italics added.) Isaiah concluded his warning to the world by alluding to two past battles. "The Lord shall rise up as in mount Perazim, he shall be wroth as *in the valley of Gibeon*, that he may do his work, his strange work; and bring to pass his act, his strange act. Now therefore be ye not mockers, lest your bands be made strong: for I have heard from the Lord God of hosts, *a consumption, even determined upon the whole earth.*" (Isaiah 28:21–22; italics added.)

"Strange" in this context means unexpected or not anticipated and refers to the Restoration and the establishment of Zion. The valley of Gibeon refers to the hailstorm sent by the Lord upon the fleeing Canaanites during the time of Joshua. "Perazim" means "bursting forth," a name given by David when he defeated the Philistines. "The Lord hath broken forth upon mine enemies before me," David said, "as the *breach of waters.*" (2 Samuel 5:20; italics added.) Armies fought in great lines of massed men. The objective was to attack at the weakest place and break through the line, much as a flood does to a dike or levee. This is the image both David and Isaiah are using. The scourge of hail and the rush of floodwaters will culminate in the end of nations and the elimination of all refuges and hiding places built on the lies and falsehoods of an apostate world. Only that refuge with Christ as its cornerstone and righteousness and judgment as the measure of its walls will withstand the hail and the flood.

Since all other refuges are based upon the lies of conquest, conquest will bring them down: "Behold, the judgments of God will overtake the wicked; and it is by the wicked that the wicked are punished; for it is the wicked that stir up the hearts of the children of men unto bloodshed." (Mormon 4:5.) If the god of destruction commands your allegiance, you should not be surprised if that god destroys you.

Ezekiel also used the image of a hailstorm to portray the sweeping away of all entities and powers built upon lies and vanity: "Because ye have spoken vanity, and seen lies, therefore, behold, I am against you, saith the Lord God." These words were directed to the false prophets of Israel, particularly those who promised peace when there would be none. "Because, even because they have seduced my people, saying, Peace, and there was no peace; and one built up a wall, and, lo, others daubed it with untempered morter." (Ezekiel 13:8, 10.) Mortar must be properly tempered, or hardened, to withstand pressure. The wall may look sturdy from the outside, but without proper temper- ing, the slightest force will bring it down. In Ezekiel's illustra- tion, the mortar represents the lies, vanity, and falsehoods taught by false prophets. A major lie states that one party is strong enough to hold back the forces of the other, thus ending up the only one standing after the contest is over. The devil can appear at times as an angel of light; little wonder that the charm and appeal of his most destructive deceptions can appear strong, reliable, and totally justifiable. (Remember that in Revelation 16, it is the lies of false prophets that lead the kings to destruc- tion at Armageddon.)

"Say unto them which daub it with untempered morter," Ezekiel continues, "that it shall fall: there shall be an overflow- ing shower; and ye, O *great hailstones, shall fall; and a stormy wind shall rend it*. . . . Therefore thus saith the Lord God; I will even rend it with a stormy wind in my fury; and there shall be an overflowing shower in mine anger, and *great hailstones in my fury to consume it*. So will I break down the wall that ye have daubed with untempered morter, and bring it down to the ground, so that the foundation thereof shall be discovered . . . and will say unto you, The wall is no more, neither they that daubed it." (Ezekiel 13:11–15; italics added.)

Ezekiel sums up God's anger toward the wall and those who build it up in words that hauntingly describe so much of what we hear in our modern world: "With lies ye have made the heart of the righteous sad, whom I have not made sad; and strengthened the hands of the wicked, that he should not return from his wicked way, by promising him life." (Ezekiel 13:22.) Such is the power of Babylon. It makes good appear evil, and evil appear good, but a day of reckoning is coming. The wall will crumble in the pounding fury of the hailstorm.

Zephaniah gives us, perhaps, the best concluding summation of Revelation 16: "Surely thou wilt fear me, thou wilt receive instruction; so their dwelling should not be cut off, howsoever I punished them: but they rose early, and corrupted all their doings. Therefore wait ye upon me, saith the Lord, until the day that I rise up to the prey: for my determination is to gather the nations, that I may assemble the kingdoms, to pour upon them mine indignation, even all my fierce anger: for all the earth shall be devoured with the fire of my jealousy." (Zephaniah 3:7–8.)

THE MOTHER OF
HARLOTS

From the battles of Armageddon and the demise of Satan's political arm, represented as the beast, John's attention is now shifted to the religious division: "I will shew unto thee the judgment of the great whore that sitteth upon many waters." (Revelation 17:1.) Later in this same chapter, we are supplied with the meaning of the many waters, for John is told directly that they "are peoples . . . and nations, and tongues." (Revelation 17:15.)

Throughout the Old and New Testaments, Christ's relationship with his people is compared to that of a bride and bridegroom or husband and wife. Mutual covenants of obedience, trust, love, and devotion are exchanged. But the bride has left her husband and broken her covenants, searching elsewhere to bestow her devotion and love. She has "committed fornication" with the "kings of the earth." (Revelation 17:2.) For these reasons she is now called the "great whore." Just as the dragon-voiced lamb of chapter 13 fostered and increased the worship of the beast, here the whore exchanges love with the kings. The images are different, but the associations and events are the same.

John is carried away "into the wilderness," where he beholds "a woman sit upon a scarlet coloured beast, full of names of blasphemy, having seven heads and ten horns." (Revelation 17:3.) This image teaches the same truth as the one above. Riding the beast suggests that she is supported by it and that she directs it, much like one riding a horse. The political and the religious are deeply connected in the opening verses of this chapter. Being in the wilderness, as mentioned earlier, indicates that the Church at that time is in a state of apostasy.

In the Doctrine and Covenants the Lord interpreted the parable of the wheat and the tares for the early Saints. He used a number of interchangeable words, all describing the same religious power: "The apostles were the sowers of the seed," he begins, "and after they have fallen asleep the great persecutor of the church, the apostate, the whore, even Babylon, that maketh all nations to drink of her cup, in whose hearts the enemy, even Satan, sitteth to reign—behold he soweth the tares; wherefore, the tares choke the wheat and drive the church into the wilderness." (D&C 86:2–3.)

No matter which word we use—*wilderness, whore, apostate, Babylon, persecutor*—the same entity is being described. The whore of all the earth, the great and abominable church, the church of the devil—all are *apostasy* in its multifaceted forms.

Nephi's account of these images is much easier to understand. He was shown "many nations and kingdoms" and was told they were "the nations and kingdoms of the Gentiles." He then saw "among the nations of the Gentiles the formation of a great church." (1 Nephi 13:1–4.) The many nations of the

241

Gentiles corresponds to the beast, with its heads, horns, and crowns, as seen in Revelation, only in 1 Nephi they are not being depicted in symbolic form.

The woman sits upon three things in Revelation 16—the beast, seven mountains, and many waters. These appear to be interchangeable. The apostasy will have control over and be in collusion with numerous political nations and kingdoms. Often the seven mountains are equated with Rome. This makes the reading very specific, however. At one time Rome was the major incarnation of the beast, but to limit the mountains to Rome is to miss a great deal of meaning. We must remember that chapter 17 is shown to us in the context of the seventh seal.

One of the best explanations of how the beast and its rider work together comes from Elder Bruce R. McConkie. "To a greater or lesser degree," he wrote, ". . . all of the governments of the earth are in league with the great whore in that, from time to time, they do such things as: prohibit the worship of God; enact laws defining religious beliefs and prescribing forms of worship; maintain state-supported false systems of religion; deny freedom of religious belief to all their citizens; impose the religious beliefs of conquerors upon conquered people; permit the mingling of religious influence with civil government; foster one religious society and proscribe another; deny to men their inherent and inalienable rights; fail to guarantee the free exercise of conscience, the right and control of property, and the protection of life; enact laws which curtail the agency of man; require the teaching of false principles in their educational systems; deny the representatives of certain churches the right to teach their doctrines or proselyte among their people; and fail to punish crime and protect the rights of their citizens, particularly unpopular minority groups." (Bruce R. McConkie, *Doctrinal New Testament Commentary*, 3 vols. [Salt Lake City: Bookcraft, 1973], 3:552–53.)

It is surely possible that one of the reasons the Lord told us we were justified in "befriending" the Constitution was its separation of church and state. (D&C 98:6.) In this decision an element of the united front of beast and harlot was weakened.

THE GOLDEN CUP

In both Revelation and 1 Nephi the woman is decorated with gold, scarlet, and precious clothing. These "are the desires of this great and abominable church." (1 Nephi 13:8.) Thus the third element of influence, economic, is interwoven with the other two. But the most important external thing about her is the wine cup, which she holds in her hand. With its contents "the inhabitants of the earth have been made drunk with the wine of her fornication." It is "full of abominations and filthiness of her fornication." (Revelation 17:2, 4.)

Wine is used in the scriptures in both a positive and negative manner. It can represent a drink in the mildest form or strongly alcoholic. The Lord prophesied of a wonderful feast he would provide for all nations. It would consist of "wines on the lees well refined." (Isaiah 25:6.) The leeward side of a vineyard is the downwind side. Grapes gathered there would be the most moist and filled with the greatest amount of juice, since the plants would transpire less.

In the Doctrine and Covenants, the above verse from Isaiah is repeated relative to the Restoration. The well-refined wine is offered in "the house of the Lord," and we are assured that it and the rest of the feast is "well prepared." (D&C 58:8–9.) Isaiah also penned the Lord's invitation to all nations when he cried out, "Ho, every one that thirsteth, come ye to the waters, and he that hath no money; come ye, buy, and eat; yea, come, buy wine and milk without money and without price." (Isaiah 55:1.) Jacob quoted this verse while encouraging his own people to greater righteousness. (See 2 Nephi 9:50.)

Wine in these instances is equivalent to truth, doctrine, teachings, principles, and ordinances—in short, all the nourishing things of the true gospel of Jesus Christ that bring joy and spiritual health. Of course, as the Lord indicated, the well-refined, richest spiritual wine is found in the House of the Lord. Drinking this pure juice of the vine creates happiness, light-heartedness, companionship, confidence, and nourishment.

However, fermented wine, that which has become strongly alcoholic, that which is distilled through the tampering of man, has just the opposite effect. When doctrines, truths, principles, and ordinances are changed from their pure form, spiritual drunkenness results. The wine in the whore's cup consists of all the apostate doctrines, creeds, and teachings, which have been spoiled and fermented. Man manipulates them for sundry reasons, often from the desire to be one with the world rather than one with the Lord. Isaiah uses this type of wine to describe the apostasy: "They also have erred through wine, and through strong drink are out of the way; the priest and the prophet have erred through strong drink, they are swallowed up of wine, they are out of the way through strong drink; they err in vision, they stumble in judgment. For all tables are full of vomit and filthiness, so that there is no place clean." (Isaiah 28:7–8.)

When one is filled with the wine of apostasy, it becomes impossible to walk the straight and narrow path. The vision of leaders is blurred as opposed to the clear insight of seers. Judgment is impaired, and tables are filled with private interpretations brought forth from individual prejudices. Remember, the golden cup is filled with the whore's own filthiness, that which came from her own sins. "Their creeds [are] an abomination," the Savior said to Joseph Smith in the Sacred Grove, "they teach for doctrines the commandments of men." (JS—H 1:19.) These are the things that fill the wine cup in the hand of the scarlet-decked woman of Revelation 17. Speaking plainly, Nephi simply said, "An exceedingly great many do stumble, yea, insomuch that Satan hath great power over them." (1 Nephi 13:29.) Spiritual control is lost through imbibing the wine of apostasy. This creates the drunkenness discussed earlier when we examined the sixth seal.

MOTHER OF ABOMINATIONS

"Upon her forehead was a name written, MYSTERY, BABYLON THE GREAT, THE MOTHER OF HARLOTS AND ABOMINATIONS OF THE EARTH." (Revelation 17:5.) In numerous translations of the Bible, "mystery" is not part of her titled name; rather, she has a name of mystery, one with a secret, private, or unknown meaning, and the title begins with "Babylon the Great."

With the help of the Doctrine and Covenants and the words of a latter-day prophet, we can better understand why she is the mother of abominations. While Joseph Smith was in Liberty Jail, he wrote a letter to the Saints in Illinois. Parts of that letter are now included in sections 121 through 123 of the Doctrine and Covenants. In section 123 Joseph instructed the Saints to create a record of all the abuses they had suffered in Missouri. He then wrote, " It is an imperative duty that we owe to God, to angels . . . to ourselves, to our wives and children, who have been made to bow down with grief, sorrow, and care, under the most damning hand of murder, tyranny, and oppression, supported and urged on and upheld by the influence of that spirit which hath so strongly riveted the creeds of the fathers, who have inherited lies, upon the hearts of the children, and filled the world with confusion, and has been growing stronger and stronger, and is now the very mainspring of all corruption, and the whole earth groans under the weight of its iniquity. It is an iron yoke, it is a strong band; they are the very handcuffs, and chains, and shackles, and fetters of hell." (D&C 123:7–8.)

Nephi also spoke of the great and abominable church as one that "slayeth the saints of God, yea, and tortureth them and bindeth them down, and yoketh them with a yoke of iron, and bringeth them down into captivity." (1 Nephi 13:5.) This yoke and these chains are the yoke and chains of ignorance of God's true doctrines. (See Alma 12:11–12.)

If we apply the Prophet's words about the suffering of the Saints in a broader manner, allowing them to cover all the grief, sorrow, and care experienced by a world of wives and children; if we include all the murder, tyranny, and oppression this isolated world has seen for the past centuries, we begin to see why the scarlet-adorned woman is called a mother.

What has supported, urged on, and upheld the tyrannies and cruelties of the past and will continue to do so in the future? It is the spirit of the apostasy, handed down from generation to generation, building momentum as the ages pass. Joseph Smith calls it the mainspring of all corruption. John calls it the mother of abominations. Why does the spirit of apostasy occupy this prominent position, creating nearly all the problems of the world?

LACKING SUFFICIENT GOOD

Joseph F. Smith provides us with answers. His comments were given during the first major world war of the past century, but their relevance to every following conflict is obvious: "We know that the spirit of strife and contention exists to an alarming extent among all the people of the world. Why does it exist? Because they are not one with God, nor with Christ. They have not entered into the true fold, and the result is they do not possess the spirit of the true Shepherd *sufficiently* to govern and control their acts in the ways of peace and righteousness. . . .

"We want peace in the world. We want love and good will to exist throughout the earth, and among all the people of the world; but there never can come to the world that spirit of peace and love that should exist, until mankind will receive God's truth and God's message unto them. . . . We will never have peace until we have truth.

"There is just one power, and one only, that can prevent war among the nations of the earth, and that is true religion and undefiled before God, the Father. Nothing else will accomplish it. It is a very common expression today that there is good in all religions. So there is; but there is not *sufficient* good in the denominations of the world to prevent war, nor to prevent contention, strife, division and hatred of one another.

"And, put all the good doctrines, in all the denominations of the world, together, and they do not constitute *sufficient* good to prevent the evils that exist in the world. Why? Because the denominations lack the essential knowledge of God's revelation and truth, and the enjoyment of that spirit which comes from God that leadeth unto all truth, and that inspires men to do good and not evil, to love and not to hate, to forgive and not to bear malice, to be kind and generous and not to be unkind and contracted." (Joseph F. Smith, *Gospel Doctrine*, 5th ed. [Salt Lake City: Deseret Book, 1939], 417–18; italics added.)

The apostasy is the mainspring of tyranny and oppression, the mother of abominations, the creator of lesser harlots, because it removed the one thing that could prevent them all: "The very conditions that exist are the results of this unbelief in the truth; and this worship of men and organizations and powers of men is divested of the power of God." (*Gospel Doctrine*, 420.) In order to win, Lucifer did not need to destroy all of the truths of the gospel, just a few "plain and precious" parts of it. (1 Nephi 13:28.) What was left was not sufficient to keep the beast at bay or the merchant city (which we will examine in the next chapter of Revelation) from exercising her sorcery upon a grasping, greedy world. The fullness of the gospel, eternal truth, is the only power sufficient to turn the tide. This fullness we have; hence our grave responsibility to share it with the world. The greatest ambassadors for peace are nineteen-year-old young men and twenty-one-year-old young women and devoted senior couples. The dragon fears these envoys of truth most of all, for their presence announces the end of his dominion. We should not be surprised that he fights their entry country by country, city by city, and neighborhood by neighborhood. We should not be amazed that the "woman [is] drunken with the blood of the saints, and with the blood of the martyrs of Jesus." (Revelation 17:6.) These had the truth, and truth is a mighty sword that can kill dragons, knock down images, slay beasts, and overthrow great cities.

Apostasy or Restoration

In light of this, it becomes apparent why Nephi concluded that "there are save two churches only . . . whoso belongeth not to the church of the Lamb of God belongeth to that great church, which is the mother of abominations; and she is the whore of all the earth." (1 Nephi 14:10.) It is either the Restoration or continued apostasy. The issue has little to do with individual religious organizations or the sincerity and goodness of numberless people upon the earth. All will be offered the supreme choice in time. Joseph Smith wrote of them when he said, "There are many yet on the earth among all sects, parties, and denominations, who are blinded by the subtle craftiness of men . . . who are only kept from the truth because they know not where to find it." (D&C 123:12.) These words come from the same section that identified the spirit of apostasy as the mainspring of all corruption. Once people find the truth, they will need to make a choice—whether to yield to its principles or remain outside its influence. "I will work a great and a marvelous work among the children of men," the Lord said, "a work which shall be everlasting, either on the one hand or on the other—either to the convincing of them unto peace and life eternal, or unto the deliverance of them to the hardness of their hearts and the blindness of their minds." (1 Nephi 14:7.) Thus, we can divide the people of the world into three main groups: those who have accepted the Restoration; those who have rejected it, choosing to remain in a state of apostasy; and those who have yet to hear the latter-day tidings imparted first to a praying youth of fourteen in a grove of trees.

"There is only one thing that can bring peace into the world," said Joseph F. Smith. "It is the adoption of the gospel of Jesus Christ, rightly understood, obeyed and practiced by rulers and people alike. It is being preached in power to all nations, kindreds, tongues and peoples of the world, by the Latter-day Saints, and the day is not far distant when its message of salvation shall sink deep into the hearts of the common people, who, in sincerity and earnestness, when the time comes, will not only surely register their judgment against a false Christianity, but against war and the makers of war as crimes against the human race." (*Gospel Doctrine*, 421.)

The Lord's ability to prophesy of future beasts, plagues, and Armageddons is basically simple. He knows what people do when the fullness of his gospel is removed from the earth. He knows the natural results when his bride is chased into the wilderness. Since John could see the apostasy beginning to take hold even in his messages to the seven churches, the whole of Revelation becomes a plea of sorts: "Can you see what will follow if you succumb to the temptations of compromise? Are you aware of the broader issue at hand? Do you wish to weaken the only chain on earth strong enough to bind the beasts that ever arise from the turbulent sea of man? Will you allow the bride of Christ to flee into the wilderness, leaving God's children at the mercy of beast, whore, and city?" John knew the answers to these questions, but he also knew that the bride would survive the wilderness to return in a radiance of light, fair as the moon and clear as the sun. And he would be shown the natural end of those who fight against and reject that welcoming light.

ONE HOUR OF POWER

The next verses of Revelation 17 are some of the most difficult in scripture to understand. They return us again to a focus on the political kingdoms of the adversary. The beast returns to center stage. Yet if we will remember what we learned in Daniel and earlier chapters of Revelation, the general sense of the next verses can be grasped. Kingdom will follow kingdom until the grip of the apostasy brings the end of all predatory nations in the great winepress of God.

When John marvels at what he has seen, the angel promises to tell him the "mystery of the woman, and of the beast that carrieth her." (Revelation 17:7.) Unfortunately for those of us who prefer the plainness of Nephi's exposition of truth, the angel uses metaphor to reveal the meaning of metaphor, and the fulfillment remains as puzzling as before: "The beast that thou sawest was, and is not; and shall ascend out of the bottomless pit, and go into perdition." Later the angel speaks of "the beast that was, and is not, and yet is." (Revelation 17:8.) There is a parody of Christ's own reality in these words, for Jesus described himself as one "that liveth, and was dead; and, behold, I am alive for evermore." (Revelation 1:18.) We are dealing with the same themes discussed in Revelation 13. We can destroy one face of evil, one crushing empire, philosophy, or ideology, but replacements are just around the corner. New horns grow out when the old ones are broken off, deadly wounds heal when the heart is left untouched, but the law of the jungle, Korihor's creed, will arise in another form. However, as we are assured by Daniel and reassured here in Revelation 17, they will have their dominion taken away as Christ's kingdom expands. Perdition will be the fate of them all.

It is with these truths in mind that we read verses 10 through 13, which speak of multiple heads, horns, and kings. Some have already fallen, some exist at present, and some are yet to appear. I am not convinced that the number of heads or horns matters in these verses in such a way that we should look for direct correspondence to literal kingdoms, movements, nations, or rulers. Collectively their message is more important than individual identification. The idea of many differing and repeating powers seems to be the relevant concern, and we will leave it at that.

That they will have their "one hour" of power is certainly troubling, but we are not deeply concerned, for their demise is certain. "These have one mind," John writes, meaning they have the same purpose and use the same means to their unholy end. As Elder McConkie explained, in one form or another they "shall make war with the Lamb, and the Lamb shall overcome them." (Revelation 17:13–14.)

CALLED AND CHOSEN

Both John and Nephi tell us how the Saints will prevail over these powerful earthly forces. "They were armed with righteousness and with the power of God in great glory," wrote Nephi. (1 Nephi 14:14.) The power of God is exercised through the magnification of priesthood. And John saw that "they that are with [Christ] are *called, and chosen,* and faithful." (Revelation 17:14; italics added.) Both of these counsels come together in the letter Joseph Smith wrote from Liberty Jail as a victim of the combined collusion of beast and whore. There he instructed the Saints about the proper use of power and influence. "There are many called, but few are chosen," began the Prophet, echoing the words of Revelation. "And why are they not chosen? Because their hearts are set so much upon the things of this world, and aspire to the honors of men, that they do not learn this one lesson—that the rights of the priesthood are inseparably connected with the powers of heaven, and that the powers of heaven cannot be controlled nor handled only upon the principles of righteousness." (D&C 121:34–36.) Nephi saw that the Saints would be armed with righteousness. Now, from the anguish of Liberty, Joseph would reveal those principles of righteousness that allow one to be called and chosen. Perhaps even more important for the topic we are discussing, those principles will give everyone who applies them personal victory over both the spirit of the age and the beast who draws strength from it.

God's way is not "to exercise control or dominion or compulsion upon the souls of the children of men, in any degree of unrighteousness." Those who use these freedom-killing methods of the beast (which were assumed by the scarlet woman as seen in any period of religious history from the Inquisition of the Counter-Reformation to the Puritans of New England to the Taliban of recent memory) are "left unto [themselves], to kick against the pricks, to persecute the saints, and to fight against God." (D&C 121:37–38.)

"Sad experience" has taught us all "that it is the nature and disposition of almost all men, as soon as they get a little authority, as they suppose, they will immediately begin to exercise unrighteous dominion. Hence many are called, but few are chosen." (D&C 121:39–40.) Perhaps the most difficult of all authority to control is that of the religious, for it carries with it the false assumption of God's favor on the forced dominion. But those John sees with Christ have not only been called but also chosen. They have learned to use authority and power in the Lord's way, and the Lord's way is always best, in time proving itself the most powerful.

Now, what are those principles of righteousness that lead to being chosen as well as called? What will give the Saints the right to rule the kingdoms of men as prophesied by Daniel? Why will "the kingdoms of this world . . . be constrained to acknowledge that the kingdom of Zion is in very deed the kingdom of our God and his Christ?" Why will those same kingdoms with all their citizens finally, gladly, willingly, and with great relief say, "Let us become subject unto her laws"? (D&C 105:32.)

The answer came out of a prison, from the pen of a man who, from the earliest periods of his life, knew by experience the persecution of beast, whore, and city. We will extend his words to include the ruling of men in all circumstances. They certainly apply to the discussion at hand: "No power or influence can or ought to be maintained . . . only by persuasion, by long-suffering, by gentleness and meekness, and by love unfeigned; by kindness, and pure knowledge, which shall greatly enlarge the soul without hypocrisy, and without guile." Such power is exercised by leaders who are "full of charity towards all men" and who "let virtue garnish [their] thoughts unceasingly." Such character leaves in their hands "an unchanging scepter of righteousness and truth; and [their] dominion shall be an everlasting dominion, and without compulsory means it shall flow unto [them] forever and ever." (D&C 121:41–46.) In the end Zion will be the only "land of peace, a city of refuge, a place of safety. . . . And it shall come to pass among the wicked, that every man that will not take his sword against his neighbor must needs flee unto Zion for safety. And there shall be gathered unto it out of every nation under heaven; and it shall be the only people that shall not be at war one with another." (D&C 45:66, 68–69.)

THE DEMISE OF THE SCARLET-CLOTHED WOMAN

But what is to become of the beast, his horns, crowns, heads, kings, and mountains? What of the Mother of Abominations? Their end is ironically fitting: "The ten horns which thou sawest upon the beast, these shall hate the whore, and shall make her desolate and naked, and shall eat her flesh, and burn her with fire. For God hath put in their hearts to fulfil his will, and to agree, and give their kingdom unto the beast, until the words of God shall be fulfilled." (Revelation 17:16–17.) The apostasy also ends at Armageddon in the self-destructive flow of the great winepress.

Lest there be any misunderstanding, Nephi clearly interprets the above passages: "I beheld that the wrath of God was poured out upon that great and abominable church, insomuch that there were wars and rumors of wars among all the nations and kindreds of the earth. And as there began to be wars and rumors of wars among all the nations which belonged to the mother of abominations, the angel spake unto me, saying: Behold, the wrath of God is upon the mother of harlots. . . . And the blood of that great and abominable church, which is the whore of all the earth, shall turn upon their own heads; for they shall war among themselves, and the sword of their own hands shall fall upon their own heads, and they shall be drunken with their own blood. And every nation which shall war against thee, O house of Israel, shall be turned one against another." (1 Nephi 14:15–16; 22:13–14.)

If we ride a beast, live the laws of a beast, exercise authority like a beast, and support the manners of a beast, we should not be surprised to die with the beast. When gentleness, charity, meekness, unfeigned love, and kindness are abandoned in favor of compulsion, power, hatred, anger, selfishness, and greed, the end is always foreseeable, whether among political, religious, or economic entities. The blinding smoke of the pit ever gives birth to the locusts of war, and in their rage and hardness of heart they gather. God does not desire it, nor does he cause it, but he knows it is inevitable—the natural end of applying anything but the principles of righteousness.

The final entry of chapter 17 is a bridge to the ideas presented in chapter 18. John shifts the imagery of the whore to that of the great merchant city: "The woman which thou sawest is that great city, which reigneth over the kings of the earth." (Revelation 17:18.) That great city is Babylon. In the turning world of Revelation's imagery, the apostate woman now assumes a new form. Here, however, the central idea is not religious apostasy or political power but the seductive lure of wealth.

REVELATION 18

THE GREAT CITY

I have had the opportunity to teach the Book of Mormon each year for the past twenty-three years. Many times as I search through its pages, I am invited to ponder why the corrupting influence of wealth is such a repeated and strongly accentuated theme. Almost every principal prophet in the Nephite records speaks about wealth. Many of them give leading addresses that warn and school their people relative to their pride and ambitions. In every age they face the same recurring problems of abundance. The heart is set on riches while the nation's spirituality dwindles.

Mormon collected his material for the Book of Mormon from countless numbers of plates detailing many problems and periods of history. He gathered his accounts under the influence and guidance of the Spirit with a view to the future. We often say that the Book of Mormon was written for our generation. Why, then, this pounding repetition regarding wealth? My reflections have intensified with the opportunity of traveling to

257

many nations of the world and visiting many members from those nations. I find it hard to believe that the Saints of Mexico, Central or South America, or even Europe need such insistent reminders. For the most part they live extremely humble lives, grateful to cover the necessities. More and more I wonder if this dominant theme was included primarily for the sake of North America. I realize that the poor can be corrupted by a desire for wealth—the sin of envy or covetouness—as much as the affluent can by its possession, yet the pointing finger of Moroni (who said, "Ye do love money, and your substance, and your fine apparel" [Mormon 8:37]) seems directed to my own nation.

The Lord needs to finance his church, to spread his gospel, to provide for the education and care of the poor, to build temples and chapels. He has given us, therefore, many opportunities to acquire the resources of the earth. The challenge he presents is thus filled with a certain ambiguity. Can we accept these things of the Lord and direct them to his purposes without falling into the spiritual decline and self-absorption of Revelation 18?

THE MERCHANTS OF THE EARTH

Almost immediately John draws into his account of the fall of Babylon "the merchants of the earth [who] are waxed rich through the *abundance of her delicacies*." (Revelation 18:3; italics added.) John uses several words that suggest the luxuries of Babylon, *delicacies* being one of them. Later we read, "How much she hath glorified herself, and *lived deliciously*." (Revelation 18:7; italics added.) The "kings of the earth, who have committed fornication . . . lived *deliciously with her*." (Revelation 18:9; italics added.) The word delicious in this context means wantonly, in excess, wastefully. "All things which were *dainty and goodly*" are available in Babylon. (Revelation 18:14; italics added.) Above all, "her costliness" is her defining feature.

Profit is the essential motive that drives the great city on. Since the pursuit of delicious, dainty, costly delicacies seems to be eternal, the great merchant city believes that her rule over the hearts, labors, and ambitions of men will continue indefinitely: "I sit a queen, and am no widow, and shall see no sorrow." (Revelation 18:7.) These words are echoes of those put into the mouth of "the lady of kingdoms" in Isaiah. (Isaiah 47:5.) They come in the midst of chapters where the Lord repeatedly tells his straying people, "I am God, and there is none else; I am God, and there is none like me." (Isaiah 46:9.) But "the virgin daughter of Babylon" claims the same loyalties, challenging the God of heaven to a duel for the hearts of men: "Hear now this, thou that art *given to pleasures, that dwellest carelessly, that sayest in thine heart, I am, and none else beside me;* I shall not sit as a widow, neither shall I know the loss of children." (Isaiah 47:1, 8; italics added; see also Zephaniah 2:15.)

Babylon's children and husband are those who have been deceived by "the multitude of [her] sorceries, and . . . the great abundance of [her] enchantments." (Isaiah 47:9.) Nothing else is quite like wealth, with all that it can buy to bewitch and mesmerize the human soul. Thus the energy and focus that belong only to the Father and Son are redirected to their chief rival for the affections of men. Sometimes we take too much pride in the ability to make money, to possess the delicacies that are ever available in the shops of Babylon. "Thy wisdom and thy knowledge, it hath perverted thee," the Lord tells Babylon, "and thou hast said in thine heart, I am, and none else beside me." (Isaiah

47:10.) As the beast "blasphemed" God in claiming it was all powerful, the harlot city claims that her beauty exceeds all other contenders for the love and loyalty of men.

When the great city falls, it is the mourning of the merchants that Revelation stresses: "And the merchants of the earth shall weep and mourn over her; for no man buyeth their merchandise any more." (Revelation 18:11.) This passage can be interpreted in at least two ways; probably both are applicable for they both have roots in Old Testament prophecies. We will see later in Revelation that Babylon's rival city, Zion, will eventually receive the honor, efforts, wealth, talents, and resources that once poured into the treasuries of Babylon's mighty men. As the people finally recognize the virtue of Zion and seek to build her up, the wares once sought for in Babylon no longer have their allure. The shopping spree is over; the dainty, delicate, costly goods are no longer craved. The spirit of consecration has humbled the power of possession. This theme will be addressed in greater detail in Revelation 21.

The second reason for the wailing cry of the merchants is derived, once again, from the words of Isaiah. No one is buying anymore because the whole structure has collapsed. It is the ultimate crash; the buying and selling of luxury ceases in the fall of the city. In the days of Isaiah, Tyre was the great merchant city of the time. Located off the coast of Lebanon, Tyre sent her ships throughout the Mediterranean, from Spain to Egypt. Caravans of trade goods from inland cities were bought and sold in the markets of Tyre. Isaiah describes the wailing that was heard at the city's destruction: "Howl, ye ships of Tarshish [Spain]; for it is laid waste, so that there is no house, no entering in: from the land of Chittim [Cyprus] it is revealed to them." (Isaiah 23:1.) The picture is of a ship loaded with goods from the far reaches of the Mediterranean. It hears, as it docks in Cyprus, that the storehouses and harbor of Tyre are no longer there. The value of their cargo has dropped drastically; there is no place to trade now.

"Who hath taken this counsel against Tyre, the crowning city, whose merchants are princes, whose traffickers are the honourable of the earth? The Lord of hosts hath purposed it, to stain the pride of all glory, and to bring into contempt all the honourable of the earth." (Isaiah 23:8–9.) *Honorable* as used in Isaiah means successful, influential, eminent, prosperous, admired for their ability to increase profits. The world of Tyre, the sister city to the great Babylon, was a place where buying and selling were more important than the need or usefulness of that which was produced. Consumption drove the economy. It mattered little what was consumed. When I hear the continual cries that the consumer must buy and buy in order to save failing or struggling economies, I feel a certain unease, especially in light of the realization that so much that is for sale consists not of necessities but of superfluities. Where will the consuming economy end?

Ezekiel also spoke about the fall of Tyre, and John derives his inventory of Babylon's wares from this earlier source. Among the markets and trading fairs of the city, Ezekiel mentions numerous nations who came to buy and sell. Everyone is there! Everything is there! The list of goods includes silver, iron, tin, brass, slaves, horses and horsemen (mercenaries), ivory, ebony, emeralds, purple and blue embroidered work, fine linen, coral, agate, wheat, honey, oil, balm, wine, white wool, spices, precious clothes for chariots, lambs, rams, goats, gems, and cedar. Even the trading ships have oaken oars, embroidered sails, ivory benches, and masts of cedar. (See Ezekiel 27.)

Business is good, profits are high, and everyone is happy, especially the governments whose subjects are contented with their ease and assets. "Thou filledst many people; thou didst enrich the kings of the earth with the multitude of thy riches and of thy merchandise." (Ezekiel 27:33.) But success has created a false god, and the masses line up to worship. Everyone wants a piece of the pie. "Because thine heart is lifted up, and thou hast said, I am a God, I sit in the seat of God, in the midst of the seas; yet thou art a man, and not God, though thou set thine heart as the heart of God." (Ezekiel 28:2.)

The Lord is not against prosperity. He has said that the resources of the earth are for the use of man, "that he might have in abundance." (D&C 49:19.) It is the emphasis, the opulence, the superfluity, the waste, the dishonesty, the disregard of the poor, and the inequalities that make the wealth of Babylon so distasteful. The Lord is not against comfort or even some luxuries. The grand dilemma is that there is no end to the list. When is too much too much? How much is enough? For Babylon knows the only way she can keep the adoration of the world is to continue to offer them new pleasures, new comforts, new delicacies, none of which have the ability to sustain happiness. The deception can continue only as long as new offerings are available in the markets of the city.

THE SOULS OF MEN

John has his own catalog of Babylon's offerings. Yet he adds one thing left out by Ezekiel, but it is one that completes the index as nothing else can. Polysyndeton is the literary device of repeated conjunctions, particularly the word "and," in a sentence or list. It is used to slow down the reader because the author wants every phrase to be weighed carefully. It is also used to show exasperation with the register or items delineated. John employs this device as he records the inventory of goods, giving a sense of impatience with the number of commodities listed: "The merchandise of gold, and silver, and precious stones, and of pearls, and fine linen, and purple, and silk, and scarlet, and all thyine wood, and all manner [of] vessels of ivory, and all manner [of] vessels of most precious wood, and of brass, and iron, and marble, and cinnamon, and odours, and ointments, and frankincense, and wine, and oil, and fine flour, and wheat, and beasts, and sheep, and horses, and chariots, and slaves, *and souls of men.*" (Revelation 18:12–13; italics added.)

Everything is for sale in Babylon, even the human soul, and life is cheap. Perhaps the greatest tragedy lies in the knowledge that a soul can be offered only by the one who possesses it. Each person lays it on the counter, walking away with the secure jingle of coins in the pocket. You can have anything you want if you have enough money. Jesus taught that there is no profit in gaining the world and losing one's soul, but in the brash economy of Lucifer's kingdom, money is all that matters, and the wailing cries of those who profited from Babylon's long run of good times reveals which god they really worshiped: "The fruits that thy soul lusted after are departed from thee, and all things which were dainty and goodly are departed from thee, and thou shalt find them no more at all. The merchants of these things, which were made rich by her, shall stand afar off for the fear of her torment, weeping and wailing. And saying, Alas, alas, that great city, that was clothed in fine linen, and purple, and scarlet, and decked with gold, and precious stones, and pearls! For in one hour so great riches is come to nought. And every ship-master, and all the company in ships, and sailors, and as many as trade by sea, stood afar off, and cried when they saw the smoke of her burning, saying, What city is like unto this great city! And they cast dust on their heads, and cried, weeping and wailing, saying, Alas, alas." (Revelation 18:14–19.)

No More at All in Thee

This is not the cry of repentance. It is not a cry of sorrow that they valued the world's wares more than God. It is not a cry of agony that their fellowman meant less to them than the latest costly, dainty delicacy. It is a lament for the city herself. It is a cry of grief that the list cannot go on forever and ever. They still have not learned what has real worth. Their source of happiness has vanished, and in their blindness they cannot visualize any other world than the old one. They can find no answer to their pitiable question, "What city is like unto this great city?" The answer is obvious: Zion will outshine Babylon as the sun diminishes the glory of a distant star. Within her borders true happiness will be enthroned in human hearts, and the cheap joys of a lesser city will be forgotten. The eerie calm of the once bustling city of Babylon testifies to this certainty. Now only the "unclean and hateful bird[s]" inhabit her desolation. Their occasional harsh cries accentuate the decease of human voice and industry. (Revelation 18:2.) As we read John's words, we can hear the stillness deepen into spectral quiet.

"Thus with violence shall that great city Babylon be thrown down, and shall be found *no more at all*. And the voice of harpers, and musicians, and of pipers, and trumpeters, shall be heard *no more at all in thee*; and no craftsman, of whatsoever craft he be, shall be found *any more in thee*; and the sound of [the] millstone shall be heard *no more at all in thee*; and the light of a candle shall shine *no more at all in thee*; and the voice of the

264

bridegroom and of the bride shall be heard *no more at all in thee:* for thy merchants were the great men of the earth; for by thy sorceries were all nations deceived. And in her was found the blood of prophets, and of saints, and of all that were slain upon the earth." (Revelation 18:21–24; italics added.)

We can hear the drum roll of her demise, her funeral song in the repeated use of the phrase "no more at all." After her dirge is sung, there is silence. The silence of her soon-to-be-forgotten temples will be the quiet of the grave, and appropriately so, for all the life blood ever spilt on earth from Abel to the present is attributed to her worship. That was the "great secret" Lucifer taught Cain (Moses 5:31)—how to exchange life for Mammon, whether immediately or drawn out in laborious years of dulling labor, whether in war, the sweatshop, or the drug-dealing back alley. It is best that this secret, like all secrets, should remain unspoken until it fades in silence from human memory.

COME OUT OF HER, MY PEOPLE

Knowing the fate of Babylon, the Lord speaks from heaven, offering the Saints good advice: "Come out of her, my people, that ye be not partakers of her sins, and that ye receive not of her plagues." (Revelation 18:4.) This has been God's counsel from the very foundations of spiritual Babylon's rise. "Come ye near unto me; I have not spoken in secret," the Lord calls to us. "Go ye forth of Babylon, flee ye from the Chaldeans, with a voice of singing declare ye, tell this, utter to the end of the earth; say ye: The Lord hath redeemed his servant Jacob." (1 Nephi 20:16, 20.)

Whatever name Babylon calls herself, it is the Lord's desire to save his people from her seductions. When we leave her, we are not to depart, as did Israel out of Egypt, constantly looking back, longing for the "flesh pots" of their former bondage. (Exodus 16:3.) "We remember the fish, which we did eat in Egypt freely," they mourned, "the cucumbers, and the melons, and the leeks, and the onions, and the garlick: but now our soul is dried away: there is nothing at all, beside this manna, before our eyes." (Numbers 11:5–6.) When we quit the environs of Babylon, we go rejoicing, singing, eager to tell the whole world the wonders of the God of Jacob. We must not itch and pine for the "good old days" of worldliness—the dainty, delicious days. Our cry must be "Alleluia," not "Alas, alas."

THE LAMB'S BRIDE

To accentuate the mourning cries of "alas, alas," chapter 19 begins with "a great voice of much people in heaven, saying, Alleluia; salvation, and glory, and honour, and power, unto the Lord our God. . . . And again they said, Alleluia. . . . And the four and twenty elders and the four beasts fell down and worshipped God that sat on the throne, saying, Amen; alleluia. . . . And I heard as it were the voice of a great multitude, and as the voice of many waters, and as the voice of mighty thunderings, saying, Alleluia: for the Lord God omnipotent reigneth." (Revelation 19:1–6.)

Whichever cry one utters will be all-revealing of his life and character. Isaiah echoed this moment of joy by writing, "The whole earth is at rest, and is quiet: they break forth into singing." (Isaiah 14:7.) The joy, however, is not just in the fall of Babylon but in the coming of the bride. The deepest joy is a welcoming one rather than a triumphant one. "Let us be glad and rejoice," John continues, "and give honour to him: for the

267

marriage of the Lamb is come, *and his wife hath made herself ready.*" (Revelation 19:7; italics added.)

The significance of this verse and its beauty did not fully strike me until I participated in the marriage preparations for our daughter. Great care was taken that every aspect of the wedding would be appropriate, sacred, inviting, and holy. I watched my daughter with a growing sense of wonder on the morning of the wedding. She rose early so that she would not be rushed. This was her wedding day, a day she had looked forward to even before she met her husband. She wanted to enjoy every minute of it. Every hair needed to be exactly right. She wanted to be beautiful for her husband.

This is the attitude of the members of the Church as they await their Savior, an attitude we should all strive to possess. No effort will be spared in our eagerness to please our Lord. Our love must reflect the depths of his own, our comeliness be equal to his sacrifice. It is the loving expectation of a bride who has "made herself ready" and greets her spouse, her friend, her beloved without hesitation, without reserve, serene in her knowledge of his love and confident in her own worth.

I recall that the choice of the wedding dress was, perhaps, the most critical and yet enjoyable decision. It was elegant, with a sweeping train of chiffon and lace. Flowers were embroidered in silk, with tiny pearls sewn onto the fabric. There had been no sparing of material in either quantity or quality. I had never seen my daughter so radiant.

The book of Revelation also speaks of the wedding dress Christ's bride will wear when he returns: "To her was granted that she should be *arrayed* in fine linen, clean and white: for the fine linen is the righteousness of [the] saints." (Revelation 19:8; italics added.) In a later entry, the bride is *adorned* for her husband."

(Revelation 21:2; italics added; see also D&C 109:74.) One does not merely *wear* a wedding dress; *adorned* and *arrayed* are the proper words to use. I must confess that this is one of my favorite images in Revelation. Our righteousness must be as lovely, as full, as carefully woven as a bride's gown. In our desire to be beautiful for our Savior, we will not spare any detail of goodness or obedience. We want sweeping trains of dignity, long veils of integrity, pearls and bows of holiness, and embroidered roses of virtue. The true bride would never say, "I am a good, decent person, but nobody is perfect"; rather, like Abraham, she would describe herself as "a follower of righteousness, desiring . . . to be a *greater follower of righteousness* . . . and desiring to receive instructions, and to keep the commandments of God." (Abraham 1:2; italics added.) She knows she has made all the preparations within her power, and yet, I suspect, she would have a lingering sense of divine discontent with her own beauty, knowing that her husband's preparations, sacrifices, and perfections have been offered at such an eternal price.

Her attitude will be one perhaps best put into words by William Shakespeare in *The Merchant of Venice*. Here Portia, the bride, greets her beloved Bassanio as he turns to accept her as his wife:

> "You see me, Lord Bassanio, where I stand,
> Such as I am: though for myself alone
> I would not be ambitious in my wish,
> To wish myself much better; yet, for you
> I would be trebled twenty times myself;
> A thousand times more fair."
> —THE MERCHANT OF VENICE, ACT 3, SCENE 2, LINES 136–41.

A personal context can be applied to the symbol of the

wedding garment. Each of us is invited to the marriage feast, but we must come dressed appropriately. Let us picture a wardrobe somewhere in the heavens, with our name upon its door. Inside hangs a single article of clothing. It is that we will put on when we present ourselves at the entrance to the supper. Each day we live, we are weaving the threads of that apparel. If our lives have been filled with service, dignity, righteousness, obedience, consecration, sacrifice, humility, and charity, when we open the door a resplendent garment will await us. We will recognize the stitching, the cut of the cloth, and its adornment, for it will reflect all the patterns of our lives. In joy we will put it on and enter the feast. But if our existence has been controlled by self-ishness, dishonesty, indulgence, anger, pettiness, pride, materi-alism, and hypocrisy, then the open door of the wardrobe will reveal the poorly stitched, scantily endowed attire that bespeaks our lives. In such vestments we will not feel comfortable in the presence of those who employed themselves in learning to be more skilled seamstresses.

THE MARRIAGE SUPPER

"And he saith unto me, Write, Blessed are they which are called unto the marriage supper of the Lamb." (Revelation 19:9.) We are to be Christ's guests when he comes to claim his bride. The image shifts from the righteous collectively as the bride, to the righteous individually as guests. What will be served at the supper?

From the Mount of Olives, Jesus told his disciples about the signs of his Second Coming. Though he revealed some things to watch for, his focus was much more centered on how to pre-pare. The preparation was not only for the actual event of his return but also how to live in the world that would precede it.

Thus it did not matter whether we were alive when he came or not; his counsels were necessary: "Therefore be ye also ready: for in such an hour as ye think not the Son of man cometh. Who then is a faithful and wise servant, whom his lord hath made ruler over his household, to *give them meat in due season? Blessed is that servant, whom his lord when he cometh shall find so doing.* . . . But and if that evil servant shall say in his heart, My lord delayeth his coming; and shall . . . eat and drink with the drunken; the lord of that servant shall come in a day when he looketh not for him." (Matthew 24:44–50; italics added.)

"Meat" in the above verse means the doctrines, principles, and commandments of the gospel. These must be shared in an appropriate manner and time. Our work, before the Lord comes, is to teach the gospel. This is how we watch for his return. May the Lord find us serving missions, teaching Primary classes, conducting family home evenings and family scripture study, sharing testimony in Relief Society or priesthood meetings, and encouraging the youth in Sunday School or seminary. This is a key to surviving the challenges of the sixth and seventh seals. The best defense is often a good offense. If we occupy our time in giving the meat of the kingdom, we will be much less prone to eat and drink with the drunken. Of course, in the last days, as discussed earlier, the people are drunk with iniquity. In truth, in light of the massive attack upon decency and righteousness that we see in the world today, giving the meat may be our only hope of resistance.

The reward of giving the meat in due season is well worth the effort, for these actions ensure that our names will be on the guest list for the Savior's marriage supper, our invitation to sit at his table. And what a feast it will be! "Let your loins be girded about, and your lights burning; and ye yourselves like unto men that wait for their lord, when he will return from the wedding; that when he cometh and knocketh, they may open unto him immediately. Blessed are those servants, whom the lord when he cometh shall find watching: verily I say unto you, that he shall gird himself, and make them to sit down to meat, and will come forth and serve them." (Luke 12:35–37.)

As we learned in Revelation 3, the Savior is not only the bridegroom, the honored patron of the ceremony, but he is also the server. Inviting us to sit at his table, he brings forth the feast. It is a meal of truth. Have we not all pondered questions for which there was no ready or revealed answer? When he comes to our position at the table and asks what nourishing truth he can offer us, will there not be questions enough for millenniums of inquiry? The Savior hinted of the entrees at his table when he told the suffering Saints of the Jackson County persecutions what awaited them if they would be true: "In that day when the Lord shall come, *he shall reveal all things—things which have passed, and hidden things which no man knew, things of the earth, by which it was made, and the purpose and the end thereof—things most precious, things that are above, and things that are beneath, things that are in the earth, and upon the earth, and in heaven.* And all they who suffer persecution for my name, and endure in faith, though they are called to lay down their lives for my sake yet shall they partake of all this glory." (D&C 101:32–35; italics added.)

Jesus said, "With what measure ye mete, it shall be measured to you again." (Matthew 7:2.) If we gave the meat of the kingdom, its edifying, nourishing truths, to others throughout our lives, it is appropriate, and in accordance with the justice of heaven, that we receive "meat" in return—the deepest meat of our Father's eternal kingdom. At the marriage supper we may expect knowledge, for we shared knowledge; truth, for we imparted truth; wisdom, for we taught wisdom; learning, for we conveyed learning; enlightenment, for we transmitted enlightenment; intelligence, for we communicated intelligence.

One reason it was so important for the Ten Virgins to have oil in their lamps was so they could contribute to the light of the marriage celebration. These celebrations often lasted long hours, even days. The combined lamps would provide the light for the festivities not only on the way to the house but inside the house also. That is why the wise virgins could not share— "lest there be not enough for us and you." (Matthew 25:9.) Before the feast and merriment were over, all ten lamps would be exhausted. Remember, the bridegroom came "at midnight." Each guest's lamp was necessary for the feast. The combination of all the burning lights made the room glorious. As a guest, each virgin wanted to be sure she had enough oil in her vessel to last the duration of the feast.

The oil is the spirit we share with each other while we wait, and which, when combined at the marriage supper, will fill the halls of heaven with resplendent light. Though our lesser lights will not exceed that of the Bridegroom himself, John gives us hope that "when he shall appear, we shall be like him; for we shall see him as he is." (1 John 3:2.) Daniel also spoke of the splendor of those who were "wise" and spent their lives sharing the gospel with others: "And they that be wise shall shine as the brightness of the firmament; and they that *turn many to righteousness* as the stars for ever and ever." (Daniel 12:3; italics added.)

RED VESTURE ON A WHITE HORSE

From the serenity and joy of a wedding, the imagery shifts to that of war, only this time the upright are the victors. Now is the time Christ will come as a conqueror, and it is fitting for that role that he appear on a white horse, the symbol of triumph. The donkey of the first coming is replaced with a king's mount. He bears his coronation names, "Faithful and True" (Revelation 19:11), just as past champions and kings were called "the Good," "the Great," "the Pious," or "the Just." "On his head were many crowns," accentuating his other title, that of "KING OF KINGS, AND LORD OF LORDS." He also bears the appellation "the Word of God." (Revelation 19:12–13.) He is the Father's messenger, he through whom God communicates his will and his love to the earth. He also "had a name written, that no man knew, but he himself." (Revelation 19:12, 16.) As indicated in an earlier chapter, the new name testifies that he is assuming a new role. It also suggests deep respect, in a manner similar to that indicated in the Doctrine and Covenants. (See D&C 107:1–4.)

He is accompanied by his "armies," who "followed him upon white horses, clothed in fine linen, white and clean." (Revelation 19:14.) They too have conquered and share in the triumph. Ever gracious and willing to share all that he was and had, his disciples are mounted with equal dignity. "Therefore will I divide him a portion with the great, and he shall divide the spoil with the strong," Isaiah inscribed. (Isaiah 53:12.)

Instead of "smit[ing] the nations" with the sword of the fist, Jesus will smite them with truth, the "sharp sword" of his mouth. Instead of ruling them with an iron rod, to beat them, he will rule with the iron rod of his word. (Revelation 19:15; see Isaiah 11:4–5.) Jesus "hath broken the staff of the wicked, and the sceptre of the rulers." Babylon, "who smote the people in wrath with a continual stroke, [who] ruled the nations in anger" (Isaiah 14:5–6), has been replaced with the gentle rule of One who "with righteousness shall he judge the poor, and reprove with equity for the meek of the earth." (Isaiah 11:4.)

Though everyone else will appear in white linen, Jesus himself is "clothed with a vesture dipped in blood, . . . [for] he treadeth the winepress of the fierceness and wrath of Almighty God." (Revelation 19:13, 15.) There are a number of symbolic reasons for this. First and foremost, his armies are in white because he has taken their sins upon himself. Blood and sin often go together in figurative language. Yet the red of these verses stands as a witness that Christ has cleansed the whole earth in another manner, and there are at least three ways the scriptures explain this staining of Jesus' garments—as a soldier in battle, a man treading grapes in a press, and a priest sacrificing animals.

THE GARMENTS OF VENGEANCE

When I was young, I used to hate running races around the track. I could never keep up with the other boys and always felt like giving up, since I had no hope of overtaking them. Sometimes in exhaustion I would fall in a heap in the middle of the track or stop and walk the rest of the way.

If we read the fifty-ninth chapter of Isaiah carefully, we will discover that a race is being described. "None calleth for justice," the Lord states, "nor any pleadeth for truth: they trust in vanity, and speak lies; they conceive mischief, and bring forth iniquity. . . . *Their feet run to evil, and they make haste* to shed innocent blood: their thoughts are thoughts of iniquity; wasting and destruction are in their paths. The way of peace they know not; and there is no judgment in their goings." (Isaiah 59:4, 7–8; italics added.) When I read these prophetic words, I cannot help but think of numerous places throughout the globe

275

where conflict rages. The fleet-footed stride of evil is ahead in the race, but who are the other participants?

"Therefore is *judgment* far from us, neither doth *justice* overtake us: we wait for light, but behold obscurity. . . . We grope for the wall like the blind. . . . We roar all like bears, and mourn sore like doves: we look for judgment, but there is none; for *salvation*, but it is far off from us." For awhile, judgment, justice, and salvation seek to overtake the rapidly hurrying feet of violence and evil, but it is no use. The people are running so fast there is no hope. "And *judgment* is turned away backward, and *justice* standeth afar off: for *truth* is fallen in the street, and *equity* cannot enter. Yea, *truth* faileth; and he that departeth from evil maketh himself a prey." (Isaiah 59:9–15; italics added.)

Judgment, justice, and salvation, with truth and equity running alongside them, seek to stay in the race. Maybe if they persevere, the feet of wickedness will tire, and they can catch up to the unhappy, roaring, mourning people. But in the end they turn away, stand in exhaustion, fall in the street, or don't even begin the race, knowing that any effort will be useless. It is a powerful image of many situations and people in the latter days. Those who try to live righteous lives only succeed in becoming victims. Those who get ahead must live the law of the jungle, eat or be eaten, prey upon others or become the prey. They must receive the mark of the beast and worship his image or be killed. The beast has risen and taken control, justified by his false prophet—the apostate, jewel-bedecked woman—and financed by the great merchant city.

But in the bleachers, another watches and is strongly dissatisfied with the way the race is progressing. "And the Lord saw it, and it displeased him that there was no judgment. And he saw that there was no man, and wondered that there was no intercessor: therefore his arm brought salvation . . . it sustained him. For he put on righteousness as a breastplate, and an helmet of salvation upon his head; and he put on the garments of vengeance for clothing, and was clad with zeal as a cloke. According to their deeds, accordingly he will repay, fury to his adversaries, recompense to his enemies." (Isaiah 59:15–18.)

A few chapters later, these same last verses are repeated, only this time in the first person—spoken by Christ himself as part of his answer to those who wonder why he is clothed in red apparel. He has decided to enter the race himself. Notice the question and answer dialogue in the next few verses.

The people: "Who is this that cometh from Edom, with dyed garments from Bozrah? this that is glorious in his apparel, travelling in the greatness of his strength?"

The Lord: "I that speak in righteousness, mighty to save."

The people: "Wherefore art thou red in thine apparel, and thy garments like him that treadeth in the winefat?"

The Lord: "I have trodden the winepress alone; and of the people there was none with me: for I will tread them in mine anger, and trample them in my fury; and their blood shall be sprinkled upon my garments, and I will stain all my raiment." (Isaiah 63:1–3.)

Edom was often used in Old Testament times as a symbol of the world. In the passage above, it occupies the same position as that of Babylon. Bozrah was a city of Edom; both suggest worldliness. The Savior answers that he has come as he promised. He always speaks in righteousness. He has come from his conquest of the world. His garments are stained by the blood of his enemies as are soldiers' in a battle. But the image of the winepress is also used. He has trodden down the grapes of wrath spoken of in chapter 14. The armies of men gathered at the winepress, and his garments were stained with the juice of that great pressing.

The Lord continues to answer the questions asked of him: "For the day of vengeance is in mine heart, and the year of my redeemed is come. And I looked, and there was none to help; and I wondered that there was none to uphold: therefore mine own arm brought salvation unto me; and my fury, it upheld me. And I will tread down the people in mine anger, and make them drunk in my fury, and I will bring down their strength to the earth." (Isaiah 63:4–6.) The importance of these verses is attested to in the Doctrine and Covenants, where they are repeated in section 133.

The Lord will not let the race go uncontested forever. Since no mortal can bring what we all long for and are striving to achieve—universal judgment, justice, truth, equity, salvation, peace, and an end to the dominion of Lucifer's laws, Christ will enter the race, fight for us in the battle, tread the winepress for us, and prepare the sacrifice. His red robes assure us of the outcome.

In an earlier chapter, Isaiah was given another image for the red clothing, that of a priest sacrificing animals. This office too would result in the staining of the priest's clothes. In this metaphor there is no question that those being offered as the sacrifice are the armies of the winepress, the gathering of Armageddon, the bold ones of Jehoshaphat's valley of decision, the locusts from the black smoke of the pit. "Come near, ye nations, to hear; and hearken, ye people: let the earth hear, and all that is therein; the world, and all things that come forth of it." With this introduction, the message must be momentous. "For the indignation of the Lord is upon all nations, and his fury *upon all their armies:* he hath utterly destroyed them, he hath delivered them to the slaughter. . . . For my sword shall be bathed in heaven: behold, it shall come down upon Idumea [another name for Edom], and upon the people of my curse, to judgment. The sword of the Lord is filled with blood, it is made fat with fatness, and with the blood of lambs and goats, with the fat of the kidneys of rams: for the Lord hath a sacrifice in Bozrah, and a great slaughter in the land of Idumea. . . . for it is the day of the Lord's vengeance." (Isaiah 34:1–2, 5–6, 8; italics added.)

The irony of the Lord's words is conspicuous. We all know of what the sacrifice consists. We also know that the destruction described is a self-sacrifice, a Jaredite type of conflict where all sleep upon their swords and wait for the daylight to begin their conflicts again.

THE SUPPER OF THE GREAT GOD

Another supper is spoken of in chapter 19. John is forever offering a choice to mankind. The choices are plain, and only a fool would abandon the marriage supper in favor of the supper of the great God: "And I saw an angel standing in the sun; and he cried with a loud voice, saying to all the fowls that fly in the midst of heaven, Come and gather yourselves together unto the supper of the great God; that ye may eat the flesh of kings, and the flesh of captains, and the flesh of mighty men, and the flesh of horses, and of them that sit on them, and the flesh of all men, both free and bond, both small and great." (Revelation 19:17–18.)

The great Goliath boasted to David that he would "give thy flesh unto the fowls of the air, and to the beasts of the field" (1 Samuel 17:44), but his own words became his epitaph. Those who devour will be devoured, no matter how mighty. The fitting irony of judgment cannot be missed.

The idea of the grand feast for the birds and beasts is frequently alluded to in the Old Testament, almost always offered in the spirit of paradox and ambiguity. The supper for the fowls of the air is often linked with the Lord's sacrifice as it was described in Isaiah. "Hold thy peace," writes Zephaniah, "for the day of the Lord is at hand: for the Lord hath prepared a sacrifice, he hath bid his guests." Those guests will include "the princes, and the king's children . . . all those that leap on the threshold, which fill their masters' houses with violence and deceit." (Zephaniah 1:7–9.) The image is one of an invading force spoiling conquered peoples in order to enrich the kings who command the pillaging armies. Of course, those with ears to hear know that the guests are in reality the birds and beasts. Doctrine and Covenants 29 adds flies to the guest list. This also fits nicely with the frequent use of Mosaic plagues when speaking of the last days. "I the Lord God will send forth flies upon the face of the earth, which shall take hold of the inhabitants thereof, and shall eat their flesh." (D&C 29:18.) The battle is over, and the natural consequences of its destruction take place.

John's representation arises mostly from the writings of Ezekiel. The link with God's sacrifice is again stressed. Ezekiel makes plain that the makers and pursuers of war are the principal agents at this paradoxical supper offered to the birds and beasts: "Speak unto every feathered fowl, and to every beast of the field. Assemble yourselves, and come; gather yourselves on every side to my sacrifice that I do sacrifice for you, even a great sacrifice. . . . Ye shall eat the flesh of the mighty, and drink the blood of the princes of the earth, of rams, of lambs, and of goats, of bullocks. . . . And ye shall eat fat till ye be full, and drink blood till ye be drunken, of my sacrifice which I have sacrificed for you. Thus ye shall be filled at my table with horses and chariots, with mighty men, and *with all men of war,* saith the Lord God. (Ezekiel 39:17–20; italics added.)

THE BEAST WAS TAKEN

Jesus bears the title "Prince of Peace." In his first epistle, John repeats many of the Savior's injunctions to his apostles at the Last Supper, focusing primarily on his commandments that his disciples learn to love each other, for therein peace is established. I have found it interesting that in this same epistle John warns against the "antichrist." There are many ways to oppose the Savior. People can deny *him,* or they can deny what he taught and stood for. Revelation's heavy emphasis on contention, discord, war, and hatred leads us to conclude that the greatest antichrist may be the general spirit of the times—when all disagreements are settled with force, and life's necessities are controlled by those with the most power. What is more antichrist than that?

I have also found it interesting that after the Savior's initial greeting to the Nephites and Lamanites, the first lesson he taught them centered on the elimination of contention: "There shall be no disputations among you. . . . He that hath the spirit of contention is not of me, but is of the devil, who is the father of contention, and he stirreth up the hearts of men to contend with anger, one with another. Behold, this is not my doctrine, to stir up the hearts of men with anger, one against another; but this is my doctrine, that such things should be done away." (3 Nephi 11:28–30.)

So the two forces meet, the gentle and the hardened, the meek and the mighty, the forgiving and the vengeful, the lion and the lamb. "The beast, and the kings of the earth, and their armies" array themselves against "him that sat on the horse, and against his army." (Revelation 19:19.) This time, however, peace, gentleness, kindness, meekness, compromise, liberty, selflessness, and goodness will not be vanquished: "The beast was taken, and with him the false prophet. . . . These both were cast alive into a lake of fire burning with brimstone. And the remnant were slain with the sword of him that sat upon the horse . . . , and all the fowls were filled with their flesh." (Revelation 19:20–21.) We must never lose sight of the certainty that truth will conquer apostasy, peace prevail over war, humility outlast pride, and the spirit of Christ silence the spirit of the world.

So ends the nineteenth chapter. It contains the wondrous, solemn beauty of the bride with her guests seated at the marriage supper, joyful in the fullness of the Bridegroom, and terminates with the fowls feasting on the self-slaughtered armies that worshiped the "god of forces." Another image has been added to the long list already delivered in Revelation. Armageddon, the winepress, the sacrifice, the supper of the great God, the harvest of the grapes of wrath, the day of the Lord's vengeance, the valley of decision, the locusts and horsemen of hell, the blinding smoke released by the burning fallen star—each adds a new dimension, each contributes to the climax of a world that has seen the red horse dominate in the affairs of men from the beginning. All that remains now is the chaining of the dragon, he who encouraged, rejoiced, inspired, and manipulated the whole business throughout the seven seals.

THE MILLENNIUM
AND BEYOND

Until the dragon himself is captured and chained, the possibility always exists that another beast, another purple and scarlet woman, another everything-for-sale, buying-and-selling city may yet arise: "I saw an angel come down from heaven, having the key of the bottomless pit and a great chain in his hand. And he laid hold on the dragon, that old serpent, which is the Devil, and Satan, and bound him a thousand years, and cast him into the bottomless pit, and shut him up, and set a seal upon him, that he should deceive the nations no more, till the thousand years should be fulfilled: and after that he must be loosed a little season. " (Revelation 20:1–3.) The security of Satan's confinement is suggested by the use of the words *key, chain,* and *seal.* There is no doubt of his detention.

This is the ultimate application of justice, using the same standard set by the individual himself. Enoch once saw the exulting Satan and his angels laughing at the Father over the misery of his children. He was shown with "a great chain in his hand, and it veiled the whole face of the earth with darkness." (Moses 7:26.) He who chained others now is chained. He who loved to spread darkness over the earth is shut up in darkness. He who dragged others into the pit descends himself into it.

Isaiah described the fall of spiritual Babylon but focused his attention on the moment when Lucifer descends into the pit that he himself has dug. It is interesting how many times in the scriptures hell is described as your "own place." It is not bottomless because God dug it that deep, but because those who "enjoy" its depths continue to burrow. (D&C 88:32.) Isaiah's description of the moment John relates in the first verses of chapter 20 is full of satiric irony and is worthy of examination, for it gives the fullest account of the chaining of the dragon and his banishment to the pit.

In our imaginations, we are to see an assemblage of despotic rulers who once held power over the nations of the earth. As the great king of Babylon, Lucifer, enters in review to join them, they speak to him, their tone filled with sarcasm. As Isaiah says, "Hell from beneath is moved for thee to meet thee at thy coming: it stirreth up the dead for thee, even all the chief ones of the earth; it hath raised up from their thrones all the kings of the nations. All they shall speak and say unto thee, Art thou also become weak as we? art thou become like unto us? . . . The worm is spread under thee, and the worms cover thee." (Isaiah 14:9–11.)

Now no royal robe of purple covers the great serpent monarch, and no red carpet is rolled out in welcome; only the worms of decay await him. Though he once claimed, "I will ascend into heaven, I will exalt my throne above the stars of God . . . I will ascend above the heights of the clouds; I will be like the most High," he is "brought down to hell, to the sides of the pit." (Isaiah 14:13–15.) Notice how his own claim to equal God was once used by his beast and harlot city.

All the children of God will reflect upon Satan's fall: "They that see thee shall narrowly look upon thee, and consider thee, saying, Is this the man that made the earth to tremble, that did shake kingdoms; that made the world as a wilderness, and destroyed the cities thereof; that opened not the house of his prisoners?" (Isaiah 14:16–17.) I cannot help but compare this entry into the realms of death with that of the Savior as portrayed by Joseph F. Smith in Doctrine and Covenants 138. Jesus, too, was welcomed by the hosts of the dead, but with songs of praise not sarcasm, with bended knee of homage, not the mockery of impossible dreams of ambitious glory. Now the doors of the prison were opened as the liberating truths of the gospel, coupled with the ordinances of the temple, rang through the halls of the spirit prison. Christ once promised to "bring out the prisoners from the prison, and them that sit in darkness out of the prison house." (Isaiah 42:7.) What a contrast to Lucifer's descent! Thousands of years of basically uninterrupted cruelty and misery, on both sides of the veil, now culminate in the imprisonment of the original warden. He has ruled the earth with blood and horror. Will his long reign be remembered?

NO HOUSE OF GLORY

I have had the opportunity over the years of visiting numerous mausoleums representing many different cultures and ages of history. The great pyramids of Egypt were built to the memory of the Pharaohs and still stand. With tense anticipation I have crawled down the interior stairway of Pacal's Temple of the Inscriptions in Mexico to see the celebrated Mayan lord's intricately carved sarcophagus. I have visited the memorials to the mighty Caesars of Roman fame and examined the beehive tombs of Mycenaean kings in Greece. I have looked into the faces of the terra cotta soldiers and horses buried to serve a Chinese emperor. It always astounds me to witness the efforts of ambitious potentates to be remembered, the audacity of their thoughts that they would continue to rule after death with the same pomp and grandeur they held for a small blink of time in mortality.

With these great monuments in mind, Isaiah continues his censure against the fallen angel: "All the kings of the nations, even all of them, lie in glory, every one in his own house [resplendent tomb]. But thou art cast out of thy grave like an abominable branch . . . as a carcase trodden under feet. Thou shalt not be joined with them in burial, because thou hast destroyed thy land, and slain thy people: *the seed of evildoers shall never be renowned.*" (Isaiah 14:18–20; italics added.) There will be no talk of the good old days of apostasy, war, and materialism; no memorials for the monarch who sponsored, urged, plotted, seduced, conspired, and devised them; no Hollywood offerings glorifying the violent heros of the defeated Babylonian kingdom. No wondering millennial tourists will gape at Lucifer's commemorative shrine, for there will be none. The seal on the bottomless pit testifies to this truth: "The Lord of Hosts hath sworn, saying, Surely as I have thought, so shall it come to pass; and as I have purposed, so shall it stand." (Isaiah 14:24.) This is God's version of "So let it be written, so let it be done!"

If this unequivocal defeat of the villainies of Lucifer, the consummate builder of tyrannical empires, will come to pass, we are warranted it will be true of all lesser sovereigns: "Then shall his yoke depart from off them, and his burden depart from off their shoulders. This is the purpose that is purposed upon the whole earth: and this is the hand that is stretched out upon all the nations." (Isaiah 14:25–26.)

John knew this to be true and attests it time and again throughout Revelation. It is good and wise that we be constantly reminded of this as each news report reaching us from the far shores of this globe assails us with ignominy, heartache, ruthlessness, and inhumanity. But the "acceptable *year* of the Lord" is coming; the "*day* of vengeance" but marks its debut. (Isaiah 61:2; italics added.) Let us be hopeful, for a year is much longer than a day. A new yoke and a new burden will be laid upon the weary world, but we need not fear the placing of this burden, for the ruler is wise and kind. "Take my yoke upon you," he entreats, "and learn of me; for I am meek and lowly in heart: and ye shall find rest unto your souls. For my yoke is easy, and my burden is light." (Matthew 11:29–30.)

THE FIRST RESURRECTION

Now the day longed for by all who are holy begins: "I saw the souls of them that were beheaded for the witness of Jesus, and for the word of God . . . and they lived and reigned with Christ a thousand years. . . . Blessed and holy is he that hath part in the first resurrection: on such the second death hath no power." (Revelation 20:4, 6.)

Abraham longed for a day of righteousness, a day enjoyed, at least within the confines of their own city, by the people of Enoch. He left the land of his idolatrous fathers and "looked for a city which hath foundations, whose builder and maker is God." (Hebrews 11:10.) He and many other holy men and women spent their lives seeking the city of Zion, the city of Peace. But they "died in faith" without seeing its jeweled walls,

287

yet they received the promise that one day the earth would know the peace of Zion and they could celebrate within her gates. They did not receive "the promises . . . [during their mortal lives], but having seen them afar off, . . . were persuaded of them, and embraced them, and confessed that they were *strangers and pilgrims on the earth.* For they that say such things declare plainly that they seek a country. . . . wherefore God is not ashamed to be called their God: for he hath prepared for them a city." (Hebrews 11:13–16; italics added.)

These words were repeated to the early Latter-day Saints who were also seeking a better city, "a city reserved until a day of righteousness shall come—a day which was sought for by all holy men, and they found it not because of wickedness and abominations; and confessed they were strangers and pilgrims on the earth; but obtained a promise that they should find it and see it in their flesh." (D&C 45:12–14.) Through the miracle of the resurrection, John knew that every righteous man and woman from Adam to the dawn of the Second Coming would enjoy that for which they yearned during their lives.

I do not expect I will live to see the Second Coming before I die. I do not anticipate I will walk through the gates of the holy millennial city in the flesh. There are times when we all feel like strangers on earth, and it is fitting that we should so feel. This is not our home, at least not yet, but an alien world that often bruises our finer sensibilities. What are we to do? We must do as Abraham did, and as John encourages us to do on almost every page of Revelation: We must embrace the future promises, be persuaded of them, and recognize that we will remain pilgrims searching for a home, for the city the Lord has prepared for all who are not ashamed to call him their God. The search may be exhausting at times and the desired rest far distant, but to reign with Christ on the earth a thousand years is surely a light bright enough to shine down the darkest tunnels of time, urging us forward.

A LITTLE SEASON

Nephi spoke of Satan's confinement in literal terms, giving us the main reason the adversary is locked, chained, and sealed in the pit: "Because of the righteousness of [the] people, Satan has no power; wherefore, he cannot be loosed for the space of many years; for he hath no power over the *hearts* of the people, for they dwell in righteousness, and the Holy One of Israel reigneth." (1 Nephi 22:26; italics added.) Though there may be external forces keeping Lucifer bound, including the reigning Lord, Nephi suggests it is the people themselves who hold the key to his captivity.

Since the heart guards the sealed doors of Satan's prison, the heart can also let him out. The Lord has revealed that "when the thousand years are ended, *and men again begin to deny their God,* then will I spare the earth but for a little season." (D&C 29:22; italics added.) What causes men to deny their God, particularly one who has been so gracious in blessing them? During the millennial era of peace, the "hearts" of the people reject the adversary, embracing the Father and Son instead. It is also in the heart that Satan will regain his hold upon men, having been "loosed out of his prison." (Revelation 20:7.) The Book of Mormon offers us a fairly detailed account to ponder relative to the freeing of the dragon.

Lucifer's greatest weapon has always been the riches of the earth. With these he has been able to purchase the armies and navies of the world along with their assortment of oppressive false priests and destroying tyrants. The book of Helaman often mentions the human heart and its relationship to wealth. The Church is always mentioned at the center of this problem of affluence and its accompanying pride: "It was among those also who professed to belong to the church of God. And it was because of the pride of their *hearts*, because of their exceeding riches." (Helaman 4:11–12; italics added.) In words we could use to describe the millennial reign, we are told, "They had not been stirred up to anger, to wars, nor to bloodshed; therefore they began to set their *hearts* upon their riches; yea, they began to seek to get gain." (Helaman 6:17; italics added.) We are told that Satan could get the people to commit "awful wickedness, from generation to generation according as he can get *hold upon the hearts* of the children of men. And now behold, he had got great hold upon the hearts of the Nephites . . . [they] did build up unto themselves idols of their gold and their silver." (Helaman 6:30–31; italics added.) Passage after passage like the ones above are scattered throughout Helaman. The heart is the key, and for "many years," according to Nephi, Satan cannot get a foothold on the hearts of the millennial citizens. Something other than wealth lies at the center of their hearts. It is the love of God and the accomplishment of his great millennial work in the temples.

Wilford Woodruff once expressed a fervent desire that gives us a glimpse into both the millennial reign and its demise: "Oh, I wish many times that the veil were lifted off the face of the Latter-day Saints. I wish we could see and know the things of God as they do who are laboring for the salvation of the human family who are in the spirit world; for if this were so, this whole people, with very few, if any, exceptions, would lose all interest in the riches of the world, and instead thereof their whole desires and labors would be directed to redeem their dead."

(Wilford Woodruff, *Discourses of Wilford Woodruff,* selected by G. Homer Durham [Salt Lake City: Bookcraft, 1946], 152.) With an eye single to the salvation and eternal binding of our great family chains, the binding chains of materialism are broken.

Book of Mormon history follows a general pattern similar to that of the last days. Many wars precede great destructions, which prepare the way for the resurrected Christ to come in glory and establish an era of peace and righteousness. In 4 Nephi, however, the old serpent is loosed. Once powerful again, he brings the people to swift destruction. It is in this account we will see the best narrative of the "little season" of Lucifer's release.

RELEASING THE DRAGON

In the first verses of 4 Nephi, six times Mormon mentions the peace of the people, stressing that "there were no contentions and disputations among them. . . . And surely there could not be a happier people among all the people who had been created by the hand of God." (4 Nephi 1:2, 16.) We are also told the reason for this joy: "There was no contention in the land, *because of the love of God which did dwell in the hearts of the people."* (4 Nephi 1:15; italics added.) To loose Satan, the people's hearts had to change, and materialism slowly but surely did its work. Notice the step-by-step progression that is outlined in 4 Nephi, from the happiest people on earth to the misery of the wars of destruction.

The trouble starts when the people "become exceedingly rich, because of their prosperity in Christ." Some then begin to be "lifted up in pride," seeking "the fine things of the world." The foundations of the great merchant city are laid again. The

291

next step is predictable: "From that time forth they did have their goods and their substance no more common among them." Consecration dies in the competitive spirit of the times. It is every man for himself, in its milder form. With the loss of consecration, the natural selection of talent and opportunity leads to their being "divided into classes." (4 Nephi 1:23–26.) The law of the jungle that gives birth to the beast now casts a distant shadow.

Knowing the inevitable consequences of the path the people were beginning to take, the Church would surely have preached against the new agenda. So a church that accepted the new order of things needed to be created: "They began to build up churches unto themselves to get gain, and began to deny the true church of Christ." They still "professed to know the Christ, and yet they did deny the more parts of his gospel." The whore has returned, and though she does not yet entangle the majority with her seductive beauty, time will see her charms desired by an ever-increasing circle of people. When compromise with one principle of the gospel has been accepted, it is not surprising that the disavowing of other doctrines and practices will follow. Now they begin to "administer that which was sacred unto him to whom it had been forbidden because of unworthiness." Undoubtedly this was done in the name of tolerance and Christian love. This last church was particularly popular and "did multiply exceedingly because of iniquity." (4 Nephi 1:26–28.)

The next phrase is revealing: "Satan . . . did get hold upon their hearts." If people continue to deny more and more parts of the gospel, eventually they will even deny the center principle that supported all the others: "Again, there was another church which denied the Christ." Now the seeds of deeper

292

division enter the society as they "persecute the true church of Christ . . . and . . . despise them." Nothing arouses the ire and animosity of one who has left the Church like the faithfulness and humility of those who remain true to it. (4 Nephi 1:28–29.)

Opposition grows with the desire to dominate and control: "They did exercise power and authority over the disciples of Jesus who did tarry with them." When the law of the jungle sur-faces again in this manner, the beast with his many heads and horns is just around the corner, and, of course his unrighteous use of power will be justified by the convenience of a false priesthood and the assurance that it all pays very well. Closing their eyes to every work of God, "the people did harden their hearts, for they were led by many priests and false prophets to build up many churches. . . . And they did smite upon the people of Jesus." (4 Nephi 1:30, 34.)

Now comes the "great division." The righteous are separated from those who "wilfully rebel against the gospel of Christ." All we need now is the billowing smoke of the pit, the hatred that blinds and rages. "And they did teach their children that they should not believe. . . . and they were taught to hate the chil-dren of God." With the opposition so appealing to the natural man and growing stronger every day, soon "the more wicked part of the people did wax strong, and became exceedingly more numerous than were the people of God." It is so hard to remain true when everyone else is bowing to the new image on the block. Before long the marking must surely begin again. When the more righteous part of the people also dwindle in unbelief, the last great battles of Mormon cannot be avoided. (4 Nephi 1:35, 38–40.)

I believe the wonderful millennial peace will end in a simi-lar fashion, with one exception—Satan's victory will not be so complete that he will eliminate the Church and kingdom of God. Zion will not be compromised, for there will be many who stand true in spite of the current flow of the times. Now the stage is set for the last great conflict between the forces of good and those of evil. John, drawing from the words of Ezekiel, will title the forces of evil "Gog and Magog." (Revelation 20:8.)

THE BATTLE OF GOG AND MAGOG

These two names come from the book of Ezekiel and detail yet another account of what we generally refer to as Armageddon. The standard charter seen so often in Revelation is applied in Ezekiel's version: The powerful will prey upon the defenseless. "I will go up to the land of unwalled villages," the boast is made. "I will go to them that are at rest, that dwell safely, all of them dwelling without walls, and having neither bars nor gates, to take a spoil, and to take a prey." (Ezekiel 38:11–12.) The aggressive party, as seen in other similar circumstances, represents a coalition of nations. Their destruction is assured through the many symbolic and natural means already discussed in earlier chapters. Ezekiel 38 speaks of "a great shaking . . . and every wall shall fall to the ground." "Pestilence . . . blood . . . overflowing rain, and great hailstones, fire, and brimstone" are all mentioned. We have seen every one of these already in Revelation. The end of Gog and Magog is brought about in the standard fashion: "I will call for a sword against him throughout all my mountains, saith the Lord God: *every man's sword shall be against his brother.*" The birds and beasts are then invited to God's "sacrifice," where he tells them, "Ye shall be filled at my table . . . with all men of war." (Ezekiel 38:19–22; 39:17–20; italics added.)

It is apparent that John's use of the terms *Gog* and *Magog*,

294

which direct us to Ezekiel, suggest that the little season will see a repetition of the conditions prior to the Savior's coming at the beginning of the Millennium. After all, Satan is not too creative—he doesn't need to be—as all his old tricks work very well in a society that has begun to deny God again in its quest for power and wealth.

But the earth has seen enough. It is time to repeat the outcome of another war that was waged before the earth was created, one spoken of earlier in Revelation, when "Michael and his angels fought against the dragon; and the dragon fought and his angels, and prevailed not; neither was their place found any more in heaven. And the great dragon was cast out." (Revelation 12:7–9.)

These verses are repeated using identical language in the Doctrine and Covenants version of the little-season battles. "Then he shall be loosed for a little season, that he may gather together his armies. And Michael, the seventh angel, even the archangel, shall gather together his armies, even the hosts of heaven. And the devil shall gather together his armies; even the hosts of hell, and shall come up to battle against Michael and his armies. And then cometh the battle of the great God; and the devil and his armies shall be cast away into their own place, that they shall not have power over the saints any more at all." (D&C 88:111–14.)

WARRING FOR THE SOULS OF MICHAEL'S POSTERITY

We might view this war as both a continuation and a duplication of previous conflicts. The one described in Ezekiel—a conflict of men and armies who will eventually meet the same fate as their predecessors, fighting among themselves while God protects his own "even unto the destruction of [his] enemies by fire" (1 Nephi 22:17; see also Revelation 20:9)—and a battle like the one in the premortal world, but this time fought for the final allegiance of all remaining unresurrected souls, those who may still merit a kingdom of glory, albeit a telestial one, if they will accept Christ as their Redeemer.

Notice that Michael as the leader of the Lord's forces casts the armies of evil into "their own place." Earlier in Doctrine and Covenants 88, the final choice for these souls was described using the same expression. After detailing the resurrection of the three kingdoms of glory, the Lord tells of the final choice of those who go with the adversary: "They who remain shall also be quickened [resurrected]; nevertheless, they shall return again to their own place, to enjoy that which they are willing to receive, because they were not willing to enjoy that which they might have received. For what doth it profit a man if a gift is bestowed upon him, and he receive not the gift? Behold, he rejoices not in that which is given unto him, neither rejoices in him who is the giver of the gift." (D&C 88:32–33.) The gift offered is the atoning sacrifice. The arm of mercy is extended even to those who were deceived by Lucifer on the earth and delivered to his captivity in the world of spirits. They can still repent, and one front of the final battle is fought to deliver these souls.

Doctrine and Covenants 138 lists Adam with many of his noblest descendants and all "faithful elders." "Mother Eve, and many of her faithful daughters" are also seen. These comprise a mighty army to combat the opposition. "The dead who repent will be redeemed, through obedience to the ordinances of the house of God, and after they have paid the penalty of their transgressions, and are washed clean, shall receive a reward according to their works, for they are heirs of salvation." (D&C 138:39, 57, 58–59.)

The great Michael is not willing to give up a single one of his descendants to the adversary without offering them the mercy of Jesus. The final climactic act in these last scenes of the old world, "before the earth shall pass away," comes when "Michael, mine archangel, shall sound his trump, and then shall all the dead awake, for their graves shall be opened, and they shall come forth—yea, even all." (D&C 29:26.) We can be assured that Michael will not sound his trumpet until the Savior knows that not a single soul under the adversary's influence will accept their Lord and Deliverer and thus end their sufferings at the hands of Lucifer.

Those who are left will go into their "own place," a hell of their own construction, "for they cannot be redeemed from their spiritual fall, *because they repent not; for they love darkness rather than light, and their deeds are evil, and they receive their wages of whom they list to obey.*" (D&C 29:44–45; italics added.) Simply put, they have rejected the first four principles of the gospel. They have no faith in Christ and want nothing to do with his atonement. Without this faith, they will not repent. In this sense, they have committed the unpardonable sin. How can pardon be granted to one who rejects the only means whereby forgiveness is possible? Without repentance they cannot be washed clean through the ordinances of the House of the Lord, as Joseph F. Smith taught in section 138. Not being washed clean, they cannot receive the Holy Ghost and inherit at least a telestial glory, presided over by the Holy Spirit. In this manner they sin even against the Holy Ghost.

Those who believe the armies of Michael laboring in the spirit world, repent of their sins, accept the cleansing ordinance of vicarious baptism, and heed the directions of the Holy Spirit will be saved: "These all shall bow the knee, and every tongue shall confess to him who sits upon the throne forever and ever . . . and every man shall receive according to his own works, his own dominion, in the mansions which are prepared; and they shall be servants of the Most High; but where God and Christ dwell they cannot come, worlds without end." (D&C 76:110–12.)

THE GREAT WHITE THRONE

The great seven-thousand-year conflict is over, and the seventh seal draws to a close. "The devil . . . [is] cast into the lake of fire and brimstone, where the beast and the false prophet are." Now is the time of judgment for all the rest. Sitting upon a "great white throne," Christ bestows the rewards of life: "I saw the dead, small and great, stand before God; and the books were opened: and another book was opened, which is the book of life: and the dead were judged out of those things which were written in the books, according to their works. And the sea gave up the dead which were in it; and death and hell delivered up the dead which were in them. . . . And death and hell were cast into the lake of fire." (Revelation 20:10–14.)

Joseph Smith commented extensively on verse 12, explaining it in the context of the saving ordinances of the temple. He leaves no doubt that the last great battle, its subsequent victory, and particularly the final judgment are closely linked to vicarious work for the dead: "John the Revelator was contemplating this very subject in relation to the dead, when he declared, as you will find recorded in Revelation 20:12 . . ." (D&C 128:6.) Joseph explains that the books that are opened contain the records of ordinances performed on earth, "whether they themselves have attended to the ordinances in their own *propria persona*, or by the means of their own agents, according to the ordinance which God has prepared for their salvation from before the foundation of the world." (D&C 128:8.)

All of us will participate in the final monumental confrontation. We will stand with the armies of Michael, our first father. We will use all the powers of persuasion and eternal truth to convince every child of God that salvation comes only in and through faith in the Lord Jesus Christ. We fought once in the premortal world, where the stakes were equally high. On earth we fight the battle as we attempt to turn others to righteousness. Our work in the temples are blows struck even in preparation for that last war when both sides gather their armies to gain the final allegiance of every soul who has been born on this earth. We will fill the books with ordinances in anticipation that the day will come, either before, during, or at the end of the Millennium, when the prison will release into the kingdoms of glory the believing, the repentant, and those who bow the knee. We will see Lucifer fall again, and with him, this time, will fall death itself as the resurrection claims its own. We will see the sufferings of hell end for all who choose to end them. This is the will of the Father, and Christ has executed it. Beast, harlot, merchant city, false prophet, dragon, death, and hell are all defeated. It is time to enter the eternal city and explore our new surroundings.

THE HOLY CITY

For the righteous—those who were not deceived by the dragon, did not worship his image, refused his mark, would not live by the beast's law of the jungle, turned from the apostate cup in the hands of the harlot, rejected the wares of Babylon's market, were not blinded by the smoke that leads to the winepress, and fought with the armies of Michael to win souls to Christ—there is a reward commensurate with their labors, sacrifices, and faith. They will experience "a new heaven and a new earth: for the first heaven and the first earth were passed away; and there was no more sea." (Revelation 21:1.) This new heaven and earth are so wonderful that Isaiah taught "the former shall not be remembered, nor come into mind." (Isaiah 65:17.) Sometimes our pains are so great we do not believe that any future joy can compensate for them. But the scriptures assure us this is not the case. In the glory of the new, the old world of distress, confrontation, and apostasy will not be recalled.

Since the Lord himself said "not one hair, neither mote, shall be lost" of all he had created, including "the fishes of the sea" (D&C 29:24–25), the reference to no sea must be understood figuratively. The disappearing sea, symbolically, can refer to the end of strife, chaos, and the turmoil of clashing nations, for, be it remembered, the beast arose out of the storm-tossed sea of humanity in chapter 13. The sea can also suggest the divisions of men, for nations and continents have been separated from each other by the seas. In the Lord's new earth there are no divisions, between men or any other aspect of creation. However, we will surely still enjoy orange and purple sunsets over a whispering surf with the call of seabirds above, the salt smell in the breezes, and the tug of retreating water at our feet.

"The holy city, new Jerusalem," the city of peace, is seen "coming down from God out of heaven, prepared as a bride adorned for her husband." A voice announces that "the tabernacle of God is with men, and he will dwell with them." (Revelation 21:2–3.) Even today, the many temples dotting the globe testify that the Lord wants to live with his people. His house is among us, and he is always home, always willing to admit us to his hospitality—and we may stay as long as we wish. These earthly temples are constant reminders of the future John describes in chapter 21.

COMFORTING HIS CHILDREN

Before entering the city, however, there is comforting to attend to. Many tears have been shed throughout the seven seals of earth's existence. Drawing upon the words of Isaiah, but improving on their power, John describes one of the tenderest scenes anywhere in scripture: "God shall wipe away all tears from their eyes; and there shall be no more death, neither sorrow, nor crying, neither shall there be any more pain: for the former things are passed away." (Revelation 21:4; see also Isaiah 25:8.) This is the second time John has quoted this particular prophecy of Isaiah. He also ended his description of our own seal, the sixth, with the promise that "God shall wipe away all tears from [our] eyes." (Revelation 7:17.) Those of us who face the challenges of the sixth seal have the personal assurance that this promise applies directly to us.

We have all seen enough tears of tragedy, pain, grief, and sorrow to last an eternity. We have shed many ourselves—tears from the anguish of physical pain endured in long, silent battles; parental tears over straying or wayward children; a spouse's tears over conflict, rejection, divorce, and disappointment; bitter tears poured forth in guilt from the repeated follies and weaknesses of the natural man within us; aching tears of loneliness offered by the friendless and unloved; empathetic tears pulled forth as we witness the cruelty of man against man; quiet tears created by the death of those who have become part of our very souls as our universal mother receives them into her earth-locked arms.

But all that is past! All things are new! The Savior has come, and, as a parent gently sweeps the tears from a child's cheeks with a finger, the Redeemer wipes them from his children's eyes in understanding sympathy. It is a gesture of deepest intimacy. Only family members would do such a thing for each other. Friendship alone is not sufficient for this level of touching. "All your losses will be made up to you in the resurrection, provided you continue faithful," Joseph Smith taught. "By the vision of the Almighty I have seen it." (*Teachings of the Prophet Joseph Smith*, 296.) This was given in the context of being reunited with family and friends. I assume that means both those we shared our earthly existence with, those we knew in our premortal life, and those we will come to love in our labors in the spirit world, particularly the past generations of our own ancestors.

Enoch was shown the day of reunion within the borders of the New Jerusalem: "The Lord said unto Enoch: Then shalt thou and all thy city meet them there, and *we* will receive them into our bosom, and they shall see *us*; and *we* will fall upon their necks, and they shall fall upon *our* necks, and *we* will kiss each other." (Moses 7:63.) Since the Lord himself is speaking to Enoch, I cannot help but notice and wonder at the constant use of "we," "our," and "us" in this verse.

"And he that sat upon the throne said, Behold, I make all things new. And he said unto me, Write: for these words are true and faithful." (Revelation 21:5.) So important is it that we understand the compassionate, healing touch of those tear-removing hands, God himself commands John to record the scene, adding his own witness that the words are true and faithful. We can count on this personal witness of our Savior's love.

Christ then announces some of his most frequently mentioned titles: "I am Alpha and Omega, the beginning and the end." (Revelation 21:6.) These two Greek letters are the first and last ones of the alphabet. Of all Christ's titles, I am most moved by this one. I did not comprehend its beauty until I asked myself the question, "What is Christ the end of? What is he the beginning of?" I found my answer in the verse quoted earlier. He is the end of tears. He is the end of death. He is the end of sorrow. He is the end of crying. He is the end of pain. Whatever sorrow or anguish we may have suffered, are presently suffering, or may yet face in the future, Christ will end it. The long, sad chronicle of earth's seven seals in the intensity of each individual's burdens of pain will end. As he said of his own intense suffering during those last moments on the cross, "It is finished," so too will we say those words of all our griefs of whatever type they may be.

If he is the end of all tears of sorrow, he is also the beginning of tears of joy. He is the beginning of all the opposites whose balance holds the universe in the scales of justice. He is the beginning of life. He is the beginning of peace. He is the beginning of happiness. He is the beginning of Godly pleasure. He is the beginning of forgiveness.

As if these greatest of all blessings to humanity were not sufficient to satisfy Christ's worlds-encompassing graciousness and mercy, he promises, "I will give unto him that is athirst of the fountain of the water of life freely. He that overcometh shall inherit all things; and I will be his God, and he shall be my son." (Revelation 21:6–7.)

When Nephi saw the images of his father's dream, he spoke of the "fountain of living waters . . . which waters are a representation of the love of God." (1 Nephi 11:25.) We all thirst for love, for it is one of the most basic of human needs. Far too many have lived in a desert of hatred. The tender touch and whispered words of softness did not encompass the daily round of their lives. But the fountain of the Father flows, and they may now "freely" drink their fill of his love. They are sons and daughters of God, and to prove their full acceptance into the divine family, they inherit all things.

Comfort having been offered and accepted, we hear a voice urge us forward with these words: "Come hither, I will shew thee the bride, the Lamb's wife." Now "that great city, the holy Jerusalem, [is seen] descending out of heaven from God." (Revelation 21:9–10.)

TWELVE GATES AND TWELVE FOUNDATIONS

The descriptions of the city speak of "precious" stones, "clear as crystal. . . . The wall of it was of jasper: and the city was pure gold, like unto clear glass. And the foundations of the wall of the city were garnished with all manner of precious stones. . . . And the twelve gates were twelve pearls . . . and the street of the city was pure gold, as it were transparent glass." (Revelation 21:11, 18–21.)

When we understand what crystal, precious gems, gold, clear glass, and pearls all have in common, we will grasp what these images are saying about the holy city. None of these decay. They have no impurities to make them tarnish, rust, spoil, decompose, or change their consistency. They reflect light. They are symbols of beauty, refinement, and uncorrupted richness, for the city is eternal and unchanging.

The city is encircled with "a wall great and high . . . [with] twelve gates, and at the gates twelve angels, and names written thereon, which are the names of the twelve tribes of the children of Israel. On the east three gates; on the north three gates; on the south three gates; and on the west three gates." (Revelation 21:12–13.) The placing of the gates follows the pattern of the encampment around the Tabernacle as Israel wandered in the wilderness. One enters the city through participation in the house of Israel. Baptism is the ordinance, the rebirth, that enables us to claim the blessings of membership in the family of Israel. It is noteworthy that the scriptures call baptism "the gate," a gate Christ himself walked through. (2 Nephi 31:9, 18.)

Brigham Young spoke of the angels who guard the gate, indicating that the ordinances of the temple are also necessary that we might pass by those watchful sentries: "Your endow-ment is, to receive all those ordinances in the house of the Lord, which are necessary for you, after you have departed this life, to enable you to walk back to the presence of the Father, passing the angels who stand as sentinels being enabled to give them the key words, the signs and tokens, pertaining to the holy Priesthood, and gain your eternal exaltation in spite of earth and hell." (*Discourses of Brigham Young,* selected by John A. Widtsoe [Salt Lake City: Deseret Book, 1954], 416.) When we complete the last edifying moment in the endowment, we are in some measure enacting our final entrance through the gates of the holy city.

A WALL GREAT AND HIGH

"The wall of the city had twelve foundations, and in them the names of the twelve apostles of the Lamb." (Revelation 21:14.) We generally speak of only one foundation for a wall. The lowest course must be the strongest and broadest, for it will bear the weight of the completed structure. Upon this founda-tion the upper courses of stone are laid. Here, however, twelve foundation layers support the wall. Obviously the wall can bear tremendous weight. These stones are the apostles. John has added another image describing the chosen twelve of Jesus: they are stars, which guide and give direction; they are eyes, which see and receive light; they are horns of authority and power, which accomplish work for the head, who is Christ; and now they are a wall of security and protection. Each stresses a differ-ent aspect of their calling, each adding to our confidence and trust in their leadership.

If we added upper courses to the wall, they would comprise the many offices of the priesthood, including both Aaronic and

Melchizedek. In Doctrine and Covenants 20, both priesthoods are to "watch over the church always, and be with and strengthen them; and see that there is no iniquity in the church." (D&C 20:42, 53–54.) Like a great wall surrounding God's people, the apostles and priesthood bearers over whom they preside protect the Church and keep it secure. With the angel guardians at the gates, there is no chance that anything unholy or impure can enter to disturb the peace, quiet, and blessedness of the Saints: "And there shall in no wise enter into it anything that defileth, neither whatsoever worketh abomination, or maketh a lie: but they which are written in the Lamb's book of life." (Revelation 21:27.)

Jesus taught his apostles, "When the Son of man shall sit in the throne of his glory, ye also shall sit upon twelve thrones, judging the twelve tribes of Israel." (Matthew 19:28.) Since one enters the holy city through the gates of the tribes of Israel, they will judge all within. "Judging" in this sense means to serve, to minister, and to bless. Jesus told Peter that he would make John "a ministering angel; he shall minister for those who shall be heirs of salvation who dwell on the earth." (D&C 7:6.)

PRAISE AND SALVATION

Much of the imagery of chapter 21 is gleaned from Isaiah 60 and 26. There the wonderful city of God is also described: "Violence shall no more be heard in thy land, wasting nor destruction within thy borders; but thou shalt call thy walls Salvation, and thy gates Praise." (Isaiah 60:18.) Earlier Isaiah wrote, "We have a strong city; salvation will God appoint for walls and bulwarks. Open ye the gates, that the righteous nation which keepeth the truth may enter in. Thou wilt keep him in perfect peace, whose mind is stayed on thee: because he trusteth in thee." (Isaiah 26:1–3.)

Salvation comes only through the redeeming work of Jesus, but the benefits of his sacrifice hinge on our acceptance of priesthood ordinances that testify of our obedience and willingness to order our lives in the ways of truth. For those who do so, the gates of praise are opened. The righteous are lauded for their righteousness; their works have been in compliance with the covenants and ordinances of the priesthood, and their names are recorded in the "books" spoken of in chapter 20. They have been true and faithful in all things. Brigham Young indicated that they have acquired all the knowledge and ordinances necessary to pass the gates, and the guardian angels recognize that they are worthy of praise as well as acceptance into the city.

In vision Joseph Smith saw the entry into the "celestial kingdom of God." He wrote, "I saw the transcendent beauty of the gate through which the heirs of that kingdom will enter, which was like unto circling flames of fire." (D&C 137:1–2.)

The apostles are a protective force, as depicted in the image of the wall, allowing the people within to be at rest. But it is not a foreboding, militaristic wall, frowning down from its battlements upon a threatening enemy. Rather, it is one that reflects from its gem-covered surface the glory of God's light: "The foundations of the wall of the city were garnished with all manner of precious stones." (Revelation 21:19.)

The stones are then named, and many of them correspond to the stones worn by the High Priest as part of his official clothing, further linking the wall to the idea of priesthood responsibility. Each stone in the high priest's ephod bore the name of a tribe of Israel, suggesting that he kept the people close to his heart. Surely the image fits that of our present apostles. I have the calm assurance that next to their hearts are the precious gems of God's inheritance.

IN THE HOLY OF HOLIES

The city is measured with "a golden reed" in John's presence: "And the city lieth foursquare, and the length is as large as the breadth: and he measured the city with the reed. . . . The length and the breadth and the height of it are equal." (Revelation 21:15–16.) The city is a giant cube. The idea of something being square indicates that it is true, exact, perfect, straight, without the least degree of variance or inclination. Alma said of the Lord, "He cannot walk in crooked paths; neither doth he vary from that which he hath said; neither hath he a shadow of turning from the right to the left, or from that which is right to that which is wrong." (Alma 7:20.) His kingdom and its inhabitants follow his example.

The temple of Solomon incorporated this idea in the dimensions of the Holy of Holies: "The oracle in the forepart was twenty cubits in length, and twenty cubits in breadth, and twenty cubits in the height thereof: and he overlaid it with pure gold." (1 Kings 6:20.) Every detail John gives us suggests the city's perfection. If it bears God's name and will become his dwelling place, it must conform to his character.

John said, "I saw no temple therein: for the Lord God Almighty and the Lamb are the temple of it." (Revelation 21:22.) In truth there need be no temple, for the whole city is a temple—in fact, the central, most sacred, and holiest part of the temple. The celestial room in our temples corresponds to the city. If we live in such a way that we can always enter this room in worthiness, it can assure us that we will one day enter the holy city of perfection. We know what we must do to enjoy the peace of the celestial room. We know the gate through which we must pass to enter. We know what we must learn and live. The ordinances of the House of the Lord are nothing less than our preparation for life in a city represented as a perfect square.

"And the city had no need of the sun, neither of the moon, to shine in it: for the glory of God did lighten it, and the Lamb is the light thereof." (Revelation 21:23.) The greatest light we can see is the sun. John now compares the celestial light of the Lamb with the brightest thing we experience. Christ's light is equal to his truth, his intelligence, for we read, "The glory of God is intelligence, or in other words, light and truth." (D&C 93:36.) The book of Revelation provides us with a metaphor for God's truth, using the mightiest light we know. That light will illuminate the holy city throughout eternity. Compared to it the sun itself is eclipsed, not by darkness but by a greater light.

In a wonderfully worded portion of *The Merchant of Venice*, Shakespeare illustrates for us the idea behind the sun and moon as described in Revelation 21:

> "That light we see is burning in my hall.
> How far that little candle throws his beams! . . .
> When the moon shone, we did not see the candle.
> So doth the greater glory dim the less.
> A substitute shines brightly as a king
> Until a king be by, and then his state
> Empties itself, as doth an inland brook
> Into the main of waters."
> —*THE MERCHANT OF VENICE*, ACT V, SCENE I, LINES 100–108.

THE GLORY OF THE NATIONS

John informs us that the gates of the city "shall not be shut at all by day: for there shall be no night there. And they shall bring the glory and honour of the nations into it." (Revelation 21:25–26.) Many of the ideas presented in Revelation 21 are first introduced in Isaiah. Isaiah gives us the details of the perpetually open gate. When Babylon ruled, all the wealth and tribute of the world flowed through its gates to enrich and beautify it. Now, however, things have shifted. Isaiah sees "the abundance of the sea . . . converted unto" Zion. (Isaiah 60:5.) The ships that used to dock and unload their wares for sale in the markets of the world now consecrate their resources to the building up of the New Jerusalem, the Zion of the Lord, his holy city.

"The multitude of camels shall cover thee . . . they shall bring gold and incense; and they shall shew forth the praises of the Lord." (Isaiah 60:6.) The image shifts from the ships of the ocean to the caravans of the deserts. From land and sea, the treasures of the nations pass through the gates to accomplish the Lord's work.

"All the flocks of Kedar shall be gathered together unto thee, the rams of Nebaioth shall minister unto thee: they shall come up with acceptance on mine altar, and I will glorify the house of my glory." (Isaiah 60:7.) Isaiah's picture now changes from a mercantile tone to a religious one. The Lord will accept the devotions of all nations who will worship him with their sacrifices—none will be excluded.

The Lord will accept the efforts of all: "The sons of strangers shall build up thy walls, and their kings shall minister unto thee. . . . Therefore thy gates shall be open continually; they shall not be shut day nor night; that men may bring unto thee the forces of the Gentiles, and that their kings may be brought." (Isaiah 60:10–11.) What is the purpose of all this stream of wealth and people? The Lord answers, "to beautify the place of my sanctuary; and I will make the place of my feet glorious." (Isaiah 60:13.)

So the gates cannot be shut for at least two reasons. First, multitudes of people and nations desire to honor God with such fervency that the flow never ceases. Second, the open gate is an invitation for all to participate; all are welcome. The open gates also suggest there is no need to fear the spoiling of an invading enemy; the city is a place of safety.

Sometimes people ask, "Does this describe the millennial New Jerusalem (the terrestrial Zion of prophecy), or the celestial city of God? Why would the Lord want such a flow of goods into his eternal kingdom?" Poetic writing has many levels of meaning. Though it sounds evasive, the answer to the questions would be "Yes!" Both are encompassed in the visions of John. However, the eternal, celestial city holds the dominant position on the stage of this prophecy. In that city all will also wish to add their glory, the wealth of their kingdoms, their gifts to the Father and the Lamb forever and ever.

✎☙✎

THE PURE RIVER AND
THE TREE OF LIFE

From the gates and walls of the city, we are invited to come inside, to the very center. Here John is shown "a pure river of water of life, clear as crystal, proceeding out of the throne of God and of the Lamb. In the midst of the street of it, and on either side of the river, was there the tree of life, which bare twelve manner of fruits, and yielded her fruit every month: and the leaves of the tree were for the healing of the nations." (Revelation 22:1–2.)

This description matches one given by Ezekiel when he saw in vision the future temple of Jerusalem. It is a beautiful lesson on the power of the temple. The fact that John uses it to portray the center of God's celestial world tells us as much about our own temples as it does about the eternal city of our Father in Heaven. Temples are symbols on earth of the realities of heaven.

Ezekiel was brought to the east doors of the newly constructed temple, where he saw a spring of water that "issued out from under the threshold of the house." (Ezekiel 47:1.) The spring formed a river that began to flow eastward through the dry desert land of the Judean wilderness before emptying into the Dead Sea.

I have been to both the Judean Wilderness and the Dead Sea, and few places on earth are more barren of life. There is no marine life at all in the Dead Sea, and only a covering of grass spotted with wild flowers appears in the desert after spring rains. Yet as the water from the temple flows, it bestows life. Ezekiel is brought to "the brink of the river. . . . Behold, at the bank of the river were very many trees on the one side and on the other. Then said he unto me, These waters issue out toward the east country, and go down into the desert, and go into the sea: which being brought forth into the sea, the waters shall be healed." (Ezekiel 47:6–8.)

The water has the power to create flourishing life from the deadness of barren soil and rock. Its virtue can heal the life-repelling desert devoid of any living thing for generation after generation. "Every thing that liveth, which moveth, whithersoever the rivers shall come, shall live: and there shall be a very great multitude of fish, because these waters shall come thither: for they shall be healed; and every thing shall live whither the river cometh." (Ezekiel 47:9.)

Ezekiel is shown fishermen surrounding the once-killing sea drying their nets and sorting their catch into many varied species, as many as those found in the Mediterranean Sea. His attention shifts back to the trees that grow along the bank. They too are unique because they do not go through the natural cycles of dormancy and production but bear fruit in one continuous harvest, month by month: "By the river upon the bank thereof, on this side and on that side, shall grow all trees for meat, whose leaf shall not fade, neither shall the fruit thereof be consumed: it shall bring forth new fruit according to his months, because their waters they issued out of the sanctuary: and the fruit thereof shall be for meat, and the leaf thereof for medicine." (Ezekiel 47:12.)

Commanded by his angelic guide, Ezekiel is told to walk down the length of the river for a distance, then wade into it and measure its depth. His first entry into the river finds that "the waters were to the ankles." Down the bank of the river he continues his march; again he is asked to wade into the flow and measure its depth: "The waters were to the knees." Continuing his journey along the bank, a third time he is commanded to measure: "The waters were to the loins." The river continues to deepen until "it was a river that I could not pass over: for the waters were risen, waters to swim in, a river that could not be passed over." (Ezekiel 47:3–5.)

Of all the scriptures that speak of the temple, this one, for me, is the most beloved, and I am deeply comforted to find it repeated in the last chapter of Revelation, describing the very center of God's eternal city. We read earlier of Nephi's analysis of what living water symbolizes so often in scripture: the love of God. Both river and tree are united in their portrayal of this quality of God. How deep is that love? Deeper than the bottomless pit that stands as its opposite. The more we wander along its banks, the deeper it is. The more we enter into its refreshing waters, the more we are invited to immerse ourselves in its healing coolness.

While we feel and hear and see the wonders of the river, there are also the trees of life, which grow in great number along its banks. In their healing shade we partake without cessation of the nourishment of God's love. Both river and trees

315

give life-sustaining nourishment and soothing healing. As with the imagery of chapter 21, there is tear-wiping comfort in the city that will make all pains, trials, suffering, loneliness, bewilderment, and guilt fade inconsequentially into the memory of a dream. We learned from those experiences; they strengthened us, proved us, and gave us power to resist every form of disobedience or opposition to eternal law. But this is a new world, the world of the river and its trees. All the hatred, variance, cruelty, and animosity of the nations are gone, all souls are healed, and all are enlivened.

But need we wait for these hope-filled blessings? The answer is no! The trees of life cast their sun-blocking shadows upon the earth, and if we listen we can hear the surging, bubbling, inviting beauty of the river in the distance. The life-sustaining, healing waters of light, love, and nourishment flow from our temples. They are earthly reminders of a home we once knew and a fulfillment we will soon share.

Somewhere in the recesses of our premortal memory is the peace of wandering calmly along the shaded waters of life. We know the taste of fruit from low-bending limbs. The temple touches these memories, and though we may not know why, and can rarely put it into words, there is a familiarity about the feel, the spirit, and the peace of the temple that is more than earthly. It is the combined force of memory and promise, the past and the future coming together in the present—the feeling that our spirits should never wander far from our eternal place of nativity.

We should not wonder at this marvel. Is it not consistent with the character of a kind Father and a loving Older Brother to concern themselves with the present thirst and hunger of those who strive to honor them—a thirst and a hunger that is eternal and can only be satisfied by a single fountain and tree? They would not leave us to travel the desert of life's labors, staring out over the dead sea of so much of human experience, without placing within our reach the healing river and fruit-laden trees. In the temple we are home, if only for a few precious moments. We feel the crystal coolness of the stream on our feet, we hold the soft sweetness of ripe fruit in our hands, and they encourage us to press forward until that greater river and those most lovely of trees, of which the earthly temple is but a foretaste, will forever grace our view and bless our lives. In that future world "there shall be no more curse," for the Fall's effects on both mankind and creation have been surmounted through the resurrection and mercy of the Atonement.

"And they shall see his face; and his name shall be in their foreheads." (Revelation 22:3–4.) In the past I have thought of this verse as applying almost exclusively to the feelings people would experience in knowing they belonged to the Father. They are his children, and he claims them. Lately, however, I have thought of the effect this knowledge might have on my attitudes toward others. Without question, the realization that all other souls in that vast assemblage of celestial beings bear the mark of the Divine Father would contribute to the love and unity each would feel for the others. It bespeaks the love of the grand celestial family, where the title "brothers and sisters" will reach its fullest felicity.

I COME QUICKLY

Twice in the last chapter of Revelation, the Savior says, "Behold, I come quickly." (Revelation 22:7, 12.) Sometimes we interpret "quickly" to mean "soon." A better interpretation would be "suddenly"; he will come unexpectedly, particularly for the unprepared. This is one reason we speak of earthquakes and tornadoes as signs of the times. They also come suddenly. If one is not already prepared for their fury, there will be no time to prepare when the moment arrives. So it is with the Savior's return; we must ever be ready. John feels he has given us much of what we need to be prepared whenever the time comes. We will also be prepared to live in the generations of the Lord's return whether we live to see the actual moment or not. "Blessed is he that keepeth the sayings of the prophecy of this book," John says. (Revelation 22:7.) The book of Revelation is thus a manual of preparation that will steady us in the days ahead.

It is wisdom in God that he does not reveal the exact hour of his return, only the general conditions that will keep us alert. Ironically, most of those conditions have existed for much of the earth's history. The Restoration is, perhaps, the best indicator that the Lord's approach is near, much more than wars, earthquakes, famines, and general wickedness.

I recall trying an experiment with a class of BYU students one semester. I told them they would need to write three papers for their final grade. I explained the details of the assignment, the length, the topics, and other expectations, but I did not tell them when the papers were due. I then began to teach the lesson for that day. It did not take long before one of the students raised his hand and asked, "Brother Wilcox, you did not tell us when the papers were due. Could you give us the due dates, please?"

I answered that I would not tell them the due dates. I would require all three papers on a single day sometime before the end of the semester. I promised them I would give them ample time to accomplish the task, but there would be no hints as to when the collecting of the papers would arrive. If they had all three done, they would receive a grade and pass the class. However, if they did not have all three finished on the day I asked for them, they would fail, and there would be no period of grace.

I remember the shocked look of disbelief on all of their faces. Someone remarked that I was not being fair. I then asked them a few questions. "How many of you, as a general rule, do your papers a few days before they are due? How many of you are working on them the last hours of the night and morning before the due date?" I was greeted with a majority of raised hands.

"How many of you worry about the paper during most of the semester, with increasing concern as the day approaches? If I do not tell you when they are due, how many of you will begin to work on them immediately? How many will have all three done sometime in the next few weeks? When they are completed, how will you feel as you enter the class with your papers in your backpacks? Would you hope that I asked for them that very day? But if you did not have them ready, you would hope and pray that I would delay one more week. Actually, I am doing you a favor by not telling you when they will be due. I am being more than fair; I am being merciful. You will get started early, complete them early, and enjoy the rest of the semester."

We then discussed why the Lord does not reveal when he will return. When I told them I was just illustrating the principle and would give them the due dates, I actually saw some disappointment in their eyes. They had understood the wisdom of an unannounced deadline.

Our Father in Heaven understands human nature completely. It is an act of mercy to keep locked within his own mind the exact time he will send his Son back into the world. If we receive his mercy, we will be always prepared and, like my students, will look forward with eagerness for his approach, greeting with joy his sudden appearance. "At last," we will say, "he has come."

I AM THY FELLOWSERVANT

Twice in Revelation, John falls at the feet of the angelic messenger with whom he is conversing—once in chapter 19 (verse 10) and once in chapter 22 (verse 8). Each time he is told, "See thou do it not: for I am thy fellowservant, and of thy brethren the prophets." (Revelation 22:9; see also 19:10.) There must be something magnificent about a resurrected, glorified body that invites worship. If the messengers are not yet resurrected, then the spirit itself is capable of astonishing radiance. We should not be surprised at this, for John himself wrote that when Christ "shall appear, we shall be like him; for we shall see him as he is." (1 John 3:2.)

Also, the visions and the wisdom John has been shown are so overwhelmingly edifying that his gratitude swells toward the messenger who has revealed it unto him. At times I have been so grateful for the knowledge imparted by a teacher that it is not hard to understand why John would fall at the feet of his celestial guides. How wonderful it is that the Lord allows us to teach each other the beautiful truths of his gospel, that such feelings of appreciation may lodge in our hearts and we may understand as students and teachers the gifts of God. Since ultimately all intelligence comes from God, expanding our souls and minds, the emotions we feel toward our earthly instructors must properly be directed to their original source. Every teacher who has imparted knowledge powerfully through the Spirit must say, "Worship God." (Revelation 22:9, 19:10.)

To Add or Diminish

Many times I have heard members of other faiths point out that the Bible ends with an injunction from John: "If any man shall add unto these things, God shall add unto him the plagues that are written in this book: and if any man shall take away from the words of the book of this prophecy, God shall take away his part out of the book of life, and out of the holy city." (Revelation 22:18–19.)

These verses are also mirrored reflections of an earlier Old Testament commandment. In Deuteronomy, Moses counseled, "Ye shall not add unto the word which I command you, neither shall ye diminish ought from it." (Deuteronomy 4:2.) The Lord certainly does not want us to add our own scriptures to those he has revealed, nor does he want us to subtract from his holy words, thus removing many plain and precious things. However, there is another interpretation that should be pondered and practiced.

The principles, ordinances, commandments, and practices of the gospel are often described as a narrow path. There is not a lot of wiggle room for us to weave back and forth from conservative to liberal in our levels of obedience. Keeping these things in balance is sometimes like walking a tightrope. We must constantly correct our behaviors and interpretations to stay on course. We do not wish to make a commandment mean more than the Lord requires, nor do we wish to reduce its power through too lenient an application. An example may help to illustrate.

In 1831 Joseph Smith sent some missionaries to the Shakers. This religious group believed that "baptism by water was not considered essential; the eating of pork was specifically forbidden, and many did not eat any meat; and a celibate life was considered higher than marriage." (Heading to Doctrine and Covenants 49.)

Notice how in each case they had added to or subtracted from the Lord's revealed laws. They had diminished from the ordinance of baptism, added to the law of health, and added and subtracted in the case of celibacy. In their eagerness to add to the law of chastity, they diminished from the law of marriage and from the command to multiply and replenish the earth. Occasionally we do similar things in the Church, particularly if we become enamored with what we sometimes call "gospel hobbies." If we study all the scriptures, they will as a whole keep us in balance. This is one reason we should not single out a particular book of scripture and study it exclusively. We are apt to add or diminish, since our perceptions will be out of balance.

Why would John be so concerned about Revelation that he would include this Mosaic warning at the close of his writings? Perhaps because of the nature of what he wrote. No other type of writing is more susceptible to adding and diminishing than that which is symbolic, figurative, parabolic, metaphorical, image-driven, or prophetic. There is always the danger that we will read things too literally or too figuratively. With a little twisting, we can make the images say what we want them to say, trying to justify a preconceived concept.

I have tried hard not to fall into this trap, hoping I have heeded the warning. If I have added or diminished from any symbol of the Revelation, it has been inadvertent. We all continue to learn, and I pray for the day when my knowledge of all scripture will be complete and balanced in the way the Lord desires. Until that day comes for us all, let us thoughtfully consider John's warning and hesitate to be too dogmatic in either direction.

THE CLOSING PRAYER

Revelation ends with a prayer and its answer: "The Spirit and the bride say, Come. And let him that heareth say, Come. And let him that is athirst come. And whosoever will, let him take the water of life freely." (Revelation 22:17.) Knowing the trauma of earth's history as revealed in the previous chapters, and knowing also the wonders of the holy city and the joys of its inhabitants, the only logical prayer to offer would be one of longing that Christ come. Let him end the conquests of hate, the lies of apostasy, the frenzied buying and selling of a materialistic world. The Spirit itself speaks through our prayers, inviting the King of Kings to come. The bride, prepared and ready, longs for the wedding. Everyone who understands the contrasting worlds presented in Revelation will add their voice to the general "amen" of that one-word prayer—"Come."

If we ask, we will receive; if we knock, the door will be opened; if we seek, we will find. The answer comes, and not only in Revelation; the whole Bible ends with Christ's own reply to the universal prayer: "He which testifieth these things saith, Surely I come quickly. Amen." (Revelation 22:20.)

Now John adds his own personal prayer. He who once lay upon the bosom of our Savior at the Last Supper, he who was called "beloved" as was his Master, he who knows the glory of a life shared with Jesus prays with us all, "Even so, come, Lord Jesus." Until that day, John speaks with hope across the centuries to us: "The grace of our Lord Jesus Christ be with you all. Amen" (Revelation 22:21.)

I have for many years loved to sing the hymn "Come O

Thou King of Kings." I think of it each time I finish reading or teaching the book of Revelation. May the words of this hymn express to every student of Revelation, and to each member of the Church, all that I long for myself and for them:

> Come, O thou King of Kings!
> We've waited long for thee,
> With healing in thy wings,
> To set thy people free.
> Come, thou desire of nations, come;
> Let Israel now be gathered home.
>
> Come, make an end to sin
> And cleanse the earth by fire,
> And righteousness bring in,
> That saints may tune the lyre
> With songs of joy, a happier strain,
> To welcome in thy peaceful reign.
>
> Hosannas now shall sound
> From all the ransomed throng,
> And glory echo round
> A new triumphal song;
> The wide expanse of heaven fill
> With anthems sweet from Zion's hill.
>
> Hail! Prince of life and peace!
> Thrice welcome to thy throne!
> While all the chosen race
> Their Lord and Savior own,
> The heathen nations bow the knee,
> And ev'ry tongue sounds praise to thee.
> —HYMNS, NO. 59.

MINE EYE
CAN PIERCE THEM

everal years ago I visited the Nazi concentration camp at Dachau, outside of Munich, Germany. Places have memories, and an intensity of feeling permeates the ground there, a heaviness that the intervening years have not dispelled. I anticipated feeling sadness as I walked this ground, which I did, but I was surprised by the impact of a truth whispered by the Spirit as I moved from site to site in my silent, lonely reveries. It was a verse of scripture from the visions of Enoch describing the sorrows of God as he looked down upon his children. He had given mankind two basic commandments, "that they should love one another, and that they should choose me, their Father; but behold, they are without affection, and they hate their own blood." (Moses 7:33.)

So much of Revelation is encompassed in those words, yet the soft voice of the Spirit continued, and one of the greatest hopes I had ever felt was born there, among the crumbling ruins of one of the most brutal cruelties practiced upon the human race. Here all the demons of Revelation's darkest hours were combined and unleashed.

"I can stretch forth mine hands," the Lord told Enoch, "and hold all the creations which I have made; and mine eye can pierce them also, and among all the workmanship of mine hands there has not been so great wickedness as among thy brethren." (Moses 7:36.) I have been familiar with this statement for much of my life and always read it negatively, asking myself why I was fated to spend my mortal years upon the most wicked of worlds—yet this day a new thought dawned. The universe is really a place of goodness, an environment of burning lights and wonderful perfections. The evils of Dachau, the devouring nature of the beast, the liquor of apostate wine, the crushing greed of Babylon's marketplaces are exceptions to the rule. No other people on any other world the Father and Son have created have known the depths of sin we have witnessed.

That night I looked into the night sky at the myriad pinpoints of light and felt a deep, satisfying, soul-cleansing comfort. The vast expanse of creation is filled with light, mercy, and compassion. We are the anomaly that proves the norm, not the mean by which we judge "worlds without number." Though I knew there must be opposition in all things, in every kingdom of the Father, no planet has faced the enemy in darker power than here. I suddenly felt at home among the spinning worlds ordered above me. The dragon has no hold upon them.

Every page of Revelation testifies that even here, on the one world that has seen the greatest wickedness, the Father and Son have everything in control. The outcome has been determined since the foundation of the world. No matter how powerful the enemy appears, no matter the level of opposition he musters, he shall not prevail. One day our earthly home, as a sea of crystal in whose central city the fountain of love and the tree of life refresh everlastingly, will take its rightful position among the gleaming stars of celestial worlds. Its galactic quarantine will end, and another bright, shining light will testify to the Father's wisdom, goodness, and mercy.

So when the beasts arise from the sea or the locusts emerge anew from the smoke of the pit; when the sun mourns in black sackcloth and the moon's blood-red anger broods in the night sky; when the gaunt face of famine and the pale green of pestilence mount their horses to stalk the nations; when the gaudily dressed harlot offers her intoxicating wine to congregations already stumbling under the influence of apostasy; when all the world seems to respond eagerly to the dragon-voiced lamb and bow before the image of the beast, accepting the law of conquest and retribution as the only way to survive; when the merchant city with its never-ending display of dainty, delicate, costly wares appears to entice us with its distracting assertion that everything is for sale and everything must be bought; when the winepress overflows with the bitter grapes harvested from the fields of hate and distrust—we know in the marrow of our bones that all of this is transitory. None of it holds an eternal grip in the broad expanse of eternity we see each night as our own bright sun sets.

Let us make correct choices, for that is the purpose for which John was shown his swirling visions of kaleidoscopic imagery. Choice leads naturally to consequence. Goodness, consecration, meekness, humility, and obedience lead to the first ingathering harvest, the adorned bride in her robes of pure righteousness, the marriage supper of truth and intelligence, the radiant city of light and purity, just as selfishness, dominance, hatred, anger, lust, and greed lead to Armageddon, the wine-press filled to the brim with the grapes of wrath, and the mournful cry "Alas, alas" at the fall of idolatrous Babylon.

Ultimately, since John borrowed so heavily from the Old Testament, the book of Revelation becomes one of its best commentaries. We are being introduced to the theme of Genesis through Malachi. Though we have used the Old Testament consistently to comment and give insight upon Revelation, if we reversed the order we would not be disappointed. It is fitting that Revelation is the last book we read as we take our journey across the roads of the Bible's landscapes.

John's message is universal. It offered hope to the Saints of his own period who saw the beast, the whore, and the merchant city holding sway in their own age and heard the hoofbeats of mounted horses who began their rides in dispensations past. It is a timeless view of life, designed to be likened to any period yet always ending in the joyful knowledge that all will be well. The Savior will execute the Father's will, the earth will be cleansed to become an orb of lights and perfections, and our tears will be wiped away as sorrow, grief, pain, and death become only memory as the cycling rounds of eternity progress from age to timeless age.

INDEX

329

Balaam, 35–36
Balak, 35
Balances (scales), 70–71
Bear, 74, 177
Beast, 175–78, 198–99
Beasts: allusion of, 5; meaning of four,
    53–56; represent conquest, 74; in
    book of Daniel, 176–78; destruction
    of, 184
Belief, 17
Bible (JST) in clarifying Revelation, 2,
    159
Big Dipper, 23
Bishops, 23
Black, color of, as famine, 70–71
Blasphemy, 181–82
Blessings of gospel, 33–34
Blood: desire for, 80–81, 223; cleanses
    earth, 111–12; water turning to,
    222
Book, little, 137
Book of life, 187–88, 298–99
Book of Mormon: clarifies Revelation,
    2–3; apostasy complete in, 167; was
    written for American Saints,
    257–58; follows pattern of last days,
    291–94
Breastplates, 126
Bride, Church as, 31–32, 160–62,
    267–69
Bridegroom, Christ as, 31–32, 160–62,
    272

꩜ C ꩜

Calf, 55
Candlesticks, 21, 147–48
Cedars of Lebanon, 118
Celestial world, 52–53. *See also*
    Jerusalem, New
Change of heart, 62–63
Chaos, 175
Chastisement, 29–30, 44
Chastity, 202

Choices, 12, 17–18
Christianity, 8–9, 167–68
Chronology, 13
Church of Jesus Christ: fighting
    against, 2; as radiant woman, 23; as
    bride, 31–32, 160–61, 267–69; as
    stone cut out without hands,
    82–84, 192–93; to rise again after
    apostasy, 142; as woman clothed
    with sun, 159; comes forth from
    wilderness, 161–62; children of,
    170
Civil War, 223–24
Cleansing of earth, 111–12
Clothing, 270, 275
"Come, O Thou King of Kings," 323–24
Comfort of Christ, 301–4
Commotion, 79–80
Compass, 68–69
Conquest, 69, 74
Consecration, 95–96, 100
Constitution, United States, 179, 243
Contention, 123
Coronation, 38
Correction, 29–30
Corruption, 246
Covenants of God, 218–19
Creation: parts of, standing for whole,
    54–55, 92, 117; worshiping God of,
    204, representation of, in plagues,
    221
Crowns: placed before the throne, 52;
    metonymy of, 118; representing
    kingly warriors, 125–26;
    representing kingdoms and
    dominions, 164–65
Crystal, 49, 52
Cyrus, 226–27

꩜ D ꩜

Dachau, 325
Dan, tribe of, 97
Daniel, book of: portrays same events,

E

F

❦ K ❦

❦ L ❦

Q

R